FLAVOR

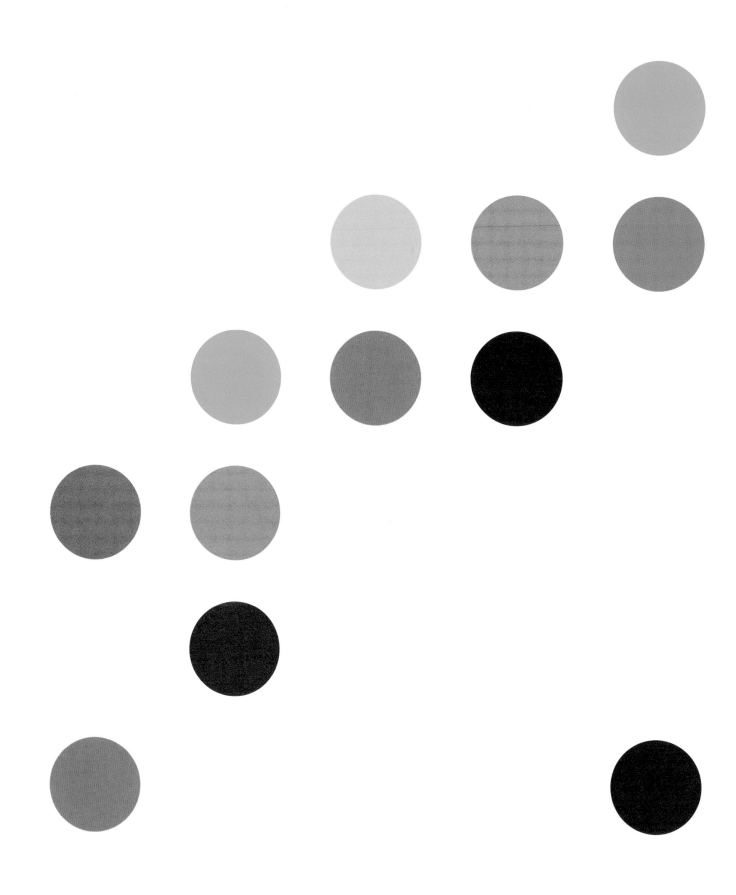

FLAVOR

ROCCO DISPIRITO WITH KRIS SHERER
PHOTOGRAPHS BY HENRY LEUTWYLER

HYPERION

NEW YORK

For information address
Hyperion, 77 West 66th Street
New York, New York 10023-6298.

ISBN 0-7868-6856-2

Hyperion books are available for
special promotions and premiums.
For details contact
Michael Rentas, Manager,
Inventory and Premium Sales,
Hyperion,
77 West 66th Street, 11th floor
New York, New York 10023
or call 212-456-0133.

FIRST EDITION
10 9 8 7 6 5 4 3 2

To my Grandma Anna-Maria, Grandma Maria, my mother Nicolina, my aunts, paisani & friends: Margarite, Maria, Elena, Isadore, Concettina, Guisseppina, Angelina, Emanuela, Raffielina, Camilla, Pasqualina, Vincenzina & all the other great women out there who give generously, cook, teach, nurture, inspire & bring the good life to the rest of us. It wouldn't be the same without you.

CONTENTS

THANK YOU, THANK YOU, THANK YOU TO: RUBA ABU-NIMAH *for her incredible eye & making this book more beautiful & functional than I ever imagined it could be;* MIGUEL ALFONSO *for his adorable intensity;* DAVID AVITAL *for his enthusiasm & exaggeration;* PHIL BALTZ *for believing;* IAN SPENCER BELL *for his beauty;* TERI BIANCO *for her hugs;* KAREN BUSSEN *for her brilliant blue eyes;* BRYAN CALVERT *for his endurance;* HELEN CANNAVALE *for introducing me to Henry;* DOMINIQUE, MICHAELE & NANCY CECILLON *for changing my life & the course of my career;* SHANE CLARKE *for being the master of all things;* DAVID COLEMAN *for his dreads & Run DMC hat;* DAVID CRAINE *for being there—for always being there;* JOSH DECHELLIS *for his generous talent & his nose for good things;* PHILIPPE FALLAIT *for his chicory bombe;* STEFAN FORBES *for his mad jokes;* MATTHIAS GAGGL *for being such a good DJ;* GYPSY GIFFORD *for her swimming;* LUCI GOTT *for how good she looks in chocolate;* JONATHAN HAYES *for tasting, tasting, tasting my food;* CRISTINA HSIAO *for being the first at everything;* DR. ERNESTO ILLY *for knowing so much;* LINDA IMMEDIATO *for her schoolgirl charm;* ABRA JACOBS *for testing recipes;* NANCY KERSHNER *for being the greatest wit & pastry chef;* GRAY KUNZ *for changing the way I think about cooking, kicking my ass & being unafraid to be who he is;* KRISTINA KUREK *for her moves & her dimples;* CARLA LALLI MUSIC *for being great at too many things to mention;* HENRY LEUTWYLER *for his inspired photography, for reading the manual in the nick of time & for treating this book like it was his own;* ROBYNNE MAII *for her helpful research;* FRANK MORALES *for being Frank;* KRISTIN OSBORN *for her pearly whites;* DIEGO PEREZ *for magic light;* FRED PRICE *for making a short story long;* DANIEL QUISHPE *for all the free food;* LON ROSEN *for returning phone calls same day;* JEFF ROSENTHAL *for figuring it all out & being the calm in the storm;* STACEY ROSSLEY *for caring, laughing, getting it done & being so damn cute;* RUTH REICHL *for "carefully considered exotica" & so much more;* ROBERT RUIZ & *family for ceviche;* ELEANOR SANTO DOMINGO *for being a rock & getting it all done;* DEBORAH SCHOENEMAN *for her honesty, advice & being such a good friend;* WILL SCHWALBE *for*

guiding, teaching, humoring &, of course, for "Will Schwalbe!"; YVONNE SCIO for being a sweet, smart, sexy woman & not being heavy; KRIS SHERER for putting my rambling thoughts into words in such a great way; SARAH SHIRLEY for the clothes on my back; THIERRY SIGHEL for opening my eyes; FRANZ STUHLPFARRER for being Austrian; CHARLIE SUISMAN for being the first; JUEL SYED for grace under fire; ROD TAYLOR for those incredible bay scallops; DAVID VIGLIANO for getting me to do it; NACH WAXMAN for the best bookstore; LESLIE WELLS for extending; GRANDMA ANNA-MARIA for her unconditional love & those ripe figs; GRANDPA ROCCO for a great name; UNCLE SILVIO for his style, UNCLE BEPPE for his strength, UNCLE AMADEO for his humor, UNCLE DAVIDE for loving my mom, UNCLE ANGELINO for teaching me about opera; MOM for her energy, smile, meatballs & for taking me to Coney Island; DAD for his intelligence, creativity & touch; MARIA for lavishing me with attention at a time when I really needed it; MIKE for getting me through college with all his credit cards; JACK for tuning my guitar & fixing my car; JAMAICA, QUEENS, for all those interesting people; YASMIN for loving everything I cook; HENRY JR. for eating kumquats at nine months; BRUCE SPRINGSTEEN for inspiration; STEVE, JEFF & PAUL for putting up & putting out; THE VERY GROOVY PEOPLE OF NEW YORK CITY for eating out five nights a week; THE NEW YORK TIMES, GOURMET, FOOD & WINE, ZAGAT & all the journalists out there for their ink; DIANE, CHARLIE, REGIS, KELLY, KATIE, MATT, AL, DAVE & all the other TV people out there who keep asking me back; THE JAMES BEARD FOUNDATION for all the nominations, dinners & promoting the culinary arts; KASHMIR for being the perfect place; ALL THE COOKS, PREP COOKS, DISHWASHERS, RESERVATIONISTS, SOUS-CHEFS, WAITERS, BUSSERS, HOSTS, MANAGERS, CAPTAINS, FOR THE YEARS, THE LATE NIGHTS, THE GRUELING WORK, THE LITTLE MONEY, THE RESPECT, THE FAITH & FOR TAKING WHAT I GAVE THEM & MAKING IT SO MUCH BETTER.

  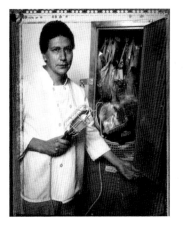 

SUGGESTED MENUS

VEGETARIAN
This is a late summer/early fall menu that uses no meat or fish.
Aromatic Tomato and Kimchee Soup (page 116)
Baby Lettuces with Pickled Zucchini Blossoms and Yogurt-Tahini Vinaigrette (page 130)
Cauliflower Bisteeya with Spiced Eggplant Purée (page 146)

NEW HOUSE
Where the heck is the food processor? Unpack the boxes later.
You can make everything on this menu with a few pans, a bowl, and a baking sheet.
Escarole with Jicama and a Rhubarb Vinaigrette (page 136)
Crusty bread
Bucatini with Summer Vegetables and a Tomato-Anise Broth (page 144)
Peach-Phyllo Strudel with Goat Cheese Cream (page 266)

BLOWOUT CELEBRATION
A long-awaited promotion, 30th birthday, or windfall from a court ruling...
whatever the event, this pull-out-all-the-stops menu is perfect for celebrating.
Jambon de Bayonne, Baby Artichokes, and Arugula (page 128)
Sautéed Foie Gras with Glazed Peaches (page 290)
White Truffle Risotto with a Gulf Shrimp Fondue (page 292)
Warm Chocolate Cake (page 256)

HOLIDAY FEAST
I had Christmas in mind when I created this menu, but it would be just as suitable
for Thanksgiving, New Year's, or any other cold-weather family gathering.
Szechuan Peppercorn–Rubbed Fillet of Beef (page 196)
Aromatic Cauliflower Soup (page 112)
Yam Purée (page 242)
Armagnac Ice Cream (page 260)

PANTS ARE TOO TIGHT
We all know the feeling. These low-fat dishes won't make them any tighter.
Heirloom Tomatoes with Orange Zest (page 46)
Organic Chicken with Beans and Crushed Red Beets
  (follow the directions for using skinless chicken) (page 210)
Mango and Papaya Carpaccio with Cilantro Candy (page 272)

1

TOO HOT TO COOK!

**It's 97° outside: next to a hot stove is the last place you want to be.
Keep cool with this light menu of no-cook and quick-cook summer dishes.**

Dungeness Crab with Avocado and Sauce Vierge (page 58)
Baby Lettuces with Pickled Zucchini Blossoms and Yogurt-Tahini Vinaigrette (page 130)
Bruschetta or crostini
Chilled Watermelon Cocktail with Yuzu (page 254)

A MIDSUMMER NIGHT'S MENU

**Here are foods at their peak in late June.
It is a fabulous picnic-under-the-stars menu.**

Soup of Sweet Peas with Crab-Stuffed Zucchini Blossoms (page 102)
Seared Wild Salmon with Spring Onions and Rhubarb (page 152)
Summer Berries in Spiced Phyllo (page 258)

BEACH HOUSE BLAST

**This spread features some of the foods you're likely to find at or
on the way to the shore: roadside produce stand fare like corn,
tomatoes, and watermelon, plus fish and shellfish.**

Yellow Pepper Soup (page 96)
Orecchiette with Pesto Rosso (page 150)
Black Cod with Corn and Spinach (page 156)
Chilled Watermelon Cocktail with Yuzu (page 254)

FUNGUS EXTRAVAGANZA

**Some of us just can't get enough of the earthy flavors
of wild mushrooms and truffles! Indulge your love of mushrooms.**

Bouillon of Forest Mushrooms with Sherry (page 98)
Jumbo Asparagus with Oyster Mushrooms and Fresh Pecorino Cheese (page 88)
Char with Pea Sprouts and Forest Mushrooms (page 170)
Truffled Taro Root (page 234)

AUTUMN HARVEST

**The September shift to cooler weather never fails to reinvigorate our desire to cook.
Good thing, since autumn is an agriculturally rich season in all parts of the country.**

Eggplant Velouté with Figs (page 100)
Calamari with Pumpkin Seeds and a Butternut Squash Relish (page 52)
Roast Loin of Pork with Cinnamon-Glazed Tart Apples (page 192)
Plum Tartlettes (page 276)

DEAD-OF-WINTER FEAST

**Start to finish, this menu will take a few hours: a perfect excuse
to go nowhere on an inhumanely cold February day.**

Grilled Duck with Watercress and a Citrus Vinaigrette (page 126)

Braised Beef Short Ribs (page 186)

Truffled Taro Root (page 234)

Warm Chocolate Cake (page 256) with Armagnac Ice Cream (page 260)

FOR CHEESE LOVERS

**Want to try several cheeses in one meal? As an alternative to the traditional
cheese tray, consider serving consecutive courses of dishes with cheese.**

Jumbo Asparagus with Oyster Mushrooms and Fresh Pecorino Cheese (page 88)

Roasted Beet Salad with Goat Cheese and Frisée (page 132)

Bucatini with Summer Vegetables and a Tomato-Anise Broth (page 144)

Sweet seasonal fruit with Fromage Blanc Sorbet (page 278)

MOTHER'S DAY

A menu for a light, elegant spring brunch or dinner.

Lemongrass Lobster Salad (page 122)

Rack of Lamb with Sour Cherry Glaze (page 208)

Baby Carrots, Thai Eggplant, and Pearl Onions (page 246)

Lavender Crème Brûlée (page 262)

SUPER BOWL SUNDAY

**Meat, potatoes, and spicy greens.
Serve as a buffet with plenty of cold beer.**

Shrimp in Spiced Phyllo with Tomato Chutney (page 70)

Miso Steak with Cluster Mushrooms (page 202)

Crushed Potatoes with Parsley and Thyme (page 244)

Indian Lime Pickle Swiss Chard (page 232)

MEETING THE IN-LAWS

**An occasion stressful enough as it is!
Go with safe dishes that are easy to make and universally liked.**

Sweet Onion and White Peppercorn Soup (page 104)

Jumbo Asparagus with Oyster Mushrooms and
 Fresh Pecorino Cheese (page 132)

Prawns with Handkerchief Pasta (page 154)

White Chocolate Risotto (page 282)

MAKE-AHEAD

Any soup

Roasted Beet Salad with Goat Cheese and Frisée (page 132)

Open-Faced Lamb Sandwich with Cucumber Raita (page 200)

Summer Berries in Spiced Phyllo (page 258)

DESIGNED TO IMPRESS

The "ooh! ah! ohhh!" quotient in each of these is high.
Perfect for entertaining royalty or closing the deal.

Lemongrass Lobster Salad (page 122)

Sautéed Foie Gras with Glazed Peaches (page 290)

Slow-Cooked Salt-Crust Salmon with Endive (page 308)

Chocolate-Caramel Panna Cotta with Espresso Foam and Caramel Popcorn (page 314)

BUSY WEEKNIGHT MEAL

Believe it or not, this meal can be whipped up in less than an hour.
Pick up something at the grocery store for dessert.

Aromatic Tomato and Kimchee Soup (page 116)

Escarole with Jicama and a Rhubarb Vinaigrette (page 136)

Quick Miso Chicken (page 142)

VALENTINE'S DAY

A very romantic, red-hued meal starring winter foods.

Roasted Beet Salad with Goat Cheese and Frisée (page 132)

Black Sea Bass with Chestnuts and Blood Oranges (page 172)

Chocolate-Caramel Panna Cotta with Espresso Foam
  and Caramel Popcorn (page 314)

COCKTAIL PARTY SPREAD

Most of these recipes were designed to feed four, but you can easily
double or triple all of them as your RSVPs roll in.

Shrimp in Spiced Phyllo with Tomato Chutney (hot) (page 70)

Goat Cheese Parfait with Grilled Leeks and Marjoram Vinaigrette (room temperature) (page 82)

Bread or crackers

Szechuan Peppercorn–Rubbed Fillet of Beef (room temperature or hot) (page 196)

Horseradish spread

Taylor Bay Scallops with Uni and Mustard Oil (room temperature) (page 60)

Crunchy Pickled Vegetables (cold) (page 248)

Bergamot and Indian Lime Pickle Cured Salmon (cold) (page 56)

PART I
TASTE BUDS IN THE KITCHEN

CHAPTER 1
FINDING
FLAVOR

"Modern American," Phil said.
"Contemporary American?"
I suggested.

"How 'bout this:
Global Fusion."

Global Fusion wasn't half bad. Phil Baltz and I were bouncing ideas off each other in a phone conversation back in 1997. I had called Phil, a whip-smart friend whom I could always count on for good ideas, in a real predicament. People of various intents—customers, purveyors, other cooks—were asking over and over, "So what exactly do you call your food, Rocco?" And I didn't have an answer. Here I had spent untold hours building and defining a personal cooking style, and yet I was stumped when challenged to categorize it.

I did know what it wasn't. It wasn't, by a long stretch, classic cuisine. Was it fusion food, that hot buzz phrase of the 1980s and '90s that describes multi-ethnic hybrid cuisine? No, not quite. Although I do get a kick out of mixing old-school techniques with ingredients from around the world, my cooking is driven more by gut feel, and less by formula, than what is generally referred to as "fusion food."

Phil and I coined a few more ineffectual two-word phrases that day. None fit very well, and in the end I decided there was only one way to describe my food: "Rocco DiSpirito cuisine." I knew this wouldn't be particularly helpful as a description, but the futility of the whole process—the attempt to pigeonhole *any* chef's work into a textbook definition—was a real eye-opener. For one thing, I saw the danger in self-branding. The mere thought of having to live up to a world-spanning title like Global Fusion Chef for the rest of my cooking days made me edgy and claustrophobic. Naming one's food may be convenient, but it

punishes the cook with a litmus test that has to be passed with every new dish. If I had to ask myself, "Now, is this what I'm supposed to be making?" every time I developed something new, I'd go crazy.

As I thought more about it, it dawned on me that a good many of America's chefs cook intensely personal food that can't be neatly labeled except in terms of that chef! There's Daniel Boulud cuisine, Nobu Matsuhisa food, Alice Waters dishes, and Charlie Trotter style. Bring up the subject of vegetable juices with another enthusiastic cook and I'll bet you that somewhere in the conversation, a phrase like "Jean-Georges food" (as in Jean-Georges Vongerichten) turns up.

I think we're basking in the golden age of American cooking. Decades of rampant experimentation have resulted in a move away from that old culinary yardstick—classical French cooking. Chefs are free to create, to tinker, to reinterpret. Thanks to improvements in shipping and the marvelous, melting-pot character of our population, America's access to diverse ingredients is matched nowhere else in the world. Restaurant service has come into its own, with a style that is increasingly less ceremonious and more genuinely hospitable. And guess what? American food is no longer the butt of jokes in other countries. Just ask that group of Japanese tourists who have a reservation at Union Pacific next week, or the German family that has made dinner at New York's Gramercy Tavern a priority after reading about Tom Colicchio's food. What is Tom's food like? (I should know: his restaurant's a few short blocks away from my own.) It's American, and yet grounded in classic French, with an unswerving reverence for the seasons ... it's ... well, the best way I can describe it is to call it Tom Colicchio food.

On one of my nights out of the kitchen, you might find me hanging out with any number of New York City chefs. Twenty years ago, camaraderie among a city's chefs simply didn't exist. Why? The fact that everyone was plating up the same French standards made for some unfriendly competition.

Just as there is my kind of cuisine, there is a style of cooking out there with your name on it waiting to emerge. You don't have to be a professional cook to lay claim to your own body of cooking; in fact, professional training has little to do with it. You are already equipped with your cuisine's informing elements. You have preferences for certain foods over others, certainly. There are probably dishes you enjoy cooking at home and others you'd rather have someone make for you. And I'd bet you probably have a good instinct for which flavors go well together, too. If you surrender to your instincts, all these predilections, combined with the whole of your life experiences—your childhood, ancestry, culture, the place you grew up, the countries you've seen, your family's holiday traditions—will swirl together to become your personal cuisine. Nurtured to its fullest form, your cooking style will be as reflective of who you are as your wardrobe is. And you will feel as comfortable pulling together your own food as you do wearing your clothes.

What I'll share with you in this chapter are the elements that have worked for me. There are aspects of my cooking that are pretty

A lifetime of cooking tools.

idiosyncratic—my love affair with yuzu juice, for example. But I wouldn't have written this book if I didn't feel that some aspects have universal appeal and benefit.

If there's one thing I can do to help that inner chef come out of hiding, it's to get you to focus more on flavor and less on producing technically flawless, picture-perfect dinners. Maybe you've heard the debate over whether cooking qualifies as an art. Here's my two cents: depending on the maker's vision, it can be an art or it can simply be a craft, just as there are furniture makers who churn out utilitarian chairs and furniture designers whose conceptualized pieces appear in modern-art galleries. Cooking, I find, has two levels: technique and flavor. In technique you find the craft of cooking, and yes, anyone who cooks needs to know a few how-tos. A cook can choose to engross herself in the details of perfect pie crusts and emulsifications and never think about anything else. Technically perfect food is satisfying in much the same way a utilitarian chair can be comfortable. But beyond technical perfection is the second level of cooking: flavor. Flavor elevates cooking from a craft to an art. It can engage you intellectually and, I believe, should also always satisfy your cravings.

Flavor has always been a part of my life. I grew up in an Italian family that adored food. My grandmother immigrated to the United States from San Nicolo Baronia, a mountain village of 600 people in the Campagna region. She had a small farm on Long Island. I still dream about her lunches: plump little figs plucked from her backyard tree; fresh tomato sauces on hand-shaped pasta heaped in a giant bowl; eggs fried over a mess of sautéed peppers, onions, and garlic. It was simple, rustic food filled with lusty, big flavors. That, more than anything, is how my Italian upbringing has influenced my food: I have always gravitated toward bold flavors. I owe the cooks in my family a second debt of gratitude, for it is from them that I learned to cook from my gut. We didn't use a lot of written recipes in my family; there was no need. Instead, my mother and her mother relied on their instincts, and their taste buds, to guide them through a pasta sauce or frittata.

Remember how I said that the place you grew up will ultimately shape your cuisine? If I had grown up in an Italian family in a small Wisconsin town, or in an Italian family in Italy, I'm sure my food today would be very different. But I grew up in an Italian family in Queens, New York, a borough within a city home to several dozen ethnic communities. When it came to eating out, my family was quite adventurous. I can remember eating Japanese food at about 9 years old, Greek at about 14, and a classic Cantonese dish, shrimp with lobster sauce, in a restaurant owned by a beautiful Chinese woman. I remember her and the flavors of that dish in great detail to this day. For me, discovering new flavors has always been an exotic part of big city life.

I went to the Culinary Institute of America after high school because I had heard that it was the best. I still believe that the education offered by the Culinary—or the CIA, as it is often called—is the best available to young cooks. The CIA's curriculum is mostly classical French, and no matter what their preferred cuisine, most cooks still elect to study French cooking. There are good reasons. Technique is central to French cooking, and technique encompasses a set of skills and ideas that can be taught in a classroom setting. Like a novice piano player who spends hours pounding out scales and one-handed drills, a new cook has to get down his knife cuts, stock making, and product identification before moving on to bigger things.

How much should technique matter to you? For home cooking, I feel that mastering a few basic techniques is sufficient. If anything, home cooks worry too much about technical details. Some of the best food I've had was lovingly prepared by my grandmother. She didn't know sauté from sautoir or baste from roast. It didn't matter. Her food was great because her palate told her so.

I continued cooking in restaurants after graduating from the CIA and then Boston University's School of Hospitality. A young, twenty-something cook with nearly a decade of professional cooking experience (I was 14 when I took my first job at a pizza shop), I defined my ambition in no uncertain terms: I wanted to be a French chef. That I hadn't imagined that there was another kind of cooking I could do is a testament to how much things have changed. I spent a year in France and then returned to the States to work with various French chefs.

In the early '90s, my career path veered off into new territory. Two things happened that would plant the seed which was to become my highly personal cuisine.

First, I got to know Southeast Asian food. Now, people living in West Coast cities are spoiled in this regard: Thai and Vietnamese restaurants have flourished there a long time. New York is much farther from Asia, and the East Coast didn't get its share of authentic Southeast Asian eateries until the late 1980s. I couldn't believe how exciting this food was. The bold, piquant flavors were matched and balanced so naturally, as if the ingredients had found their own way to one another. It resembled the Chinese and Japanese food I already knew well, but it had a vibrant brashness uncommon in other Asian cuisines. I knew right away that this was the kind of flavor I wanted in my own food. Something happens in certain ethnic cuisines that almost never does in European. The components of a dish may not taste all that good on their own. Put a bite of pad thai in your mouth, and the voices of the individual ingredients bellow on their own for a few moments before singing together in a harmonious, resounding chord. Fish sauce, lime juice, peanuts, eggs, and cilantro compete, then coalesce on the palate. It's an exciting tension followed quickly by a resolution—almost as if the cook is offering his diners a puzzle, and then the solution. Southeast Asian and Indian dishes best exhibit this tension and resolution.

Could this kind of effect be duplicated in food with a more European bent? I wondered.

The second turning point in my cuisine occurred when I went to work for Gray Kunz, the chef of the then-brand-new Lespinasse in New York. I was not the only French-trained cook intrigued by Southeast Asian flavors. Swiss-born Kunz had spent years in Asia, and his refined cuisine incorporated the many ingredients he had worked with there. His food was not merely delicious in the way a perfectly executed sole meunière hits the mark. Kunz's food was exciting. One day I paid close attention to a sauce I thought was outstanding, and I had an epiphany. The sauce was successful because it had a logical complexity, and all the elements countered one another. There was tension and contrast among the ingredients, but because each opposing ingredient had been painstakingly balanced, the sauce was neither too sweet, too sour, too salty, nor too bitter.

From the day I opened my first restaurant, Annabelle, in 1995, exciting flavors and taste balance have been the crux of my food. I've tweaked and honed and played around, just as any chef does. Some flavor combinations have resonated strongly for me, and these I come back to season after season, year after year. I think the food we served in the early days of Union Pacific was perceived to have a distinct Asian aesthetic. As my palate has broadened, so has my food, and today the accent is less specifically Asian.

My lifelong mission to uncover new ingredients continues. I visit Chinatown produce stands and Indian markets in Jackson Heights, Queens, and I've cultivated a network of purveyors who constantly introduce me to new ingredients. Every time I meet a new food, I am both humbled and inspired by the reminder that it would take three lifetimes to get to know all the ingredients of this world.

Why do I hunt so enthusiastically for new ingredients? What fascinates me about products like Indian mustard oil, sumac, and huitlacoche (a Mexican fungus)? It's simple: I'm a naturally curious person who never tires of new experiences. For my customers, novel flavors add another level of interest to their dining experiences. Just as some vacationers return to their favorite destination every year while others never

BITTER

go to the same place twice, most of my diners prefer surprise to familiarity. But to tell you the truth, not all the dishes at Union Pacific include exotic or unusual ingredients. Some, like my eggplant with fig soup, rest on a combination of common products rounded up at the Union Square Greenmarket just a few blocks from Union Pacific's front door. Yet, you'd probably find that my dishes made from everyday ingredients have the same personality—the same taste profile—as my dishes that contain unusual foods. How does this happen?

There is a thread that connects my menu's offerings, running through and stringing together dishes with vastly different-sounding names. The cohesiveness exists because when I create a new dish, I know the taste profile I want to achieve before a single raw ingredient is prepped. In a nutshell, I want forthright, expressive flavors that flank a balanced juxtaposition of sweet, sour, salty, and bitter tastes. Whether I'm fiddling with a lobster salad or developing a chilled fruit soup, I zero in on balance and big, stand-up-and-be-noticed flavors—an aesthetic similar to Southeast Asian food. Many Westerners are titillated by Thai and Vietnamese food. Ask them why, and I suspect most people would credit flavors experienced for the first time. In my opinion, newness is only half the phenomenon: the way flavors work together in Southeast Asian recipes is sheer magic. This premise, basic and empowering, is never far from my mind.

We use Western technique, not Asian, at Union Pacific. Tour our kitchen, and you'll see all the standard French tools and tricks being put to work: sizzling sauté pans, giant simmering stockpots, and cooks getting their sauces ultrasmooth by passing them through elongated strainers called "chinois."

My Union Pacific staff and I thoroughly enjoy the process of developing new dishes. Our menu is reprinted daily, so we have the ability to add and remove dishes whenever the mood strikes or product availability dictates. In a particularly productive week, we may come up with as many as 15 development-stage prototypes. Inspirations come to me from many sources and at many times of the day. Most often, a single ingredient is the catalyst. Our lamb supplier tells us the first spring shipment is two weeks away, for example, so we scramble to find a lamb preparation to showcase her superior product. One time it was rhubarb:

I was motivated by a conviction that rhubarb has been unfairly typecast as a pie filling. I was determined to use it in a savory dish. I paired a rhubarb purée with Copper River salmon, an extraordinary, enormous Alaskan fish available only for a few weeks in June and July. I dream about food pretty often; occasionally, I can harness the ideas that come to me when I'm sleeping and turn them into recipes.

Whatever the initial source of inspiration, we develop dishes according to a list of checkpoints of descending importance: balance, flavor integration, texture, and presentation. I don't mean to imply that how a dish looks isn't important—that's not the case at all. But we can always give a beauty makeover to a dish after it's cooked. Conversely, I'd have trouble making a gorgeous plate of food taste good after the fact. Besides, I've found that food that tastes the way I want it to needs very little cosmetic enhancement. Delicious food tends to be great-looking food.

If you were to walk in on a dish-development session in my kitchen, the conversation you'd hear would revolve primarily around the four tastes (bitter, sweet, salty, sour). "It's too sweet," my sous-chef might say. "Right; let's get some bitter in there," another cook will chime in. Or, I might be unhappy with the salt content of a particular dish. We balance the level of sour, salty, sweet, and bitter the way a record producer mixes tracks of guitar, bass, drums, and vocals in a song. To suit your personal preference, at times you may need to amplify one track, at other times, muffle another.

SOUR

A dish typically goes through several drafts before I introduce it to the menu, and much of the retooling process is about nailing the balance. For me, there is a pretty specific arrangement that I look for; I'll rework a dish until I hit it. Each of the four tastes has got to have a presence, but none can dominate. When I'm focused on balance, I look exclusively to my palate for approval.

My target arrangement is by no means universal. It's yet another subjective component of a highly personal cuisine. You might taste a sauce that I find to be perfect and decide that it's too acidic (sour). That's fine! No two personal cuisines are identical. Differences in what you and I perceive to be "balance" in a dish result from differences in genetics (your taste buds might be more sensitive to bitter substances, for example) and established preferences.

Once you've internalized these ideas, taste balance becomes easier to work into your everyday cooking. Your taste buds are your best friend here. Whether out of guilt or stage fright, many of the home cooks I know put off testing their creations until it's too late. My advice is to taste frequently and at every stage of cooking. Did I mention you should taste your food constantly? Tasting the food you make while you are making it is paramount to producing food you love. Sounds silly, but it is one of the most difficult habits to form. It's unfortunate that written recipes rarely instruct cooks to stop and check for balance. Do it anyway.

UMAMI

Umami is the phantom fifth flavor – some people detect it; some don't.
Taste the above ingredients and decide for yourself.

SPICY

Spicy is not actually a flavor but a chemical reaction that causes a sensation of fullness
that changes the mouthfeel of food.

If you're making a tomato sauce, sample one of the tomatoes before you start. What initial judgments can you make? Are the tomatoes super juicy and sweet? You may want to use a splash of vinegar or lemon juice eventually. Taste the sauce as it's simmering. Is it salty enough for you? Too salty? The only remedy for saltiness is dilution—in this case, you'd add more tomatoes or water. Be alert; stay focused. In better restaurant kitchens, you'll see tasting spoons standing in water baths to the side of every cook's station. It's also important for professional cooks to test dishes by consuming them whole, since a dish can taste quite different at bite two than at bite twenty. Desserts, in particular, have an uncanny ability to come across as pleasantly sweet at the outset but cloyingly so by the end.

Ingredients become like numbers in a mathematical equation when you're seeking taste equilibrium. Let's say you determine that your sauce is too tart. You'll want to add a little sweetness. But what sweet food to use? There are more than one hundred! In this book, I've provided lists of sweet, sour, salty, and bitter ingredients to give you suggestions. Over the years, I've come to rely on just a handful of ingredients to balance dishes. Narrowing down the universe of foods to a few that I know intimately has made me a more efficient cook. I use citrus fruits, tart fruits, and flavored vinegars for sour; seaweed, sea salt, and cured fish for salty; sugar, honey, and browning for sweet; and charred skins, mustard, and bitter greens like chicory for bitter. Although I have my favorites, I still experiment with new foods. In fact, one of the benefits of using the flavor system to cook is that you can experiment readily.

Perfect balance between the four tastes, of course, does not alone make a great recipe. Flavor brings food to life. Whereas taste happens on the tongue, aromas perceived in the nose are responsible for flavor and as much as 80 percent of what makes foods "taste" the way they do. Unlike taste balance, which for me is a hit-or-miss thing, flavor cannot be expressed as "right" or "wrong," "on" or "off." Think of reactions you've had to different perfumes. You can like a flavor (or flavor combination) or hate it; find it timid or overpowering; or think it's boring or bizarre. A flavor may evoke memories or emotions. I suggest you think about the four tastes quantitatively, but flavor qualitatively.

An analogy: when each of us gets dressed every day, we are more or less obliged to put on certain articles of clothing. A man will pick out a shirt, pants, and shoes. If one of those items is missing, he may get some strange looks at the office. Similarly, I don't consider any dish to be fully "dressed" until it is garbed with appropriate amounts of sweet, salty, sour, and bitter. After that, I'm tuned in to nuances of flavor. How they complement one another. How they contrast one another. Provoke. Pacify. Intrigue. Do the individual flavors come together to make a new flavor? All the details that flavor brings to the mix are like the colors, patterns, fabrics, and other design details that make an outfit work.

Which flavors go best together? You could spend a lifetime traveling the world in pursuit of a catalog of answers. There are tons of classic food pairings—apples and cinnamon, chocolate and bananas, tomatoes and basil, and champagne and caviar are familiar ones. In their book *Culinary Artistry*, Andrew Dornenburg and Karen Page came up with lists of tried-and-true "food pals." (Their book is full of valuable advice for cooking professionals, and I highly recommend it to anyone considering a kitchen career.) Food pairings are and have always been the most elusive culinary information I know of, perhaps because there are no clear right or wrong answers. I remember begging my CIA instructors for published resources. Unfortunately, *Culinary Artistry* and books like it didn't exist at the time.

Classic food pairings are a great source of inspiration. After all, they've become classic for a reason. But you'll be rewarded for your efforts to come up with unique combinations. Over the years, I've developed my own mental lists of "food pals." To my palate, celery flavors partner phenomenally with mackerel. I find that taro root and truffles, two earthy flavors, are natural bedfellows. Sometimes I'll update a classic food match by substituting one of the ingredients with a similar ethnic one. Tomatoes and basil were to my Italian childhood what peanut butter and marshmallow fluff were to some other people. Now I make a summer salad with local heirloom tomatoes and Thai basil (the recipe is on page 286).

In her review of Union Pacific, Ruth Reichl, editor-in-chief of *Gourmet* magazine and former restaurant reviewer for *The New York Times*, wrote that I "think of food in ways no one else does." I am still not sure if that was meant as a compliment, but it is exactly what I want you to do. Think outside the box. If you've never imagined chocolate outside its standard dessert context, challenge yourself to incorporate it into a savory dish. Unsweetened chocolate is unbeatable as a bitter note. (Many versions of Mexican mole sauce, by the way, contain unsweetened cocoa.) Think popcorn is just a movie snack? On page 314, the crispy texture of caramel popcorn contrasts nicely with creamy panna cotta. In desserts, experiment with spices, herbs, and other traditionally savory ingredients. There really are no right or wrong food associations. Only your imagination will limit the possibilities.

Once you settle on what flavors are going to commingle in a dish, you're left to decide how. Layering a single flavor in a dish is a strategy I use a lot, and one that anyone can pick up. Sometimes I want to feature a flavor prominently without having to work a big portion of it onto the finished plate. If anise flavor is what I want, I might use Pernod or licorice stick in the stock, make a fennel purée, and dust the plate with anise seed. It's a subtle way to drive home a flavor.

Texture comes next. A variety of textures is what I go for. A lot less guesswork is needed here. Since the flavor scheme has usually been determined before we get to thinking about texture, we pick the technique that will achieve the desired effect in the product. In Halibut with Young Ginger and Shallot Crackling on page 304, the buttery soft flesh of the halibut begs for a toothsome topping. Easy enough! I serve the fish with a generous sprinkling of crispy pan-fried shallots.

As you've probably gathered, creativity plays an enormously important role in my food. I thrive on it, and in turn a stream of new ideas allows me to serve food that jolts my customers' often-jaded taste buds and gives diners something to indulge in conversationally as well as gastronomically. But creativity for creativity's sake is never the point. A plate of esoteric ingredients that falls flat on the palate is just weird, not interesting. I don't award badges of success to dishes unless they wow me and at least a handful of guinea pigs. It's as simple as that.

We are spoiled at Union Pacific. We have consistent access to top-notch produce, spices, fish, and meat. I know that every cookbook reader has come across this piece of advice at least several times before, so I'll be quick: buy the best products you can find and afford. Yes, they will make a difference, and often a big one. Local farmers' markets are not only a reliable source for superior products but also a great way to support small-scale agriculture. Educate yourself about things like egg and beef grades, and buy free-range, organic chickens if you find, as I do, that their rich poultry flavor is worth the higher price.

Buy the best you can, but never let doubts about a product's quality stop you from cooking it with purpose! One of the secrets I want to share with you is that *any* ingredient can be turned into a delicious dish. In fact, there are no bad ingredients, just poorly conceived or executed dishes. Don't make an ingredient your fall guy the way a bad carpenter blames his tools. A bagged bunch of celery from a grocery store, balanced and flavored respectfully, has knockout potential. A great dish comes down to flavors. Taste the celery, recognize that it is bitter, and decide what you need to do to find its flavor sweet spot.

I have a respect for the seasonality of produce but not a dogged devotion to it: I'm not, in other words, a seasonal purist. For the most part, I am impressed by the quality of food that is hothoused in colder months or imported from warmer climates, and I am grateful that it's available. Two that come to mind are winter beefsteak tomatoes from Florida and citrus fruit shipped from California during the height of summer. I wouldn't shy away from a perfect nectarine just because it was grown in Mexico and just because it is November. There are some foods I can't get out of their natural seasons; many of these I anticipate eagerly every year. Ramps, morels, fava beans, soft-shell crabs, Nantucket bay scallops, heirloom tomatoes, and game like woodcock and hare are truly seasonal treats. Nab them when you see them!

Like any cook, I have my favorite ingredients. Some I have adored all my life, while others have revealed their usefulness only recently. Here are a few foods that are important to me, as well as a few that are less useful to me than they are to other cooks.

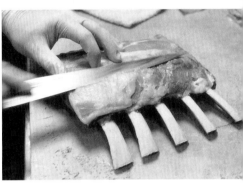

CITRUS. In my world, there are three basic spices: salt, white pepper, and citrus juice. All citrus fruits—lemons, limes, oranges, grapefruits, plus their lesser-known tropical cousins—are at least a little bit sour and tart ("tart" refers to astringency on the tongue). There is something about citrus that not only brightens and enlivens a dish but also primes the other ingredients. I think of citrus as that base layer of paint that goes on a canvas. Yuzu juice, the juice of a small Japanese orange, has an incredible fragrance that makes it one of my favorite sour agents. You can find bottles of yuzu juice at Japanese markets.

FISH. Night after night, fish represents the lion's share of the menu at Union Pacific. There are always a few fish appetizers, and at least half of the entrées are finfish or shellfish. It reflects the lighter, healthier way that people eat today.

For me, fish is the ultimate in diversity. There aren't many fish I don't enjoy working with. Each has its own personality. Black cod is ultrarich and becomes even more luxurious with fruit like pear. Mackerel has an assertive, fishy flavor that goes well with delicate celery. Skate, a relative of stingray, has a special ropy texture. With the incredible variety of flavors and textures that exist among species, fish are a cook's playground.

Another reason I favor fish is that it's very gratifying to work with pure, unadulterated products, an opportunity that poultry and larger animals don't present. Examining our fish for freshness, admiring their exterior markings, and filleting them ourselves make my staff and me feel privileged with a direct connection to the ocean.

BEEF. At 2 A.M. after a grueling night in the kitchen, I crave a cheeseburger like nothing else. And I'll never tire of the classic bistro dish *steak frites* (steak with french fries). As much as I enjoy eating beef, it's not nearly as much fun to work with as fish, poultry, game, or vegetables. Beef limits me to an abbreviated group of rich, dark flavors that will stand up to it. Furthermore, its fibrous texture doesn't permit a lot of manipulation.

OFFAL. Too many cooks overlook offal. It's a shame. Humble organs like liver, tongue, kidneys, and pig's trotters are absolutely packed with deep, deep flavor. Sure, these meats can come on strong, but countered with the right other foods, their flavors can be tamed. Try the recipe for chicken liver salad on page 124 to see what I mean. If for no other reason, appreciate offal for its super value.

CREAM. I cook with plenty of butter but almost no cream. In my opinion, cream is a bit of a culinary anachronism. In French and other dairy-loving cuisines, it's depended upon as a thickener to provide smooth texture and rich mouthfeel. Unfortunately, cream also masks flavor instead of amplifying it. In my kitchen, we rely on purées made from leek, roasted garlic, sweet onion, parsley, dill, tarragon, root vegetables like celery root and parsnips, butternut squash, fennel, mango, pineapple, corn, and ginger to thicken sauces, vinaigrettes, and vegetables. In addition to adding body, these ingredients layer in complexity and underscore nuances in flavor. Using fruit and vegetable purées and juices is an example of today's lighter methods, with a focus on fresh, vibrant flavors.

Ethnic ingredients that have become staples in my larder include Thai basil, uni (sea urchin), kaffir lime leaf, yuzu juice, miso, and fish sauce.

I get a rush from confronting an array of unfamiliar products. In some Chinese markets, there are as many as 30 types of greens for sale! In Latin American markets, bins are piled high with strange-looking hairy roots like ñame, batata, malanga, and yucca. Let your curiosity lead you to your city's ethnic markets. These days there are Chinatowns and ethnic markets of all kinds in the smallest cities. Recently I came across a wonderful Chinese district in Kansas City, Missouri. Start small. Pick out just one new ingredient, and buy it in quantity. Ask the salesperson about the item. Collect some ethnic food reference books, and consult them for guidance. Taste your ingredient. What is this food's personality? Is it tough, sour, velvety, or sweet? Cook it by a few methods and see what you get. Try sautéing it, sweating it, baking it, frying it, pickling it. The possibilities for your new discovery will become apparent.

The way you choose to cook an ingredient will greatly affect its flavor. Until a few years ago, I didn't fully realize just how much technique can nudge the flavor of something in one direction or another. If I'm working on a fish dish and need a bitter component to bring things into balance, I will char the skin of the fish. Sweating spring onions for a long time in a small amount of fat or liquid concentrates their natural sugars and transforms them completely. Acquainting yourself with the properties of different techniques may take some time, depending on your level of experience. Pay attention to how raw ingredients change as a result of the cooking method.

My personal cuisine has developed over 20 years, and it's still changing. I've had mentors along the way who have encouraged me to think independently (although I can't mention them without being reminded of the chefs who wished that I had been a little less curious). Because of the family I grew up in, cooking from my gut has always come naturally, and I'm thankful for it.

Do you cook from your gut? Let your nose and taste buds lead the way. Use recipes as guidelines, and let your instincts and passion take care of the rest. Improvise in the kitchen when you feel up to it. For some cooks, the transition may be awkward. Letting go of rules is difficult.

Try this as an experiment. Go into your kitchen and pull out your favorite pot or pan. Grab those onions sitting in the bottom drawer of your refrigerator. Peel and cut them into any shape you like. Heat the pan, put some butter in it, and when the butter has melted, add enough onions to just cover the bottom of the pan in a single layer. Season them with salt and pepper. Now peek into your fridge and cupboards and pull out your favorite sweet—maybe it's honey or port—and add some to the pan. Now locate your favorite sour, like lemon juice or maybe some fresh rhubarb from your garden. Chuck it into the pan. Let the flavors mingle for a few minutes. It's time to taste your work in progress. I mean really taste it! Put a big spoonful of it in your mouth and see what you've got. (Please don't burn your mouth, though; you'll need it for the rest of this experiment.) As you chew, think about what's going on in your mouth. What does your dish need next? Something bitter? OK, get out that jar of orange marmalade you never use and put some in. Go easy, though; orange marmalade is also quite sweet. How does it taste now? Does it please you? Or does it need more tweaking? You get the picture. You can do this. Take this active approach every time, and I mean *every* time, you cook. You will be amazed by the results.

This kind of cooking is rewarding in and of itself. When you cook from your gut, you engage all of your senses—your nose, mouth, ears, eyes, and fingers are all indulged and stimulated. Flavors and smells come into sharp focus. The food you create is tailored for you, and you're bound to love it.

Will your personal cuisine be like mine? Or will it be more like that of the chef you saw on TV last night? Will it remind you of your grandmother's cooking? (Maybe that's the last thing you want.) Know what? It doesn't matter. Let your personal cuisine emerge and be whatever it will.

CHAPTER 2
SOME TIPS
FOR USING THIS
BOOK

GROUND PEPPER. In my kitchen, we use white pepper almost exclusively. I find the flavor of black peppercorns to be a bit too assertive, and I use them only when I need a punch of heat. White peppercorns, which are nothing more than black peppercorns with their skins rubbed off, deliver just a hint of heat with a more refined flavor. Though the pepper called for in most of my recipes is simply "ground pepper," I strongly urge you to keep a peppermill (Peugeot's wooden 9-inch is my favorite peppermill) filled with white peppercorns on hand when you cook from this book. Filling peppermills with whole spices like fenugreek and coriander is another trick.

SALT. I recommend that you use sea salt as your everyday salt. Fine sea salt has none of the funny metallic taste common in mined "table salt" (do a side-by-side taste test to see what I mean). As an added bonus, it dissolves faster: when you add sea salt to a sauce, you'll notice the increase immediately. With other salts, you have to wait for the salt to dissolve before adding more, or risk oversalting. Kosher salt, in fact, is best for drawing out moisture from proteins because it was designed to dissolve as slowly as possible. Sea salt also has a lower sodium content than table salt; it's a less salty salt. Keep it in a shallow bowl or wooden container near your oven rather than in a shaker, and use your fingers to do the sprinkling.

BUTTER. Swear off salted butter right now. Permanently. You want to be the one who controls how much salt goes into your food, not some manufacturer. Land O'Lakes sweet (unsalted) butter is an excellent, high-butterfat supermarket brand.

SEASONING. I guess I can't say it enough: put your taste buds to work when you cook! I have tried to write in many seasoning pit stops. Don't wait for a cue, though: taste and season things frequently with salt, pepper, lemon juice, sugar, or whatever you feel the food's lacking. The only time to season conservatively is when you're making a reduction. Then it's best to wait until the liquid has reduced to its final volume and concentration before seasoning.

EQUIPMENT. Most of the equipment in this book is basic and low-tech, but there are a few pieces of specialized equipment that will come in handy as you cook your way through *Flavor*.

HATE

LOVE

CHINOIS. A chinois is an elongated, cone-shaped strainer with fine holes. We pass many of our soups and sauces through chinois strainers to get them ultrasmooth. Some come with their own stands.

FLAMEPROOF ROASTING PAN. A large roasting pan that can go in the oven and tolerate the direct heat of a stovetop is great when you want to turn pan juices into a sauce. Without one, you'll have to transfer the juices into a saucepan, and if the yummy browned bits stick to the bottom of the roasting pan, you'll have to go through the trouble of scraping them up with a little warm tap water.

FOOD MILL. Once ubiquitous in American kitchens, manual food mills have been largely replaced by food processors. It's a shame, because food mills can do things that food processors can't. In a food mill, food is churned through a layer of fine holes to separate tough solids from liquids or purées. There is no better way, for example, to juice pomegranate seeds. A potato ricer is a type of food mill.

MEAT THERMOMETER. Seems like a fancy professional tool, right? Actually, a meat thermometer is more essential to the amateur cook than the pro. One of the things career cooks master quickly is learning to gauge meat's internal temperature by pressing the flesh. If you don't know how to do this, estimating doneness can be very hard without a thermometer. I like instant-read, digital models.

SOUS VIDE MACHINE OR TOP-QUALITY PLASTIC WRAP. Most of the poultry dishes I've chosen to share are cooked sous vide— that is, wrapped in plastic wrap or sealed in a vacuum-packing machine and then gently poached. If using plastic wrap without the help of a sous vide machine, it's important to use a plastic wrap that really clings. In testing the recipes for this book, we found that cheaper plastic wraps sometimes come loose in hot water—a very bad thing!

MICRO PLANE CITRUS ZESTER. I know that a lot of home cooks use box graters to make lemon zest. And for some purposes, a grater works just fine. However, I'm going to recommend that any zest you use for my recipes be very finely grated—thin enough so as not to be annoyingly toothsome in the final dish. Invest in a good micro plane zester, which looks a bit like a woodworking rasp. They produce very tender filaments of zest. Best of all, even a top-of-the-line zester is cheap!

FISH BROWNING. You'll see that for most of the fish recipes, I ask you to season only one side of the fish with salt and pepper before the fish goes in a hot pan. The reason for this is that salt draws out moisture, and you want to keep the surface of the fish being cooked as dry as possible to maximize caramelization. Season the first side with salt and pepper and move the fish right away into that hot pan, seasoned side down. When it's time to flip, dab off beads of moisture from the top side with a wadded paper towel, season the top side with salt and pepper, and flip quickly. Another important step is to be sure the fish is room temperature to start with. Cold fish will release moisture into the pan when cooked and will also cool the pan itself.

NONREACTIVE MATERIALS. I use a lot of citrus juice and vinegar. When working with anything acidic, use mixing bowls and cooking pans that will not react chemically with acid—the result can be a funky, metallic taste. Nonreactive materials include glass, ceramic, stainless steel, and plastic. The prime culprits in the reactive category are aluminum and copper.

INGREDIENT SOURCES. Stumped by an ingredient? I have chosen not to weigh down the ingredient lists with shopping tips. Instead, you'll find lots of helpful information on finding and buying unusual ingredients in the Ingredient Guide with Sources. It starts on page 330.

PREPPING. Some cookbooks advise you to have all your ingredients peeled, cut, and otherwise prepped before you begin a recipe. In professional kitchens, we call this *"doing your mise en place."* I ask you to use your best judgment; it doesn't always make sense to do all the peeling and dicing ahead of time. For example, when making Calamari with Coconut Curry and Green Papaya (page 86), you'll save time by getting the rice on the heat first, then using the 30 minutes it steams to prep the papaya, apple, lemongrass, and calamari. Wait until the end of the recipe to chop the cilantro. Herbs should be cut seconds before using them because their aromas are volatile and dissipate quickly. The more delicate the herb's leaf, the more this holds true.

PART II
RECIPES

CHAPTER 3
APPETIZERS

HEIRLOOM TOMATOES WITH ORANGE ZEST

Minimalist dishes like this one, believe it or not, take a lot of discipline to create. As a chef, the urge is always to create, to layer, to complicate. But late-summer heirloom tomatoes are so dazzling in appearance and flavor that more than just a little of anything would be an insult.

- 4 large heirloom tomatoes, sliced thin
- Finely grated zest of 2 large or 3 small oranges
- 1 1/2 tablespoons sherry vinegar
- Coarse sea salt and ground pepper to taste

Shingle tomato slices on plates. Scatter orange zest over tomatoes and dress with vinegar, salt, and pepper.

- sour
- salty
- sweet
- bitter

10 mins
TOTAL TIME

10 mins
ACTIVE TIME

DIFFICULTY

4
PORTIONS

RIESLING
KABINETT

SWEET & SOUR TAMARIND SHRIMP ON ROSEMARY SKEWERS

Marinating foods is an easy way to saturate them with flavor and change their texture. You can get away with using only two or three ingredients in a marinade if those ingredients themselves are complex and have good balance. Goofing around at home one day, I created this quick recipe for grilled shrimp by grabbing what I could find in my refrigerator: sweet-sour orange marmalade and tart tamarind. But what would lend a bitter note? The peppery bite of arugula seemed perfect.

- 6 thick, woody branches fresh rosemary
- 18 large or 30 medium raw shrimp, shelled and deveined
- 1/4 cup liquid tamarind concentrate, or 1 tablespoon tamarind paste mashed with 3 tablespoons hot water
- 1/4 cup orange marmalade
- 1/4 cup extra-virgin olive oil
- 1/8 teaspoon salt
- Ground pepper to taste
- 1 bunch arugula

1. Pick off the rosemary leaves near the base of each branch. To skewer the shrimp, place shrimp flat on their sides on a cutting board so that they look like letter *C*s. Insert a rosemary branch through the tail end of the first shrimp (the bottom of the *C*) and push it through to pierce the head end (the top of the *C*). Continue skewering the shrimp, dividing them evenly among the skewers. Place skewers in a baking dish or on a large plate.

2. Place tamarind concentrate or softened paste in a small bowl. Add orange marmalade and olive oil and stir to combine. Brush skewered shrimp with mixture. Cover with plastic and refrigerate for 15 minutes.

3. Light a grill or preheat a grill pan over high heat. Season marinated shrimp with salt and pepper. Place as many skewers as will fit on grill. Cook until shrimp are firm to the touch and opaque, 2 to 3 minutes per side. Repeat with remaining skewers.

4. Spread arugula over a large serving dish. Arrange shrimp skewers over arugula. Serve immediately.

- sour
- salty
- sweet
- bitter

35 mins
TOTAL TIME

35 mins
ACTIVE TIME

DIFFICULTY

4
PORTIONS

CHENIN BLANC

CLAMS WITH GREEN ONIONS, NORI & SESAME

I've been eating clams all my life. They were brought home on Fridays for pasta sauce and eaten raw with lemon juice at holiday feasts and fairs. Clams are sweet, briny, and just chewy enough to make me salivate as I write this recipe. Widely available and ridiculously inexpensive, they make a great appetizer or light entrée all year round.

- 24 littleneck or cherrystone clams in their shells
- 2 tablespoons cornmeal
- 1/2 sheet sushi nori (square-shaped seaweed used to roll sushi)
- 2 teaspoons sesame seeds
- 15 scallions, roots trimmed, white and pale green sections cut into 2-inch lengths, plus 2 tablespoons finely sliced dark green scallion tops
- 2 tablespoons light (low-sodium) soy sauce or 1 teaspoon regular soy sauce
- 1/4 cup plus 3 tablespoons rice wine vinegar
- 1/3 cup mirin
- Several drops extra-virgin olive oil

TECHNIQUE
CLEANING CLAMS

Have you ever chewed on a grainy clam? It's probably right up there with overcooked, tough lobster on the Worst Shellfish Experiences list. Clams live on ocean floors and ingest quite a bit of sand and other grit, so before cooking them it's important to persuade the critters to expel any funky stuff. "Chipping" clams is easy: place live clams in a large bowl and cover them with cold water. Add 2 tablespoons of cornmeal and let stand for 1 hour, shaking the bowl gently every 15 minutes or so. Fooled into thinking they're being fed, the clams will purge any sand—you'll see it at the bottom of the bowl. Lift the clams gingerly from the water so as to avoid stirring up the settled sand.

- sour
- salty
- **sweet**
- bitter

1. Chip clams for 1 hour (see sidebar). Remove clams from water and keep in refrigerator.

2. Light a gas burner or heat an electric burner until hot. Lightly grasp a nori sheet with tongs and pass quickly several times through flame or over electric burner, stopping when nori gives off a faint toasted seaweed odor. The nori should not change in form or color. Coarsely chop nori and set aside.

3. Heat a sauté pan over medium-low heat and add sesame seeds. Toast seeds, shaking pan frequently, just until fragrant and golden brown, 3 to 5 minutes. In a spice mill or mortar with pestle, grind nori and sesame seeds together until crushed fine. Transfer to a small bowl and stir in chopped dark green scallions.

4. In a stockpot, combine soy sauce, vinegar, mirin, and 1/4 cup water. Bring to a simmer and add 2-inch white and pale green scallion pieces. Cook until crisp-tender, about 3 minutes. Add clams to stockpot, cover, and cook just until all the clam shells have opened, about 8 minutes. Stir midway through so that clams buried at the bottom get an equal shot of steam. Discard any clams that do not open.

5. Put 6 clams in each of 4 shallow bowls. Distribute scallions and ladle cooking broth into the bowls. Dash a few drops of olive oil on the surface of the broth. Sprinkle with sesame-nori-scallion mixture. Serve hot.

1 hr 45 mins
TOTAL TIME

35 mins
ACTIVE TIME

DIFFICULTY

4
PORTIONS

RIESLING

CALAMARI WITH PUMPKIN SEEDS & A BUTTERNUT SQUASH RELISH

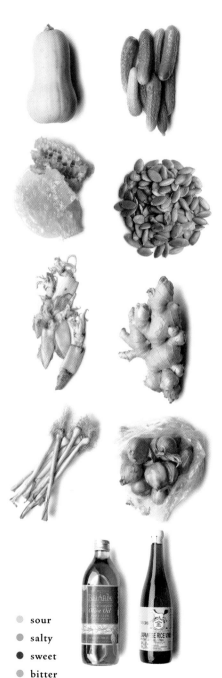

Quick-cooking in a hot pan or deep-fryer has been the tried-and-true method for years. I've found that the texture of calamari varies a lot, so to accommodate tougher squid I've had to adjust my cooking method. Try cooking calamari the "long" way: after a prolonged, gentle sweat, the flesh is buttery soft and sweet.

- 1/2 cup plus 4 tablespoons grapeseed or olive oil
- 1 cup peeled, diced butternut squash (about 1/4 medium squash)
- 1 small cucumber, peeled and diced
- 1/4 cup plus 2 tablespoons rice wine vinegar
- 1/4 cup plus 1 tablespoon honey
- Salt and ground pepper to taste
- 1 tablespoon minced fresh ginger
- 1/4 teaspoon minced fresh garlic
- 1 pound squid, cleaned and cut into rings about 1/2-inch thick, tentacles separated
- 3 shallots, minced
- 1 tablespoon minced fresh parsley
- 1/4 cup salted pumpkin seeds (also called "pepitas")

1. In a sauté pan over medium heat, warm 2 tablespoons of the oil. Add squash to pan and sauté 3 minutes. Add cucumber and sauté another 3 to 5 minutes, until squash is firm but no longer crunchy. Add 1/4 cup plus 1 tablespoon rice wine vinegar and cook 2 minutes, stirring. Add honey and cook until liquid has thickened and squash is tender. Separate the relish from its cooking liquid by straining the pan's contents into a saucepan. Taste relish and season with salt and pepper.

2. Place the saucepan with the cooking liquid over medium heat, add ginger, and cook for 2 minutes, stirring frequently, until liquid is reduced to a syrupy glaze. Transfer mixture to a blender, add garlic and remaining 1 tablespoon vinegar, and blend until smooth. With motor running, pour 1/2 cup oil through the blender's feed hole in a slow, steady stream to produce an emulsified vinaigrette. Add salt and pepper to taste.

3. Lay the calamari rings on a flat surface and salt on both sides. In a sauté pan over low heat, warm the remaining 2 tablespoons oil. Add the calamari and cook just until rings have turned from milky white to bright, opaque white, about 10 minutes, being careful not to overcook. Remove calamari from pan, leaving oil in pan. Increase heat to medium, add shallots, season with salt and pepper, cover pan, and sweat for 2 minutes. Remove pan from heat and add calamari, squash relish, parsley, and the vinaigrette. Toss gently to coat all ingredients. Center one quarter of the mixture on each of 4 small plates. Finish by garnishing with pumpkin seeds.

- sour
- salty
- sweet
- bitter

1 hr
TOTAL TIME

1 hr
ACTIVE TIME

DIFFICULTY

4
PORTIONS

PINOT
AUXERROIS

CHICKEN WINGS WITH APRICOT-TRUFFLE VINAIGRETTE

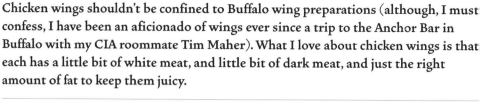

Chicken wings shouldn't be confined to Buffalo wing preparations (although, I must confess, I have been an aficionado of wings ever since a trip to the Anchor Bar in Buffalo with my CIA roommate Tim Maher). What I love about chicken wings is that each has a little bit of white meat, and little bit of dark meat, and just the right amount of fat to keep them juicy.

- 1/4 cup chopped dried apricots, preferably Turkish
- 2 heads Belgian endive, halved lengthwise, cored, and sliced widthwise into 1/2-inch strips
- 1 teaspoon fresh lemon juice
- Salt and ground pepper to taste
- 2 tablespoons sherry vinegar
- 1/2 cup black truffle juice
- 1/4 cup extra-virgin olive oil
- 1/2 cup corn oil
- 16 to 20 chicken wings, preferably boneless
- Fresh tarragon leaves to yield 1 teaspoon when chopped, held whole

1. Place apricots in a medium saucepan and add 2 cups water. Bring to a boil, reduce heat, and simmer until liquid is a thick syrup, 30 to 40 minutes. Proceed with step 2 while apricot syrup cooks.

2. In a mixing bowl, toss together endive, lemon juice, and salt and pepper. Hold aside.

3. Stir vinegar into the apricot syrup and heat just until mixture is warmed through. Remove pan from heat and stir in truffle juice and olive oil. Season to taste with salt and pepper.

4. In a high-sided sauté pan, heat corn oil until very hot. Season chicken wings on one side with salt and pepper. Working in batches, pan-fry wings until deep golden brown, 3 to 5 minutes for first side. Season just before flipping, then cook 3 to 5 minutes on second side. Drain on paper towels.

5. Chop the tarragon. In a large bowl, toss together the endive salad, apricot-truffle vinaigrette, tarragon, and chicken wings. Transfer to individual bowls. Serve immediately, while wings are still hot but endive is still raw and crunchy.

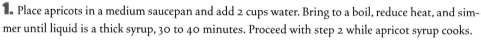

- sour
- salty
- sweet
- bitter

1hr
TOTAL TIME

1hr
ACTIVE TIME

DIFFICULTY

4
PORTIONS

MEDIUM-
BODIED
CHARDONNAY

BERGAMOT & INDIAN LIME PICKLE CURED SALMON

TECHNIQUE CURING

Curing is a whole family of time-honored
preservation tricks. Salt-curing, air-drying,
brining, smoking, pickling—yep, they're all
curing techniques. Each was developed in
a different region of the world to deal with
a very universal culinary challenge: organic
decomposition. Depending on the method
used, curing's effect on flavor can be gentle
(cured salmon is just a richer, saltier version
of fresh salmon) or radical (the flavor of olives
is transformed completely in brine). My favorite
of the bunch is probably pickling. At Union
Pacific, we pickle all kinds of vegetables—
squash blossoms, ramps, garlic...you name it!
Sometimes I'll add chopped pickles when
a dish is lacking acid, and I love to use some
pickling liquids in sauces. Turn to page 248
for a recipe for basic vegetable pickles.

- sour
- salty
- **sweet**
- bitter

The method of curing fish was developed centuries ago as a way to preserve fishermen's catches. But despite the fact that everyone has a refrigerator, curing remains popular because of its ability to impart flavor to proteins. Curing fish concentrates the fat through elimination of moisture, making the flesh exceedingly tender. My version incorporates strong citrus flavors: bergamot, the small orange that flavors Earl Grey tea, and Indian lime pickle.

- 1 1/4 cups sugar
- 1/2 cup kosher salt
- 1/4 cup brewed Earl Grey or other bergamot-flavored tea
- 1/4 cup Indian lime pickle (I recommend Patak's mild)
- 1 tablespoon dry sherry
- 2 tablespoons chopped fresh oregano
- Zest of 1 orange
- 1 large skinless, boneless salmon fillet, 10 to 12 ounces, preferably a thick center cut
- 1 cup plain yogurt
- 1/2 medium cucumber, peeled and finely diced
- 1 tablespoon chopped fresh dill, plus several sprigs for garnish
- Salt and ground pepper to taste

1. In a large mixing bowl, combine sugar, kosher salt, tea, Indian lime pickle, sherry, oregano, and orange zest. Blend well. Shoot for a consistency similar to wet cement; add a bit of water to the cure if needed.

2. Place salmon on a sheet tray lined with parchment or wax paper. Rub cure into one side of salmon fillet, covering all visible flesh. Place cure side down on sheet tray. Cover top side with generous amount of cure. Refrigerate uncovered for at least 24 hours. The texture of the flesh should be melt-in-your-mouth tender. Let it cure for additional hours if not ready.

3. Combine yogurt, cucumber, and chopped dill in a small mixing bowl. Mix gently. Season with salt and pepper to taste. Refrigerate for at least 30 minutes.

4. Remove salmon from sheet tray, scrape off cure with a butter knife, and rinse salmon under cold water for 10 minutes. Pat dry. Using a very sharp knife, slice fillet on the bias into very thin, transparent pieces. (This takes some practice. Don't worry; your salmon will taste great even if the slices are a bit thicker.)

5. To serve, pool some of the yogurt-dill sauce on each plate. Drape 6 to 8 slices of salmon on each plate. Garnish with dill sprigs.

24hrs 40mins

TOTAL TIME*

40mins

ACTIVE TIME

DIFFICULTY

4

PORTIONS

CHAMPAGNE

* 24 hours
for curing

DUNGENESS CRAB WITH AVOCADO & SAUCE VIERGE

For cooks, there are two groups of crabs. One group is best suited for flavoring stocks and sauces, but their meat isn't top-notch eating meat. Blue crab (except soft crabs) and spider crab fall in this group. The second group is what cooks turn to for chunks of sweet, delicious crabmeat: Dungeness, king, snow, stone, and Peekytoe crabs make good eating, but their shells are worthless. Dungeness crab, a gem of the Pacific Northwest waters, has a rich shellfish flavor and, in my opinion, the best yield per crab of any in this group.

TECHNIQUE
BOILING CRABS

Whenever you boil your own crabs, do it in highly flavored water. Salt, vinegar, veggies, and bay leaves are all good stuff to throw in.

- 1 pound Dungeness crabmeat from about 4 boiled crabs, carefully picked over (you can substitute the meat of stone or Peekytoe crabs [see sidebar on boiling crabs] or use packaged lump crabmeat)
- 3 tablespoons minced shallots
- 1 teaspoon chopped fresh parsley
- Juice of 2 lemons
- Salt and ground pepper to taste
- 2 ripe avocados
- 1/2 cup extra-virgin olive oil
- 1 heaping teaspoon chopped fines herbes (a mixture of chervil, chives, parsley, and tarragon), or any one of or combination of the 4 herbs
- Zest of 1 lemon

1. Reserve several larger pieces of crab for garnish. Mix together remaining crabmeat with 2 tablespoons of the shallots, parsley, and half the lemon juice. Taste and season with salt and pepper.

2. Peel the avocados and scrape fresh into a small mixing bowl. With a fork, mash well the avocado with remaining lemon juice. Season with salt and pepper.

3. In a small mixing bowl, make a sauce vierge by whisking together oil, remaining 1 tablespoon shallots, fines herbes, and lemon zest. Season to taste with pepper. Mound a quarter of the avocado mixture in individual shallow bowls, top with a quarter of the crab mixture, and pour 2 tablespoons of sauce vierge over the whole thing. Display reserved crabmeat on top. Serve chilled or at room temperature.

- sour
- salty
- ● sweet
- bitter

45 mins
TOTAL TIME

25 mins
ACTIVE TIME

DIFFICULTY

4
PORTIONS

CHENIN BLANC

TAYLOR BAY SCALLOPS WITH UNI & MUSTARD OIL

1

MUSTARD OIL

2

TOMATO WATER

3

UNI

4

SCALLOPS

○ sour

● salty

● sweet

● bitter

No dish encapsulates the theme of this book better than this one does. It's the result of inspiration from great ingredients (the sweetest, freshest bay scallops I've ever tasted) and trial-and-error experimentation during my first days as a head chef. Scallops are sweet, tomato water is sour, uni is salty, and mustard is bitter. When you slurp one of these back in one go, you see the result of balance and integration. At first it's chaos in the mouth. Slowly, the flavors flirt, mingle, and finally coalesce. They form an amalgam of flavor that isn't scallop, urchin, tomatoes, or mustard, but a whole greater than the sum of its parts.

- 4 overripe tomatoes, coarsely chopped
- 1 teaspoon sea salt
- 2 teaspoons mirin
- Pinch cayenne pepper
- 4 cranks freshly ground pepper in a mill
  Crushed ice, for presentation
- 20 bay scallops in their shells, shucked, shells rinsed well and reserved, or 5 large "dry" sea scallops (see Scallop Classifications on page 163), cut into quarters, plus 20 oyster, clam, or mussel shells
- 20 lobes of sea urchin (also "uni")
- 1 tablespoon mustard oil, or more to taste
- Coarsely ground black mustard seed

1. In a food processor, pulse tomatoes with sea salt until chunky. Line a strainer or coffeemaker basket with a coffee filter and transfer tomatoes to the coffee filter. Set strainer over a large nonreactive bowl or coffeemaker carafe. Refrigerate this contraption at least 12 hours: the tomatoes' intensely flavored, clear juices will filter into the bowl. To the tomato water, add mirin, cayenne pepper, and ground pepper.

2. Cover a dish with crushed ice. (If serving this as an appetizer, use dinner plates. A large serving tray or tiered platter would work well if these are to be served as hors d'oeuvres.) For an individual appetizer, arrange 5 shells in a ring on the ice. Place a scallop (or piece of scallop) and uni lobe side by side in each shell. Spoon seasoned tomato water into each shell to cover the shellfish, 1 1/2 to 2 teaspoons per shell. Drizzle several drops of mustard oil over each, and garnish with a pinch of black mustard seed. Serve immediately.

12hrs 45mins
TOTAL TIME

45mins

ACTIVE TIME

DIFFICULTY

4

PORTIONS

GRÜNER
VELTLINER

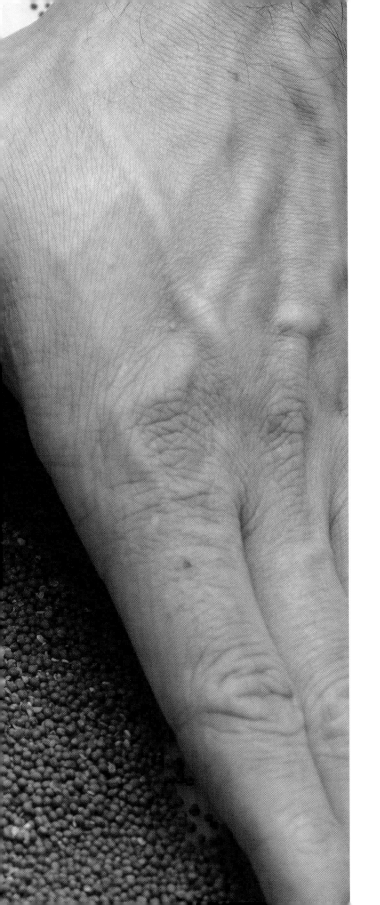

2
TOMATO
WATER

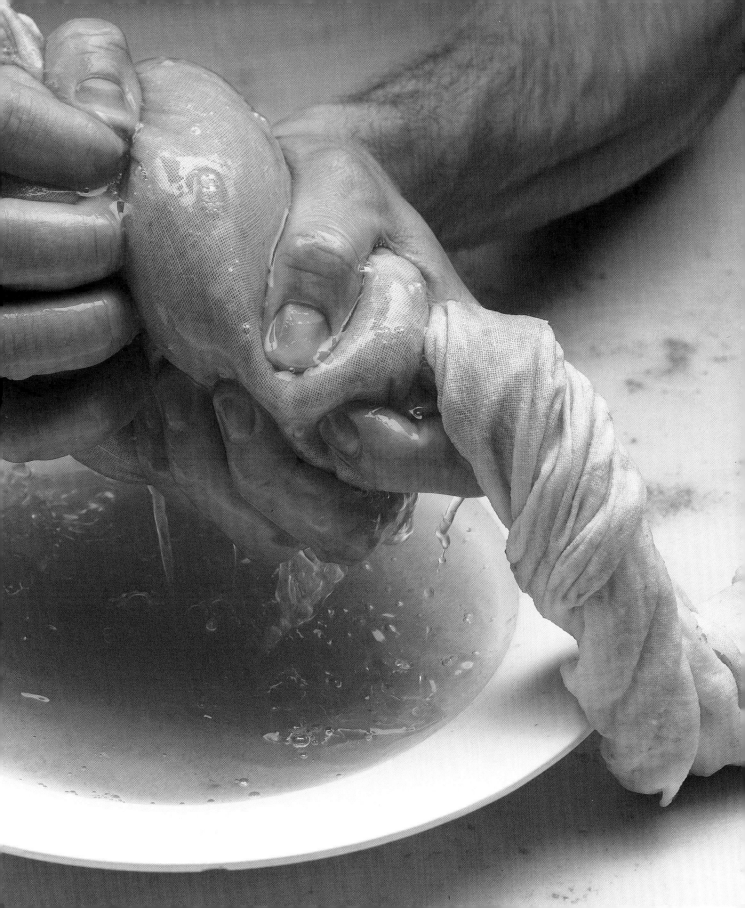

3
UNI

4
SCALLOPS

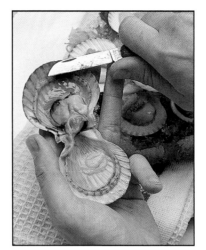

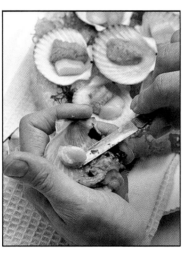

68   **FLAVOR** APPETIZERS

SHRIMP IN SPICED PHYLLO WITH TOMATO CHUTNEY

Shrimp are extremists. They do best when either barely seasoned or flavored powerfully. These are flavored powerfully.

- 4 tablespoons (1/2 stick) unsalted butter
- 1 teaspoon finely chopped fresh ginger
- 2 teaspoons finely chopped shallot
- 3/4 cup finely chopped tomatoes
- 1 1/2 teaspoons sugar
- 1 teaspoon fresh lime juice
- 1/4 cup chopped fresh cilantro
- 1/4 teaspoon salt
- 10 hazelnuts, shelled
- 4 sheets phyllo dough
- 2 teaspoons garam masala
- 12 medium (21 to 26 per pound) raw shrimp, shelled and deveined

1. Melt 2 tablespoons of the butter over medium heat. Add ginger and shallots and sauté for 2 minutes. Add tomatoes, sugar, lime juice, cilantro, and salt, and cook until sauce is thickened, stirring frequently. Taste the chutney and add more lime juice or salt if desired. (The chutney can be made 2 days in advance and refrigerated.)

2. Preheat oven to 375°F.

3. Heat a sauté pan over medium-high heat. Add hazelnuts and cook, shaking pan continuously, until they look and smell toasted, 5 minutes. Use a kitchen towel to gently rub skins off. Finely grind cooled nuts.

4. Melt the remaining 2 tablespoons butter. Roll out a sheet of phyllo onto a clean counter, and brush with half of the melted butter. Keep phyllo pile covered with a damp tea towel to prevent it from drying out. Sprinkle with half the garam masala and half the ground nuts. Place second phyllo sheet squarely over first. Brush with butter, saving a bit to be used later, and sprinkle with remaining garam masala and hazelnuts. Cut phyllo stack crosswise into 8 equal strips. (The strips should measure 1 to 2 inches in width.) Place a shrimp at the end of a strip and roll it up, changing the direction as necessary to totally envelop the shrimp. Repeat with remaining shrimp, and place rolls seam side down on a lightly greased baking sheet. Dab tops of rolls with butter. Bake until golden brown, 8 to 10 minutes.

5. Dollop some chutney over each roll and serve right away.

- sour
- salty
- **sweet**
- bitter

50 mins
TOTAL TIME

40 mins
ACTIVE TIME

DIFFICULTY

4
PORTIONS

RIESLING
KABINETT

CEVICHE OF TUNA, SWEET ONIONS & LIME

In the most traditional ceviches, chunks of fish are marinated in citrus juice, a process that changes the fish's texture pretty radically. I've reinterpreted things just a bit by marinating onions in lime and then dousing thin slices of tuna with the citrusy onions; this way, the fish stays closer to raw. Think of a cross between Japanese sashimi (thin slices of raw fish) and South American ceviche.

- 1 1/2 sweet onions, peeled, halved, and finely sliced
- 1/2 cup fresh lime juice (about 4 limes)
- 1/4 cup plus 1 tablespoon sugar
- 1 cup kosher salt for blanching
- 2 bunches fresh cilantro, leaves only
- Salt and ground pepper to taste
- 12 ounces sashimi-grade tuna, sliced into paper-thin rounds
- Extra-virgin olive oil to garnish
- 1/4 cup cilantro sprouts or picked cilantro leaves

1. Place the onions in a small nonreactive bowl and cover with lime juice. Marinate at room temperature for at least 1 hour.

2. Make a simple syrup: in a small saucepan, combine sugar with 1/4 cup water and place over medium heat. Stir to dissolve the sugar and bring to a boil. Remove pan from heat and set aside.

3. Fill a pot with water, bring to a boil, and add 1/2 cup kosher salt. Prepare an ice bath in a bowl and stir into it the remaining 1/2 cup kosher salt. When hot water has returned to a rolling boil, add cilantro leaves and cook 1 minute, until just tender and still bright green. Drain immediately and submerge cilantro in the ice bath for 2 minutes. Gather cilantro into a clump and squeeze as much water out of the leaves as possible. Put the cilantro in a blender and start motor. Pour simple syrup through the blender's feed hole, adding just enough to turn the cilantro into a purée and pausing as necessary to scrape cilantro off sides of blender. The resulting cilantro syrup should be pleasantly sweet, bright green, shiny, and perfectly smooth. Season syrup with salt and pepper.

4. Salt and pepper the fish and cover plates with a single layer of fish slices. Scatter the onions with their lime juice over the tuna. (Where the lime contacts the fish, the fish will turn opaque, making it appear cooked.) Drizzle cilantro syrup over the fish (you may have extra), and scatter the sprouts or cilantro over the entire dish. Serve immediately.

TECHNIQUE CEVICHE

Citric acid has the ability to turn soft, translucent proteins opaque and firm. Fish doused with lime juice looks cooked when in fact it is quite raw. It's a classic South American preparation for fish and shellfish that is now common the world over. I love making ceviches because they combine my favorite protein—fish—with citrus, one of my favorite flavor families.

- sour
- salty
- **sweet**
- bitter

1hr 15mins
TOTAL TIME

1hr
ACTIVE TIME

DIFFICULTY

4
PORTIONS

RIESLING
HALBTROCKEN

TUNA TARTARE
WITH YUZU & WASABI

This may come as a surprise: the best-tasting tuna is not colored solid ruby red, but is rippled with white swaths of fat—a fact that has been the secret of sushi chefs and connoisseurs for too long. A fatty tuna like bluefin should be chosen for this dish, as its richness will mellow the heat of the wasabi. Yuzu is a small Japanese citrus fruit, and its juice is a staple in Union Pacific's kitchen. It is the Normandy sea salt of citrus juices!

- 1/2 mango, peeled
- 8 ounces fresh pineapple (presliced by your grocer or from about 1/2 medium pineapple)
- 1 to 2 teaspoons wasabi paste
- 2 tablespoons yuzu juice, or 1 tablespoon grapefruit juice plus 1 tablespoon lime juice
- 1 teaspoon fish sauce
- Pinch cayenne pepper
- Pinch salt
- 12 ounces sashimi-grade tuna, skinned and cut into 1/2-inch dice
- Ground pepper
- 1/2 cucumber, peeled, seeded, and cut into thin squares 1/4-inch by 1/4-inch
- Small fresh cilantro sprigs to garnish

1. Cut flesh from mango half into small (about 1/4-inch) dice. Measure and reserve 3 tablespoons of mango scraps.

2. Separate about one-third of the pineapple and cut into small dice, the same size as the mango dice. Combine diced mango and diced pineapple in a bowl and toss to combine.

3. Coarsely chop remaining pineapple and place in a blender along with reserved mango scraps and 1 teaspoon of the wasabi paste. Purée until smooth. Add yuzu juice (or grapefruit juice plus lime juice), fish sauce, cayenne pepper, and salt. Whir to combine. Taste. Purée should be tangy and pleasantly sweet; incorporate more mango for sweetness if necessary.

4. Place diced tuna in a bowl and season with salt and pepper. Add the pineapple-yuzu purée, diced mango, and diced cucumber, and toss to coat. Plate immediately: in the center of a plate, make a circle with a quarter of the tuna. If you have a round cookie cutter or ring mold, use it to build your stack. Place tiny dots of wasabi paste in a random pattern over the tuna. Spoon some diced mango and pineapple over the fish, and layer cucumber squares on top of the fruit. Garnish with the cilantro sprigs. Assemble 3 more appetizers and serve immediately.

- sour
- salty
- sweet
- bitter

1 hr
TOTAL TIME

1 hr
ACTIVE TIME

DIFFICULTY

4
PORTIONS

RIESLING
KABINETT

Wasabi is a fresh root that grows in cold streams, not a pale green powder in a can.

Wasabi is grated on a piece of dried shark or stingray skin glued to a board.

CEVICHE OF DIVER SEA SCALLOPS WITH TAMARIND & POPCORN

Popcorn with raw fish? Believe it or not, spiced popcorn is served as a side in ceviche bars throughout Ecuador and Peru. Its crisp crunch is a great textural counterpoint to the soft flesh of raw fish and shellfish. The cumin that dusts the popcorn in this ceviche lends an earthiness reminiscent of tobacco that balances tart, bright tamarind and the natural sweetness of sea scallops.

- 1 tablespoon dark miso or soy sauce
- 1/2 tablespoon liquid tamarind concentrate
- 1 teaspoon honey
- 1 tablespoon fresh lime juice (about 1 lime)
- 2 tablespoons extra-virgin olive oil
- 8 large "dry" diver sea scallops (see Scallop Classifications on page 163)
- 2 scallions, dark green parts only
- 2 tablespoons popcorn kernels
- 3/4 teaspoon ground cumin
- Salt to taste
- Mustard oil to taste

1. Make the marinade by whisking together miso, tamarind, honey, lime juice, and 1 tablespoon of the olive oil in a bowl.

2. Slice each scallop thinly to make 1/8-inch-thick rounds. Place scallop slices in a shallow glass container (like a pie plate), pour in marinade, and jiggle and shift container to coat scallops. Refrigerate for 15 to 30 minutes.

3. Cut scallions into 2-inch segments. With a sharp knife, julienne the segments into thin strips. Submerge in ice water and hold aside.

4. If cooking the popcorn in oil, heat remaining 1 tablespoon oil in a deep pot with a lid. Add one kernel as a test. When it pops, add the remaining kernels, cover, and cook, shaking occasionally, until the time between pops is 4 seconds. Transfer popcorn to a paper bag, season with cumin and salt and shake bag vigorously. As an alternative, you can use popcorn popped in an air popper or unseasoned microwave popcorn. With either, coat the popcorn with 1 tablespoon oil before it goes into the bag (the cumin will not adhere to totally dry popcorn).

5. Remove scallop slices from marinade and fan some out on each plate. Drizzle lightly with mustard oil. Garnish with scallion strips and serve with the popcorn around the edges of the plates.

- sour
- salty
- sweet
- bitter

1hr 30mins
TOTAL TIME

1hr 30mins
ACTIVE TIME

DIFFICULTY

4
PORTIONS

GRÜNER
VELTLINER

JAPANESE HANDKERCHIEFS

The inspiration for this dish came to me when I was filleting a wild yellowtail and admiring its glistening, multicolored flesh. It seemed a shame that my customers would never know its beauty. And so I cut a wide, thin square of the yellowtail and loosely draped it on a plate. A few "handkerchiefs" cut from other fish soon joined the yellowtail, and we seasoned the whole thing with chunky soybean purée, excellent soy sauce, and fresh wasabi.

- 1 orange
- 1 cup pear juice, either store-bought or from about 1 pear
- 2 tablespoons light (low sodium) soy sauce
- 2 teaspoons sesame oil
- 1 tablespoon fresh lime juice
- Sea salt and ground pepper to taste
- 1/2 cup fresh soybeans or fresh or frozen lima beans
- 2 teaspoons wasabi paste
- 1 tablespoon sesame seeds
- 12 ounces assorted skinless sashimi-grade fish, such as tuna, halibut, red snapper, or fluke, sliced against the grain into paper-thin slices (include both rich and lean fish in your assortment)
- 1/4 cup fresh cilantro leaves

1. Peel and segment orange with a knife, holding orange over a bowl so that both the segments and juice are captured. Squeeze the juice out of the orange skin. Reserve fruit and its juice separately.

2. If pear juice is homemade, pass through a fine mesh sieve. Place pear juice in a small saucepan over medium-high heat and reduce until thick, syrupy, and medium brown. Stir in soy sauce, sesame oil, lime juice, and 1/4 cup of reserved orange juice. Taste, and season with salt and pepper.

3. Bring a pan of salted water to a boil. Cook soybeans or lima beans until tender. Drain, reserving 1/2 cup of the blanching water. Transfer beans with reserved water to blender and purée until smooth, adding more water if needed to get blender going. Add wasabi paste and blend until combined. Season bean purée with salt and pepper to taste.

4. Toast sesame seeds in a hot, dry pan until tan and fragrant, about 5 minutes. Crush in a mortar and pestle or pulse several times in a spice grinder.

5. Dollop a bit of bean purée on each plate. Drape fish handkerchiefs to the sides of the purée. Arrange several orange segments on each plate, and spoon pear sauce over the fish and orange. Garnish with ground sesame seeds and cilantro leaves. Serve.

- sour
- salty
- sweet
- bitter

1 hr 5 mins
TOTAL TIME

1 hr 5 mins
ACTIVE TIME

DIFFICULTY

4
PORTIONS

MONTLOUIS*
OR VOUVRAY

*a Chenin Blanc
wine from the
Loire Valley

GOAT CHEESE PARFAIT WITH GRILLED LEEKS & MARJORAM VINAIGRETTE

Goat cheese can come on as overly "goaty." So my idea for this appetizer was to lighten up the cheese both in texture and taste. We start with fresh, very soft goat cheese and fold in meringue until the volume of the cheese has nearly doubled. You get to enjoy the flavor of goat cheese without feeling like you've fallen face-first onto a barn floor.

- 1 cup loosely packed fresh oregano leaves
- 1 cup loosely packed fresh marjoram leaves
- 2 tablespoons red wine vinegar, preferably aged
- 1 tablespoon minced shallots
- 1/4 cup plus 2 teaspoons extra-virgin olive oil
- Salt and ground pepper to taste
- Fresh lemon juice, as needed
- 2 egg whites
- 8 ounces fresh (not aged) goat cheese, at room temperature
- 4 tablespoons (1/2 stick) unsalted butter, at room temperature
- 4 tablespoons kosher salt for blanching, plus more to taste
- 4 large or 8 small leeks, white and pale green parts only, halved lengthwise
  1/4 cup canola oil
- 1 pound taro root, peeled and grated on a box grater with large holes

1. Purée oregano, marjoram, and vinegar until smooth and pour into bowl. Stir in shallots and olive oil. Taste and season. Refrigerate overnight.

2. Beat egg whites to soft peaks. In a separate bowl, beat goat cheese with butter and 2 tablespoons hot water with an electric mixer until fluffy, about 5 minutes. Fold egg whites into cheese-butter mixture. Season with salt and pepper to taste.

3. Fill a large pan with water and bring to a boil. Prepare an ice bath in a bowl. Add 2 tablespoons kosher salt to both the boiling water and the ice bath. Bundle leek halves with kitchen string. Immerse in boiling water and cook 2 minutes. Move to ice bath for 2 minutes. Cut string. Pat the leeks dry. Drizzle leeks with remaining 2 teaspoons olive oil and season with salt and pepper. Heat a grill pan or wide skillet to hot and place as many leeks as will fit on the pan. Grill, flipping periodically, until leeks are nicely charred, about 5 minutes. Keep warm. Grill any remaining leeks.

4. In a high sauté pan over high heat, heat canola until smoking. Fry taro until golden, 10 minutes.

5. Curl 2 or 4 grilled leek halves on each plate. Top with a scoop of goat cheese mixture and spoon vinaigrette over leeks and cheese. Pile some fried taro on top and serve.

- sour
- salty
- sweet
- bitter

13 hrs 15 mins
TOTAL TIME*

1 hr 15 mins
ACTIVE TIME

DIFFICULTY

4
PORTIONS

SANCERRE

* 12 hours
refrigeration

STEAMERS IN PARSLEY BROTH

Steamers are a popular East Coast variety of soft-shell clams. With long "necks" (siphons) that extend wormlike from their shells, you're unlikely to miss them at a fish market. What's neat is that you can use the siphons as handles to dip the clams in the broth.

- 48 steamers or littlenecks, or 12 large clams
- 2 tablespoons cornmeal
- 1/4 cup olive oil
- 2 teaspoons chopped fresh garlic
- 2 tablespoons chopped shallots
- 1/2 cup picked fresh flat-leaf parsley leaves
- 1 1/2 cups dry white wine

1. Chip clams in cold water with cornmeal (see "Cleaning Clams" on page 50) for 1 hour.

2. Warm the oil over medium heat in a large stockpot with a tight-fitting lid. Add garlic and shallots and sauté until barely golden, about 2 minutes. Add parsley and cook 1 minute, stirring. Place clams in pot and add wine. Cover. When all clams have opened, about 12 minutes, remove clams with tongs to a serving platter, being sure to leave any grit behind.

3. If you wish, you may reduce the clam broth by one-third, and you may also opt to remove and discard the top shell from each clam. Divide clams in their half shells among 4 shallow bowls. Ladle parsley broth directly over clams. Serve hot.

- sour
- salty
- sweet
- bitter

1hr30mins
TOTAL TIME

20mins
ACTIVE TIME

DIFFICULTY

4
PORTIONS

PINOT GRIS*

*from Oregon

CALAMARI WITH COCONUT CURRY & GREEN PAPAYA

Green papaya is actually an immature Southeast Asian papaya. The fruit looks giant compared to a Western Hemisphere papaya. What's great about green papaya is its barely sweet, crossed cucumber-melon flavor and watermelon rind texture.

- 1 cup white wine vinegar
- 3/4 cup plus 1 tablespoon sugar
- 1 green (underripe) papaya, peeled, halved, seeded, and cut into 1/2 cup's worth of matchsticks
- 3 tablespoons unsalted butter
- 1 green apple, diced
- 2 tablespoons mild curry powder
- 1 1/2 tablespoons fresh lime juice
- One 14-ounce can unsweetened coconut milk
- 1 stalk lemongrass, coarsely chopped
- Salt and ground pepper to taste
- 1 1/2 pounds cleaned calamari, cut into 1/4-inch rings and tentacles
- 1 cup sushi rice, cooked
- 1/4 cup chopped fresh cilantro

1. In a small saucepan, combine vinegar with 3/4 cup of the sugar and bring to a boil over high heat. Add papaya. When liquid returns to a boil, remove pan from heat and let stand uncovered for 30 minutes.

2. Melt 1 tablespoon of the butter in a saucepan over medium-low heat. Add apples, cover pan, and cook 5 minutes, until barely softened. Sprinkle apples with remaining 1 tablespoon sugar, and sauté until sugar has dissolved. Add curry powder to pan, stir to coat, and cook until fragrant, 1 to 2 minutes. Add lime juice, coconut milk, and lemongrass. Simmer until sauce has reduced to the consistency of heavy cream. Strain sauce and return it to the pan. Taste, and season with salt and pepper. Cover pan to keep warm.

3. Melt remaining 2 tablespoons of butter in a sauté pan over very low heat. Sprinkle calamari with salt and pepper, add to pan, cover, and cook, stirring periodically, for 6 to 8 minutes or until calamari are opaque and very tender. Fold calamari into pan containing coconut-curry sauce; cover.

4. With a slotted spoon, remove papaya from its cooking liquid and fold it into rice. Taste mixture and stir enough of the papaya's cooking liquid into it to make the rice sticky and sweet-sour. Salt to taste.

5. Form a bed of papaya rice in each of 4 shallow bowls. Spoon calamari with sauce over rice. Garnish with cilantro. Serve immediately.

- ○ sour
- ◑ salty
- ● sweet
- ◔ bitter

1hr 15mins
TOTAL TIME

1hr 15mins
ACTIVE TIME

DIFFICULTY

4
PORTIONS

PINOT
AUXERROIS

JUMBO ASPARAGUS WITH OYSTER MUSHROOMS & FRESH PECORINO CHEESE

Grated Pecorino Romano is what we're most familiar with in this country. For this recipe, seek out the fresh pecorino that's imported from southern Tuscany. While salty like the grated stuff, it has a much different flavor. It pairs phenomenally with fresh green vegetables.

- 1/2 cup extra-virgin olive oil
- 2 tablespoons finely chopped shallots
- 1 heaping teaspoon chopped fines herbes (a mixture of chervil, chives, parsley, and tarragon), or any one of or combination of the 4 herbs
- Zest of 1 lemon
- Ground white pepper to taste
- 3/4 pound cleaned and trimmed fresh oyster mushrooms
- 6 sprigs fresh thyme
- 2 to 4 tablespoons kosher salt for blanching
- 16 spears jumbo asparagus (about 1 bunch), or 28 medium spears
- Salt to taste
- 1/2 cup sherry vinegar
- 1 cup mushroom stock (optional)
- 4 ounces young pecorino cheese (look for a 6-month Pecorino Toscano)

1. In a medium bowl or baking dish, whisk together oil, shallots, herbs, and lemon zest. Season to taste with pepper. Add mushrooms and thyme sprigs and toss. Let the mushrooms marinate at room temperature for 10 minutes or overnight in refrigerator.

2. Bring a large stockpot of water to a boil and add 2 tablespoons kosher salt. For this dish, you can serve the asparagus warm or at room temperature. If serving at room temperature, prepare an ice bath with 2 tablespoons salt dissolved in water.

3. While water comes to a boil, prep the asparagus spears. Trim them by gently breaking stalks where they naturally snap a few inches from the base. If using jumbo asparagus, peel them to about 1/2 inch below the tip. Bundle spears with kitchen twine and cook in the boiling water until they are tender throughout when pierced with a cake tester, about 5 minutes. Drain the asparagus. If serving at room temperature, shock in ice bath. If serving warm, don't shock. Discard twine.

4. Heat a large, 10- to 12-inch skillet over high heat. Lift the mushrooms out of their marinade directly into the pan to form a single layer of mushrooms (don't overcrowd the pan). Season with salt and pepper, and cook until browned and tender, then move onto a plate and tent with foil. Wipe oil from pan and repeat with any remaining mushrooms. When all mushrooms have been cooked,

- sour
- salty
- sweet
- bitter

55 mins
TOTAL TIME*

45 mins
ACTIVE TIME

DIFFICULTY

4
PORTIONS

PROSECCO

*longer with
overnight
marinating

ull pan off heat and add 2 tablespoons of the vinegar. Scrape up and dissolve any browned bits.
Pour this pan sauce over the mushrooms.

5. Make a dressing by seasoning the remaining 1/2 cup marinade with vinegar to your taste; you
may not need all the remaining vinegar. If using mushroom stock, reduce stock to 1 tablespoon in a
saucepan over high heat, lowering heat as volume of liquid shrinks. Whisk reduced stock into dressing. Season with salt and pepper.

6. To serve, divide asparagus spears among 4 plates or arrange on a serving platter. Top with the
mushrooms and shave pecorino over salad (a vegetable peeler works great for this purpose).
Douse everything with dressing and finish with a dusting of ground pepper.

CHARRED SPANISH MACKEREL WITH PEAR & SWEET SPICE

TECHNIQUE CHARRING

This dish wouldn't work without the sweet-bitter tension between the charred fish skin and the sweet dressed pear and celery root salad. I admit the idea of scorching something intentionally may seem strange. Probably you've flame-roasted bell peppers and discarded their blackened skins. I'll let you in on one of my secrets: sometimes that skin—just a tiny bit of it—tastes great when worked into a sweet soup or sauce. "Blackened," a popular dish description on menus, is another word for "charred."

- sour
- salty
- sweet
- bitter

Mackerel, a strong-tasting, oily fish full of cancer-fighting omega-3 fatty acids, is popular in Europe but unappreciated in the U.S.: I think cats probably enjoy more mackerel per year than the average American. But if you think of strong flavors as a boon rather than an obstacle, mackerel will find its way onto your list of favorites.

- Salt to taste
- 1 celery root, peeled and cut into 1-inch matchsticks
- 3 teaspoons light (low-sodium) soy sauce
- 1/4 teaspoon fish sauce
- 2 teaspoons fresh lemon juice
- 1 1/2 teaspoons honey
- 1/4 teaspoon ground star anise, plus more for garnish
- 1/4 teaspoon ground cinnamon, plus more for garnish
- Ground pepper to taste
- 1/4 cup plus 2 tablespoons olive oil, plus more to coat pan
- 2 ripe, firm Anjou pears, cut into 1-inch matchsticks
- 6 Spanish mackerel fillets, about 5 ounces each, skin on

1. Bring a pan of water to a boil and salt it generously. Add celery root and boil until just tender, 8 to 10 minutes. Strain.

2. While celery root is cooking, make dressing: in a nonreactive bowl, combine soy sauce, fish sauce, lemon juice, honey, star anise, cinnamon, and 1 crank pepper from a mill. Whisking continuously, add oil in a slow, steady stream to produce a creamy, emulsified vinaigrette. Taste, and season further if desired. Add celery root and pears to bowl, and gently toss to coat. Chill until ready to serve.

3. Heat a large sauté pan over high heat until very hot. Season the mackerel fillets with salt and pepper on skin side only. Tilting and rotating the pan, pour just enough oil into it to evenly coat the bottom. Place as many fillets as will fit in the pan skin side down. Sauté until skin is blackened and interior is cooked medium, 5 to 8 minutes. Do not flip the fillets. Keep cooked fish warm while you sauté remaining fillets.

4. Using a very sharp knife, cut fillets on bias into slices about 1 inch thick. After slicing each fillet, gently compress the stack of slices between your knife and fingers and move it to a small plate. When released, the slices will loosely overlap. Top fish with pear and celery root salad. Dust plates with ground cinnamon and star anise. Serve immediately.

1 hr
TOTAL TIME

1 hr
ACTIVE TIME

DIFFICULTY

4
PORTIONS

SCHEUREUBE
SPÄTLESE

CHAPTER 4
SOUPS

YELLOW PEPPER SOUP

I got tired of cutting up yellow peppers for salads. They're so much more than that! When I want to feature a large quantity of a single vegetable, soup is where I start. The end result? A vivid yellow, velvety, sweet-sour, smoky soup.

- 4 yellow bell peppers
- 1/2 cup pear juice
- 1/4 teaspoon mustard powder
- 2 teaspoons rice wine vinegar
- Salt and ground pepper to taste
- Sour cream or crème fraîche to garnish (optional)

Roast peppers over a flame or in an oven for 45 minutes at 375°F. Cool in a paper bag. When completely cool, peel, seed, and chop peppers coarsely. Purée peppers in a blender until smooth. Pass purée through a wide mesh sieve into a pan over medium-low heat. Add 1 1/2 cups water, pear juice, mustard powder, vinegar, and salt and pepper to taste. Heat, stirring, until warmed through. Garnish servings, if desired, with a dollop of sour cream or crème fraîche.

- sour
- salty
- sweet
- bitter

1 hr 10 mins
TOTAL TIME

10 mins
ACTIVE TIME

40 mins
TOTAL TIME

25 mins
ACTIVE TIME

| | | | | | | |

DIFFICULTY

4
PORTIONS

VOUVRAY

BOUILLON OF FOREST MUSHROOMS WITH SHERRY

I developed this bouillon with a specific aesthetic reference firmly in mind: I wanted a soup that smells and tastes like a fertile forest floor—woodsy and intensely savory. Maximum flavor is extracted from the mushrooms through slow-cooking and a final steeping period.

- ● ● 20 ounces fresh cultivated mushrooms, such as white button or cremini
- ● ● 12 ounces fresh wild mushrooms, such as morel, chanterelle, or porcini
- ● 4 tablespoons (1/2 stick) unsalted butter
- ● 2 shallots, peeled and minced
- ● ● 1 clove garlic, peeled and minced
- ● Salt and ground pepper to taste
- ● ● 1/2 cup port, preferably white port
- ● 1 cup chicken stock
- ● ● 2 tablespoons finely chopped fresh chives
- ● ● 2 tablespoons sherry

1. Chop cultivated and wild mushrooms together. Cut them any size you like, as long as they fit in a spoon when finished (remember that they will shrink while cooking). Small mushrooms may be used whole.

2. In a large pot over medium heat, melt butter. Add shallots and garlic, season, and cook until translucent and soft, about 3 minutes. Lower heat and add all mushrooms. Season, cover, and sweat, stirring occasionally, until mushrooms are soft and fragrant, about 20 minutes.

3. Add port to the pot. Use a wooden spoon to loosen any brown bits from the bottom of the pot. Raise heat to medium and cook 5 to 7 minutes, until very little port is visible. Add chicken stock and 3 cups water, bring to a boil, then remove pot from the heat. Steep uncovered for 20 minutes. Season with salt and pepper to taste.

4. Ladle bouillon into soup bowls and garnish with chives. Float several dashes of sherry on the surface of each bowl of bouillon. Serve immediately.

- ● sour
- ● salty
- ● sweet
- ● bitter

1 hr 15 mins
TOTAL TIME

35 mins
ACTIVE TIME

DIFFICULTY

4
PORTIONS

PROSECCO

EGGPLANT VELOUTÉ WITH FIGS

The essence of autumn, this soup stars eggplant and figs. It's one of the first dishes I crave when the air turns crisp and leaves start to change color. While any variety of eggplant will work here, do use white eggplants if they're available. Their creaminess will make the soup live up to its name (*velouté* means "velvety").

- 1 1/2 pounds white eggplant (about 2 medium) or other eggplant
- 1/4 cup extra-virgin olive oil
- 1 large onion, peeled and coarsely chopped
- 2 1/2 cups coarsely chopped fennel (about an 11-ounce bulb)
- 6 cloves garlic, peeled and sliced
- 1 tablespoon minced fresh ginger
- Salt and ground pepper to taste
- 1/2 cup port
- 1/4 cup sherry vinegar
- 2 tablespoons honey
- 4 fresh figs
- Walnut oil for garnish (optional)

1. Remove caps and stems from eggplants. Cut in half lengthwise. Heat a cast-iron griddle over high heat until smoking hot. Lay eggplants on hot griddle. Rotate them frequently until skins are thoroughly charred and blackened and meat is cooked through, about 15 minutes. Transfer eggplants to a bowl and set aside until cool enough to handle. Without removing charred skin, chop eggplant into medium chunks.

2. In a large, heavy-bottomed pan over medium heat, heat 2 tablespoons of the olive oil. Add the onion, fennel, garlic, and ginger, stir to coat with oil, season with salt and pepper, and cover pan. Cook, stirring occasionally, until vegetables are aromatic and softened, 6 to 8 minutes. Add eggplant and 1 quart water. Simmer for 20 minutes. Working in batches, purée the eggplant-vegetable mixture in a blender until smooth, then pass through a wide mesh sieve. Season soup to taste.

3. In a small saucepan over medium-high heat, bring port, vinegar, 1/2 cup water, and a pinch of salt to a simmer. Stir in honey. Add figs and boil until figs are tender and liquid has reduced to about 1/4 cup syrup, 23 to 26 minutes. Reduce heat toward the end to avoid scorching the syrup.

4. Gently reheat soup in a covered pan. Observe consistency: if soup seems too thick, add water. Remove stems from figs. Make fig "flowers" by carefully quartering each fig to within 1/4 inch of its base. Ladle soup into 4 bowls and center a fig on the surface of each soup. Drizzle with walnut oil (if using) and finish with a ring of port syrup. Serve immediately.

- sour
- salty
- **sweet**
- bitter

SOUP OF SWEET PEAS WITH CRAB-STUFFED ZUCCHINI BLOSSOMS

My Italian grandmother would feed me fried, battered zucchini blossoms that she'd gathered from her garden. I've never forgotten them. The zucchini blossoms in this soup are little cachepots, jewel boxes stuffed with some of my favorite summer flavors.

TECHNIQUE
DEEP-FRYING

Did you know that when you deep-fry something, it's not the hot oil that does the cooking? OK, the oil is responsible for a French fry's crispness and beautiful golden tan. But steam trapped inside does the rest. With these zucchini blossoms, the batter cooks instantly, and then steam builds up quickly beneath the breading. It is critical that frying oil always be 380–400°F. Cooking food in oil below this temperature range results in greasy food and soggy crusts that fall off. Frying—both deep and pan—accentuates sweetness.

- 20 ounces frozen or fresh peas (2 packages if using frozen)
- 2 to 3 tablespoons sugar, depending on sweetness of peas
- 1 cup whole fresh tarragon leaves, plus 1 teaspoon finely chopped tarragon (about 1 bunch total)
- 1/8 teaspoon salt, plus more to taste
- 2 cranks black pepper from a mill, plus more to taste
- 8 ounces crabmeat (1 cup), carefully picked over
- 2 tablespoons mayonnaise
- Zest and half the juice of 1 lemon
- Pinch cayenne pepper
- 4 large zucchini blossoms
- 2 cups frying oil, such as canola or corn
- 1 cup all-purpose flour
- 2 eggs

1. Bring 2 1/2 cups water to a boil, add peas and sugar, and blanch 2 minutes. Transfer peas with cooking water to a blender. Add tarragon leaves and purée until smooth. Season to taste.

2. In a small bowl, combine crabmeat, mayonnaise, lemon zest, lemon juice, cayenne pepper, and chopped tarragon. Toss to combine. Season to taste with salt and pepper. Stuff each zucchini blossom with a quarter of this mixture, leaving the opening free of stuffing so that the blossom can be folded over.

3. In a high-sided sauté pan, heat oil until very hot but not smoking. While oil heats to frying temperature, place flour in a shallow bowl. In a separate shallow bowl, whisk together eggs, 1 tablespoon water, 1/8 teaspoon salt, and 2 cranks ground black pepper. Dredge zucchini blossoms in flour, keeping openings folded over, and shake off excess. Follow by rolling each blossom in the egg, coating generously, and then immediately drop blossoms in frying oil. (There should be enough egg on each blossom so that strings of fried egg batter form in the oil: think Italian tempura!) Fry until golden brown on each side, about 2 minutes per side. Drain on paper towels. Sprinkle with salt and pepper. Snack on the golden batter strings.

4. While blossoms stand for a minute, gently reheat the soup over low heat in a covered pan. Ladle soup into 4 individual bowls and garnish each serving with a stuffed zucchini blossom.

- sour
- salty
- sweet
- bitter

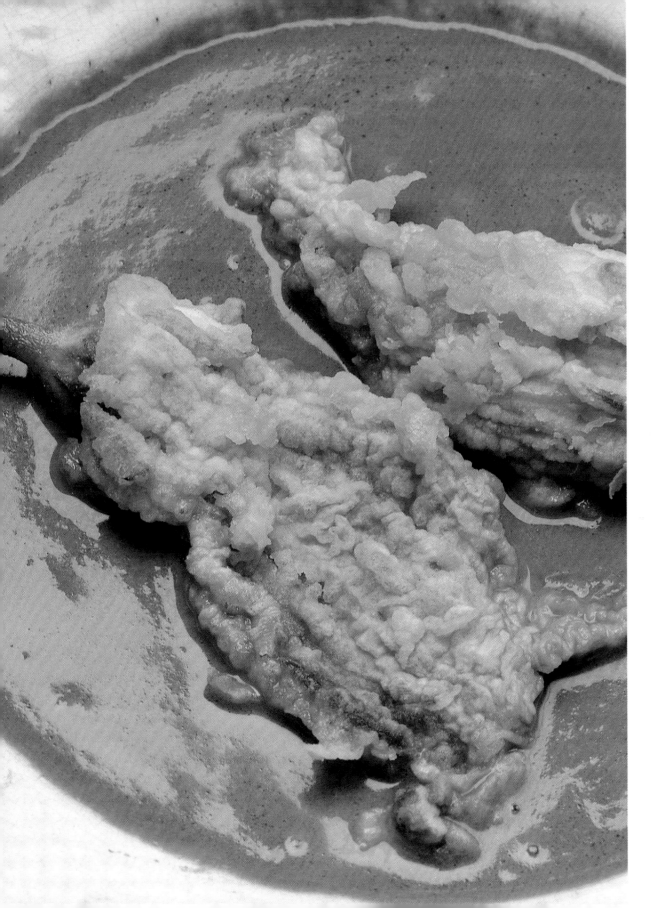

1 hr
TOTAL TIME

1 hr
ACTIVE TIME

DIFFICULTY

4
PORTIONS

SAUVIGNON
BLANC

SWEET ONION & WHITE PEPPERCORN SOUP

At Union Pacific, nothing is wasted. This soup is a noble use of all the sweet onion scraps left over after a day of chopping and slicing. I find that sautéed, puréed onions need surprisingly few additions to taste great—a little pepper and port turn scraps into a sophisticated soup.

TECHNIQUE SWEATING

This is a technique I use a lot. If it's a new kitchen word for you, it'll be easy to remember: sweating means forcing a food to perspire by cooking it in a covered pan over low heat, and then using that flavorful liquid as the cooking medium. Mushrooms and peppers give up their liquid very quickly; fibrous vegetables like fennel are a bit more stubborn and have to be sweated longer. This technique produces very tender, moist food with no color change and little if any caramelization.

- 1/2 cup (1 stick) plus 2 tablespoons unsalted butter
- 4 large Vidalia, Mayan Sweet, or Maui onions, peeled and sliced thin
- 7 cloves garlic, peeled and sliced thin
- 8 ramp or scallion bulbs, sliced into thin rounds
- Salt and ground white pepper to taste
- 4 slices day-old brioche
- 8 white peppercorns, tied in a cheesecloth sachet and lightly pounded
- 1/4 cup white port, or 1/4 cup white wine plus 2 tablespoons sugar

1. In a large casserole or soup pot, melt 1 stick of the butter over medium heat. When it begins to foam, add onions, garlic, and ramps or scallions. Season well with salt and white pepper. Mix well, reduce heat to low, and cover. Sweat the alliums, stirring every 15 minutes, until onions are meltingly tender, about 45 minutes. Do not let onions brown.

2. While onions cook, make croutons: stack the brioche slices and cut stack into strips about 1/2 inch wide. Turn the stack 90° and repeat, cutting bread into 1/2-inch squares. Heat a sauté pan over medium heat and add remaining 2 tablespoons butter. When butter foams, add brioche squares and cook, stirring frequently, until croutons turn golden brown. Arrange in a single layer on a tray lined with paper towels, season with fine salt, and let cool.

3. Add peppercorn sachet to pot containing onions, and stir. Add white port and simmer 15 minutes, or until about 75 percent of the port has cooked off. Add enough water to just cover onion mixture, about 1 1/2 cups. Simmer for 20 minutes. Remove sachet. Working in batches if necessary, transfer soup to a blender, cover, and purée until smooth. The soup can be eaten at this stage, or passed through a fine mesh sieve or chinois for a luxuriously smooth texture.

4. You may wish to reheat the soup over low heat, especially if you've taken the time to pass it through a strainer. Before ladling it into soup bowls, check its seasoning a final time and adjust accordingly with salt and white pepper. Garnish each bowl of soup with a handful of croutons and serve hot.

- sour
- salty
- sweet
- bitter

1hr 55 mins
TOTAL TIME

1hr
ACTIVE TIME

DIFFICULTY

4
PORTIONS

GRÜNER
VELTLINER

BEEF SHABU-SHABU

If you think any dish with beef must be a heavy one, think again. This soup, which resembles Vietnamese pho, may be the lightest incarnation of beef you've tasted. The beef itself is sliced very thin and cooked gently in a broth that dances with the bright flavors of lime, ginger, and Thai basil.

- 2 tablespoons extra-virgin olive oil
- 2 tablespoons finely shredded fresh ginger
- 2 teaspoons minced fresh garlic
- 2 tablespoons orange marmalade
- 1/2 cup fresh lime juice plus 2 limes cut in half from top to bottom
- 1/4 cup tamari
- 4 1/2 cups chicken stock
- 2 tablespoons hoisin sauce
- Salt and ground pepper to taste
- 1 pound beef tenderloin, all exterior fat and nerve trimmed off and sliced paper-thin by your butcher
- 20 whole fresh Thai basil leaves plus 10 leaves roughly chopped
- 1 cup bean sprouts

1. In a medium saucepan over low heat, warm oil. Add ginger and garlic, and sauté until fragrant, about 1 minute. Stir in orange marmalade, 1/4 cup lime juice, tamari, chicken stock, and hoisin sauce, increase heat to medium-high, and cook 10 minutes. Season to taste.

2. Pile beef slices in 4 large soup bowls. Place 5 basil leaves in each bowl. Reheat broth until it is boiling hot, add 1/4 cup lime juice and chopped basil, and then fill bowls with broth. Garnish each bowl of soup with a small mound of bean sprouts and serve with lime halves on the side.

- sour
- salty
- sweet
- bitter

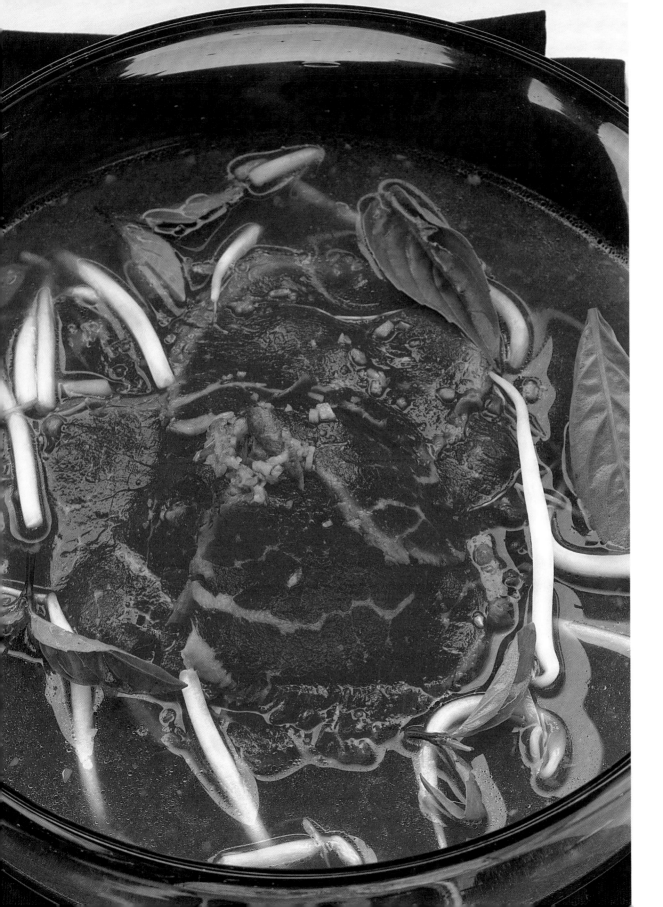

35 mins
TOTAL TIME

35 mins
ACTIVE TIME

DIFFICULTY

4
PORTIONS

SPRING GARLIC SOUP WITH BACON

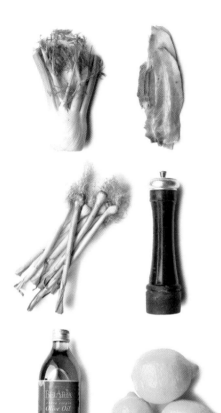

Spring garlic is one of those foods to look for vigilantly in farmers' markets in late spring and early summer. Just-harvested garlic is tender and mild-tasting, with none of the bitterness that develops in older, dried garlic. On a trip to Thailand, I was amazed to learn that there it's harvested year-round. I'm jealous!

- 4 ounces bacon (4 slices), minced
- 12 ounces spring garlic (about 5 bulbs), stems trimmed and bulbs quartered
- 2 cups chopped fennel
- 1 cup chopped onion
- Salt and ground pepper to taste
- 2 tablespoons fresh lemon juice
- Extra-virgin olive oil to garnish

1. Add bacon to a large stockpot over medium heat. Sauté until much of the bacon's fat has been rendered but well before bacon is crispy, about 6 minutes. Reduce heat to low and add garlic, fennel, and onion. Season lightly with salt and pepper, cover pot, and sweat until all ingredients are very tender, 11 to 14 minutes. Add 1 quart water, bring to a simmer, and simmer soup for 1 hour.

2. Working in batches, transfer pot's contents to a blender and purée until very smooth. Pass through a wide mesh sieve into a clean pan. Stir in lemon juice. Season to taste. Garnish small bowls of spring garlic soup with squiggles of olive oil.

- sour
- salty
- sweet
- bitter

1 hr 20 mins
TOTAL TIME

20 mins
ACTIVE TIME

DIFFICULTY

4
PORTIONS

CROZES-
HERMITAGE
BLANC

SAFFRON-SCENTED SEAFOOD SOUP WITH POTATOES

My adaptation of bouillabaisse, the classic south-of-France fish stew. Pay attention to the licorice and saffron flavors in it; they are the batteries that charge the soup.

- 1 cup olive oil, plus more to garnish
- 2 fennel bulbs, trimmed and cut into squares
- 1 large onion, diced
- 20 cloves garlic
- Salt and ground pepper to taste
- Heaping 1/2 teaspoon crumbled saffron
- 2 cups Pernod or other anise-flavored liqueur
- Three 14-ounce cans plum tomatoes
- 1/2 bottle dry white wine
- 1 or 2 whole firm-fleshed ocean fish (about 6 pounds total), such as bass, cod, monkfish, porgy, perch, rouget, snapper, or whiting, scaled and gutted
- 4 large or 8 small Yukon gold or fingerling potatoes, peeled
- 1 1/2 pounds skinless fillets of any firm-flesh ocean fish (see suggestions above)
- Fleur de sel or other coarse sea salt (optional)

1. In a large stockpot, heat oil over medium-low heat. Add fennel, onion, and garlic. Season with salt and pepper, and cover pot. Sweat until fragrant and tender, stirring occasionally, about 15 minutes. Add saffron and Pernod; stir. Cook uncovered until most liquid has cooked off, about 15 minutes. Add tomatoes with their juices, wine, and whole fish. Season. Bring to a gentle simmer, and simmer for 50 minutes. Add potatoes and continue to cook 40 minutes, or until potatoes are firm, tender. Remove potatoes and hold aside.

2. Working in batches, transfer contents of pot (including whole fish) to a blender and purée. Alternatively, use an immersion blender. Outfit a manual food mill with a fine-holed disc and pass purée through the food mill into a clean pan over low heat. Bring to a simmer, then immerse fish fillets (halve them first, if necessary to fit them in pan) and cooked potatoes in soup. Poach until fish is opaque and potatoes are rewarmed, 6 to 10 minutes. Reduce heat to low. With a slotted spoon, remove fish and potatoes. Check and adjust seasoning of soup.

3. Divide potatoes among 4 shallow bowls and quickly crush with the back of a fork. Cut fish into bite-size chunks and add to bowls. Ladle soup over potatoes and fish, and garnish each serving with fleur de sel and a squiggle of olive oil. Serve warm.

- sour
- salty
- sweet
- bitter

2 hrs 50 mins
TOTAL TIME

1 hr 20 mins
ACTIVE TIME

DIFFICULTY

4
PORTIONS

ALBARINO

AROMATIC CAULIFLOWER SOUP

If you want to be really clever, grate the head of cauliflower against a box grater. The mini florets look a little like couscous. Use them to garnish the soup along with pine nuts and basil syrup.

- 3 tablespoons plus 1/4 cup corn or vegetable oil
- 1 large Vidalia onion, peeled and chopped
- Salt and ground pepper to taste
- 2 quarts cauliflower florets (from about 1 large head)
- 1/4 cup sugar
- 3 cups fresh basil leaves
- 1/2 cup pine nuts
- 2 tablespoons ground coriander

1. Warm 3 tablespoons of the oil in a large soup pot over low heat. Add the onion, season with salt and pepper, cover pan, and sweat onion for 10 minutes. Add the cauliflower, season, and stir well to coat. Increase heat to medium and cook uncovered another 10 minutes, stirring frequently. Add 1 quart water and increase heat to high. When water reaches the boiling point, immediately reduce the heat so that the soup simmers. Simmer 20 minutes or until cauliflower is completely tender. Working in batches, transfer the soup to a blender and purée until smooth. Pour the soup through a wide mesh strainer into a clean pot and keep it warm.

2. While soup simmers, make a simple syrup by heating sugar with 1/4 cup water until sugar is dissolved. Transfer syrup to a blender.

3. Bring a small pan of salted water to a boil. Submerge the basil and boil for 3 minutes. Drain basil in a colander and immediately run colander under cold tap water until leaves are cool. Place basil in blender with the syrup and purée for 2 minutes. Strain, sprinkle with salt, and set aside.

4. Heat the remaining 1/4 cup corn oil in a shallow pan over medium-low heat. Add the pine nuts and cook, shaking the pan frequently, until nuts turn golden brown, about 1 minute. Place pine nuts on a plate lined with a paper towel to drain. Sprinkle with salt, pepper, and coriander. Whisk 2 tablespoons of the pine nut–flavored cooking oil into the basil syrup.

5. To serve, ladle the hot soup into bowls. Drizzle a few spoons of basil syrup around the perimeter and pile some pine nuts on the surface of each bowl of soup. Serve hot.

- sour
- salty
- sweet
- bitter

55 mins

TOTAL TIME

55 mins

ACTIVE TIME

DIFFICULTY

4

PORTIONS

CHENIN BLANC

SPICED CRAB RAGOUT

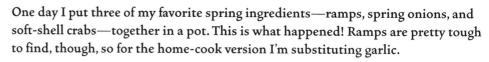

One day I put three of my favorite spring ingredients—ramps, spring onions, and soft-shell crabs—together in a pot. This is what happened! Ramps are pretty tough to find, though, so for the home-cook version I'm substituting garlic.

- 14 cloves garlic, peeled, 12 kept whole and 2 smashed under blade of a heavy knife
- 1/2 cup olive oil
- 1 cup red wine vinegar
- 12 small live blue crabs, chopped (if you don't relish the idea of chopping live crabs, ask your fishmonger to do the job!)
- 3/4 cup chopped onions
- Salt and ground pepper to taste
- 1 tablespoon fennel seed
- 1 teaspoon fenugreek
- 3 tablespoons tomato paste
- 1 bottle Riesling or other high-acid white wine
- 8 ounces (1 cup) chunk crabmeat, picked over carefully
- Crème fraîche to garnish

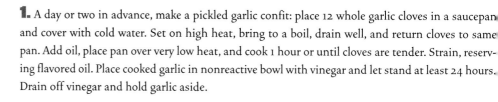

1. A day or two in advance, make a pickled garlic confit: place 12 whole garlic cloves in a saucepan and cover with cold water. Set on high heat, bring to a boil, drain well, and return cloves to same pan. Add oil, place pan over very low heat, and cook 1 hour or until cloves are tender. Strain, reserving flavored oil. Place cooked garlic in nonreactive bowl with vinegar and let stand at least 24 hours. Drain off vinegar and hold garlic aside.

2. In a large stockpot over medium heat, warm 1/4 cup of the garlic oil. (Reserve the rest of the oil for another use; garlic oil is great in vinaigrettes and with pasta.) Once the oil is hot, add blue crab pieces. When crab has turned pink, add smashed raw garlic and onions, sprinkle with salt and pepper, and sauté 3 minutes. Add fennel seed and fenugreek, and sauté 1 minute. Add tomato paste and sauté 5 minutes, or until paste is dried. Add wine, bring to a boil, cover pan, reduce heat to low, and simmer 45 minutes. Strain contents of pot through a fine mesh sieve into a clean pan set over medium-high heat. Cook until reduced to a medium-bodied soup. Season to taste.

3. Ladle soup into 4 bowls and garnish each serving with a heap of crabmeat, 3 pickled garlic cloves, and a dollop of crème fraîche.

- sour
- salty
- sweet
- bitter

26 hrs 15 mins
TOTAL TIME*

2 hrs 15 mins
ACTIVE TIME

DIFFICULTY

4
PORTIONS

LIGHT-BODIED
GEWÜRZ-
TRAMINER

*1 day for
pickling, plus 2
hours and 15
minutes

AROMATIC TOMATO & KIMCHEE SOUP

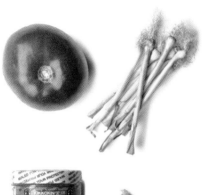

I first met kimchee in a Korean restaurant on New York's East 34th Street, and right away, I wanted to make it my own. I wasn't deterred when I learned that the food is basically cabbage stuffed in jars and left to rot. The challenge of working kimchee into cuisine with a European aesthetic is in finding ways to temper its powerful heat and pickle. After tasting this soup for the first time, everyone in Union Pacific's kitchen agreed: "Not bad for rotten cabbage!"

- 2/3 cup extra-virgin olive oil
- 2 tablespoons minced fresh garlic
- 3/4 cup prepared kimchee made from cabbage and green onions
- 2 1/2 pounds heirloom beefsteak tomatoes, coarsely chopped
- Salt and ground pepper to taste
- Sugar as needed
- Fresh lemon juice as needed
- 1/2 cup chiffonade of fresh Thai basil or other basil

1. In a large saucepan over medium heat, warm 1/3 cup of the olive oil. Add garlic, cover pan, cook 3 minutes, and add kimchee. Cover and cook until kimchee is very tender and fully cooked, about 5 minutes. Add tomatoes, season, reduce heat to low, and simmer for 30 minutes, stirring occasionally. Pass contents of pan through a food mill into a clean pan. Alternatively, purée mixture in a blender or with an immersion blender, and then strain purée through a mesh strainer into a clean pan.

2. Set pan over low heat and stir in remaining 1/3 cup olive oil. Taste and season with salt and pepper. Since the taste profile of tomatoes ranges dramatically, you'll want to adjust for your tomatoes' acidity by adding a pinch of sugar if the soup is too acidic or a squeeze of lemon juice if it's too sweet.

3. Ladle soup into bowls and garnish with Thai basil. Serve warm.

- sour
- salty
- sweet
- bitter

1 hr
TOTAL TIME

30 mins
ACTIVE TIME

DIFFICULTY

4
PORTIONS

RIESLING
KABINETT

CHAPTER 5
SALADS

RADISHES WITH CRANBERRIES & GOAT CHEESE

I made a faux pas the first time I ordered *radis beurre* at a Paris bistro. I remember sitting for a short eternity, staring at the plate of breakfast radishes with tiny ramekins of butter and salt, before finally being assured that, yes, the whole dish had been delivered to the table. I've gone a step or two beyond the bistro classic by folding sour and sweet flavors into the mix.

- 1/3 cup dried cranberries
- 1 1/2 cups radishes, trimmed and quartered (about 15 radishes or 1 average bunch)
- 2 teaspoons extra-virgin olive oil
- Salt and ground pepper to taste
- 1/3 cup crumbled goat cheese

1. Place the cranberries in a small bowl and cover with hot water. Let stand 30 minutes. Drain.

2. Toss together radishes and plumped cranberries. Add olive oil, toss, and season to taste with salt and pepper. Fold in crumbled goat cheese, being careful not to crush the cheese into a paste. Serve at room temperature or chilled.

- sour
- salty
- **sweet**
- bitter

45 mins
TOTAL TIME

15 mins
ACTIVE TIME

DIFFICULTY

4
PORTIONS

SANCERRE

LEMONGRASS LOBSTER SALAD

Lemongrass is lipophilic: its molecules bind with oil, but not with water. To capture its essence, we infuse oil with lemongrass, and then use the flavored oil to make a mayonnaise. This lobster salad would make a perfect opening to an elegant summer brunch or dinner.

- 2 stalks lemongrass, chopped small
  1/2 cup neutral-flavored oil, preferably grapeseed
- 1 egg yolk
- 1 teaspoon prepared mustard
- 1 tablespoon plus 1 teaspoon fresh lime juice
- 1/4 teaspoon salt, plus more to taste
- 2 cranks ground pepper in a mill, plus more to taste
- Shelled meat from 4 small "chicken" lobsters, about 12 ounces total
- 1 1/2 cups diced, peeled European seedless cucumber (about 1/2 cucumber)
- 2 tablespoons minced fresh cilantro
- 2 slices brioche, lightly toasted and cut in quarters

1. Place lemongrass and oil in a small saucepan. Warm over low heat until small bubbles appear on oil's surface. Remove pan from heat and allow oil to infuse for 1 hour. Strain through a fine mesh sieve and discard solids. Allow oil to cool to room temperature before proceeding with mayonnaise.

2. In a medium bowl, whisk together egg yolk, mustard, 1 tablespoon lime juice, 1/4 teaspoon salt, and 2 cranks ground pepper. Whisking constantly, slowly beat in the lemongrass-infused oil to create a thick emulsification. Season the mayonnaise to taste.

3. In a bowl, combine lobster meat, cucumber, cilantro, and remaining 1 teaspoon lime juice. Fold in 2 tablespoons of lemongrass mayonnaise, gently turning to coat. Taste, and season with salt and pepper as desired, plus more lime juice if you want.

4. Divide salad among 2 to 4 plates, and garnish with brioche croutons.

- sour
- salty
- sweet
- bitter

1 hr 30 mins
TOTAL TIME

15 mins
ACTIVE TIME

DIFFICULTY

4
PORTIONS

COTEAUX DU LAYON

CHICKEN LIVER & CORN SALAD

Strong flavors beg to be tempered! Chicken liver takes on a new personality when combined with a bright, acidic vinaigrette, sweet corn, and bitter watercress.

- 2 ears sweet corn
- 2 teaspoons whole fennel seed
- 1/4 cup turbinado sugar ("sugar in the raw"), if you own a gas torch
- 1 1/2 tablespoons sherry vinegar
- 1/4 cup extra-virgin olive oil
- Salt and ground pepper to taste
- 1 tablespoon finely chopped fresh chives
- 1 large bunch watercress (about 4 ounces), torn apart and thick stems removed
- 3 strips bacon
- 3/4 pound chicken livers (about 8 livers)

1. In a large pot of salted boiling water, cook the ears of corn until fork-tender, about 10 minutes. Remove from water and set aside to cool.

2. While corn is boiling, heat a sauté pan or skillet over medium heat. Spread fennel seeds in pan and cook, shaking pan continuously, until seeds are toasted, 2 to 3 minutes. Transfer seeds to a mortar and crush with pestle.

3. Using a sharp knife, strip corn kernels off cobs in long bars about 3 kernels wide. (This technique takes an attempt or two to master! Don't worry if some kernels separate.)

4. Sprinkle the corn sections with sugar. Using a gas torch, burn the sugar until bubbly and dark, much as you would a crème brûlée. (If you don't have a gas torch, skip the sugaring step.)

5. Prepare vinaigrette: place vinegar in a small mixing bowl and, whisking continuously, pour olive oil in the bowl in a slow, steady stream. Taste, and add salt and pepper to your liking. Stir in chives. Toss watercress with all but 2 tablespoons of the vinaigrette. Throw in crushed fennel seeds; toss.

6. Place a pan over medium heat and add bacon. Cook until brown and crispy and transfer to paper towels to drain, leaving pan with rendered bacon fat over medium heat. Season chicken livers with salt and pepper on both sides. Add livers to the pan and sauté on both sides until medium rare, 2 to 3 minutes per side. Cut each liver on the bias into several pieces.

7. Divide the corn bars among 4 plates. On the corn, stack some chicken liver pieces and then watercress, then more chicken liver and more watercress. Crumble bacon over salads. Drizzle the remaining vinaigrette around each plate. Serve warm.

- ○ sour
- ○ salty
- ● sweet
- ○ bitter

1hr 30mins
TOTAL TIME

1hr 10mins
ACTIVE TIME

DIFFICULTY

4
PORTIONS

COTEAUX DU
LAYON

GRILLED DUCK WITH WATERCRESS & A CITRUS VINAIGRETTE

sour
salty
sweet
bitter

This is essentially duck à l'orange, updated, lightened up, and given my special twist. Though we've suggested using grapefruit, orange, and lime juice, any combination of citrus juices will work.

- 2 ruby red grapefruits, 1 juiced and 1 peeled and segmented (see directions for segmenting citrus fruit on page 164)
- 2 navel oranges, 1 juiced and 1 peeled and segmented
- Juice of 1 lime
- 1 cup vegetable or canola oil
- 2 tablespoons sesame oil
- 1 tablespoon soy sauce
- 2 tablespoons minced fresh mint
- 1 tablespoon sugar
- 2 teaspoons minced shallots
- 1 teaspoon salt, plus more to taste
- 4 cranks of fresh ground pepper in a mill, plus more to taste
- 4 skin-on duck breasts, preferably White Pekin, about 8 ounces each, excess fat trimmed
- 1 pound watercress, thicker stems removed
- Sesame seeds for garnish

1. In a medium nonreactive bowl, combine grapefruit juice, orange juice, lime juice, vegetable or canola oil, sesame oil, soy sauce, mint, sugar, shallots, 1 teaspoon salt, and 4 cranks pepper. Place duck breasts in a nonreactive baking pan and bathe with marinade. Refrigerate 30 minutes.

2. Remove duck from marinade. Strain the marinade and divide, transferring about half to a small saucepan and reserving the rest. Place the saucepan over high heat, bring to a boil, and boil 1 minute. Check seasoning. Set aside to cool.

3. Preheat a grill with briquettes banked around edge. Alternatively, preheat a grill pan over medium-high heat. When it is too hot to hold your hand 6 inches above grill for more than a few seconds, it's ready. Place duck breasts skin side down on grill and cook, brushing flesh side with uncooked marinade occasionally, until skin is dark brown and crisp and most of the duck's fat has been rendered, about 7 minutes. Flip and brush with more marinade. Grill until meat is medium rare, 3 to 5 minutes. Transfer to a cutting board and let stand 5 minutes.

4. In a large bowl, toss watercress with half of cooked marinade. Divide watercress among 4 plates. Slice duck breasts on the bias and place slices on top of salad. Scatter citrus segments over entire dish. Drizzle remaining cooked dressing over the top and sprinkle with sesame seeds.

1 hr 20 mins
TOTAL TIME

45 mins
ACTIVE TIME

DIFFICULTY

4
PORTIONS

MEDIUM-
BODIED
CABERNET
FRANC

JAMBON DE BAYONNE, BABY ARTICHOKES & ARUGULA

I first visited Spain in 1999. Now, the hot list of what to bring back from Spain will depend on who you're talking to, but if you ask me, no item is more worthy of being smuggled back than an aged Spanish ham. Looking at the pig's hoof sticking out of my carry-on as I drove away from Kennedy Airport (how is it that no customs official noticed that trotter?), I was already scheming up dishes.

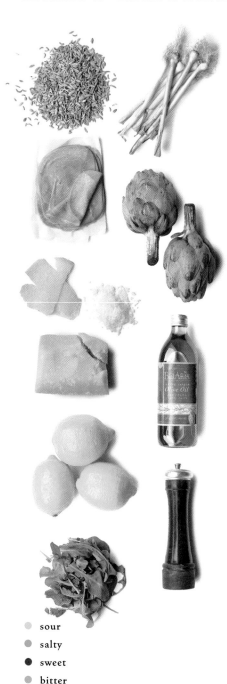

- 3/4 cup plus 2 tablespoons olive oil
- 1/2 medium onion, peeled and chopped
- 4 cloves garlic, peeled and lightly smashed under the blade of a heavy knife
- 1 teaspoon black peppercorns
- 1/2 teaspoon fennel seeds
- 1/2 cup white wine
- 1/4 cup fresh lemon juice (about 2 lemons)
- 12 baby artichokes
- Salt and ground pepper to taste
- 2 bunches arugula, washed and dried
- 12 thin slices Jambon de Bayonne or prosciutto, torn into bite-size pieces
- 4 ounces Parmigiano-Reggiano cheese, shaved thin

1. In a medium saucepan over medium heat, heat 2 tablespoons of the olive oil and sweat the onion and garlic until tender, 5 to 7 minutes. Add the peppercorns and fennel seeds, and cook for 2 minutes. Add the white wine and remaining 3/4 cup olive oil and simmer for 20 minutes.

2. Fill a bowl with water and add 2 tablespoons of the lemon juice. Cut off artichoke stems. Remove the outermost leaves by rotating the artichoke against the blade of a sharp knife. Trim off any leaves still attached to the bottoms. Cut the top third off each artichoke and discard. As you finish each artichoke, place immediately in the water bath. The citric acid will help retard discoloration (oxidation).

3. After the olive oil mixture has simmered for 20 minutes, strain it into a clean saucepan, discard spices, and return liquid to medium heat. Add the artichokes and cook, uncovered, stirring occasionally, until the artichokes are completely tender, 30 to 40 minutes. Transfer artichokes to a bowl. Cover bowl with plastic and refrigerate until ready to compose the salad.

4. Strain artichoke cooking liquid into a measuring glass. Discard the rest. To this whisk in remaining 2 tablespoons lemon juice a little at a time. Taste, and season with salt and pepper. Add more lemon juice if necessary: vinaigrette should be well balanced and not too acidic.

5. Toss arugula with half the vinaigrette and plate. Drape pieces of ham over greens. Slice each artichoke in half and scatter pieces over greens and meat. Finish salads with shavings of cheese and vinaigrette.

- sour
- salty
- **sweet**
- bitter

1 hr 15 mins
TOTAL TIME

45 mins
ACTIVE TIME

DIFFICULTY

4
PORTIONS

PROSECCO

BABY LETTUCES WITH PICKLED ZUCCHINI BLOSSOMS & YOGURT-TAHINI VINAIGRETTE

As with all the recipes in this book, I want this salad to give you ideas for creating your own signature dishes. Take a familiar dish, like a simple green salad, and apply your creativity and preferences. Simple green salads with oil-and-vinegar dressings never offended anyone, but frankly, they're boring. With a few quick additions of foods I love—pickled zucchini blossoms, yogurt, and tahini—this salad is out-of-the-ordinary and something I get excited about eating!

- 3 cups white vinegar
- 1 1/2 cups sugar
- 1 tablespoon kosher or sea salt for pickling
- Generous pinch of saffron threads
- 12 medium or 16 small zucchini blossoms, stems trimmed
- 1/2 cup goat yogurt or plain yogurt
- 1/4 cup tahini
- 2 tablespoons extra-virgin olive oil
- 1/2 teaspoon prepared Dijon mustard
- 3 tablespoons fresh lemon juice (from about 1 lemon)
- Salt and ground pepper to taste
- 10 ounces mixed salad greens

1. In a small saucepan over medium heat, combine vinegar, sugar, 1 tablespoon salt, and saffron threads. Bring to a simmer, stirring to dissolve sugar. Remove pan from heat and let stand at room temperature until liquid is the temperature of comfortably warm, drinkable tea. Arrange zucchini blossoms in nonreactive bowls or baking dishes or in a large glass pickling jar or jars. Pour warm liquid over the blossoms. When completely cool, cover. Let stand at room temperature for at least 12 hours. Remove pickled blossoms from the liquid and pat dry with paper towels.

2. Combine yogurt, tahini, olive oil, mustard, and lemon juice in a bowl. Whisk by hand until well mixed. Taste, and season vinaigrette with salt and pepper. (This recipe yields more vinaigrette than you'll need for the salad, but it keeps well and doubles as a dip for crudités.) Place salad greens in a large mixing bowl and toss with just enough vinaigrette to lightly coat the leaves, about 5 table spoons.

3. Divide dressed greens among 4 plates. Top each salad with an equal number of pickled zucchini blossoms. Serve at room temperature or chilled.

- sour
- salty
- sweet
- bitter

12 hrs 30 mins
TOTAL TIME

30 mins
ACTIVE TIME

DIFFICULTY

4
PORTIONS

PROSECCO

ROASTED BEET SALAD WITH GOAT CHEESE & FRISÉE

You have to go no further than the name of this salad to see the four-taste formula at work. Beets are incredibly sweet; goat cheese is both salty and tangy (sour); and frisée is bitter. And while I could have stopped there, I decided to incorporate walnuts—not for their mildly bitter taste, but purely for their nutty flavor.

- 3 large beets (about 1 1/2 pounds), stems and roots trimmed
- 3 tablespoons oil, any variety, or enough to just coat beets
- Salt to taste
- 1/2 cup shelled walnuts
- 1/4 cup red wine vinegar
- 1 tablespoon prepared Dijon mustard
- 1 tablespoon finely grated grapefruit zest
- 1 tablespoon chopped fresh tarragon
- 1/2 tablespoon sugar
- 1/2 cup walnut oil
- Ground pepper to taste
- 8 ounces fresh goat cheese, crumbled
- 2 cups frisée (from a 4-ounce head), torn by hand

1. Preheat oven to 425°F.

2. Rub beets with a thin film of oil, sprinkle with salt, and wrap each separately in aluminum foil. Place on a baking sheet and roast in oven 1 hour, or until they are tender throughout when pierced with a skewer.

3. Spread walnuts on a baking sheet, sprinkle with salt, and toast in oven (with beets) for 6 minutes, stirring several times, until darker brown and fragrant. Set aside.

4. In a mixing bowl, whisk together vinegar, mustard, grapefruit zest, tarragon, and sugar. Pour walnut oil into bowl in a slow, steady stream, whisking vigorously to create an emulsification. Season to taste with salt and pepper.

5. Once beets have been roasted, remove from oven and let stand. When cool enough to handle, pull off beet skins and slice beets across into 1/4-inch-thick rounds. Fan several beet slices on each of 4 plates; season with salt and pepper. Layer crumbled goat cheese, frisée, and walnuts over beets. Just before serving, dress entire salad with the walnut-tarragon vinaigrette. Serve at room temperature or chilled.

- sour
- salty
- sweet
- bitter

1 hr 35 mins

TOTAL TIME

40 mins

ACTIVE TIME

DIFFICULTY

4

PORTIONS

SAUVIGNON
BLANC

SCALLOPS WITH BEETS & MÂCHE

Make this dish if only to pick up a new technique. It's a good one. Here's the technique: brown a little butter, then roll the scallops around in the butter until they're fully cooked and encased in a golden, caramelized crackle that comes from the scallops' natural sugars. Pushing the taste of an ingredient as far as it will go is one of the cornerstones of my cooking style.

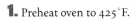

- 3 large beets (about 1 1/2 pounds), stems and roots trimmed
- 3 tablespoons olive oil, or enough to just coat beets
- Salt and ground pepper to taste
- 1 pound small scallops, preferably "dry" bay scallops (see Scallop Classifications on page 163)
- 3 tablespoons unsalted butter
- Finely grated zest and juice of 1 lemon
- 1 quart mâche or other delicate-flavored greens
- Small piece Parmigiano-Reggiano cheese

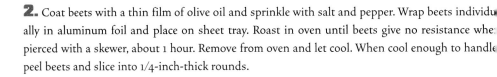

1. Preheat oven to 425°F.

2. Coat beets with a thin film of olive oil and sprinkle with salt and pepper. Wrap beets individually in aluminum foil and place on sheet tray. Roast in oven until beets give no resistance when pierced with a skewer, about 1 hour. Remove from oven and let cool. When cool enough to handle, peel beets and slice into 1/4-inch-thick rounds.

3. Dry scallops thoroughly with paper towels. Heat a cast-iron sauté pan until smoking hot. (If you don't own a cast-iron pan, any material that isn't nonstick will work.) Add butter. When butter foams, sprinkle scallops on both sides with salt and pepper and, once seasoned, transfer immediately to hot pan. For first 30 seconds, do not disturb scallops. After 30 seconds, loosen scallops with a spatula and gently swirl pan in a circular motion to roll scallops, encouraging all surface areas of scallops to come in contact with bottom of pan. Cook until golden brown all over, about 3 minutes. Remove to a plate and cover to keep hot.

4. Add lemon juice to same pan and stir vigorously with a wooden spoon to release browned bits. Season to taste. Return scallops to pan and gently swirl pan to coat scallops with lemony sauce.

5. Fan beet slices on plates. Arrange scallops with their sauce over beets. Pile mâche on scallops and garnish salad with lemon zest. Sprinkle with salt and pepper and grate a bit of Parmigiano-Reggiano over each plate. Serve while scallops are warm.

○ sour
◐ salty
● sweet
◑ bitter

1 hr 30 mins
TOTAL TIME

25 mins
ACTIVE TIME

DIFFICULTY

4
PORTIONS

SAUVIGNON
BLANC

ESCAROLE WITH JICAMA & A RHUBARB VINAIGRETTE

It wasn't until I got into professional kitchens that I witnessed escarole being steamed, wilted, and braised. When I told other cooks that my Italian family eats raw escarole as salads, they thought we were nuts. Look, I know it's bitter. But it's also delicious raw! All it needs is a good dose of something sweet, like a tangy rhubarb vinaigrette and juicy, sweet jicama. Another great thing about this sturdy green is that it keeps in the fridge much longer than lettuce.

- 1 head escarole, 9 to 10 ounces (see cleaning instructions below)
- 1/3 cup plus 1 tablespoon extra-virgin olive oil
- 1 cup chopped rhubarb (from a 4-ounce stalk)
- 1 1/2 tablespoons sugar
- 1 1/2 tablespoons sherry vinegar or white wine vinegar
- 1 1/2 tablespoons chopped fresh tarragon
- 1 teaspoon Dijon mustard (the more potent the better: I recommend Maille and Coeur Savage brands)
- Salt and ground pepper to taste
- 1/2 cup small-cubed jicama (from a 3-ounce piece)

1. Separate leaves of escarole. Do not discard stems. Rinse in several changes of water until water runs clear. (A good way to check for grit in water is to scoop a bit in a white teacup or other white vessel: imperfections stand out.) Spin the escarole in a salad spinner or lay leaves flat on paper towels and pat dry. Chop or tear the leaves into small bite-size pieces.

2. In a saucepan over low heat, warm 1 tablespoon of the oil. Add rhubarb and 2 tablespoons water and stir to combine. Cover the pot and cook for 7 minutes, or until rhubarb has broken down. Remove pan from heat.

3. Off the heat, add sugar, vinegar, tarragon, and mustard, and stir until sugar has dissolved. Add remaining 1/3 cup oil all at once and whisk vigorously to incorporate. Season with salt and pepper.

4. In a large salad bowl, combine escarole, jicama, and rhubarb vinaigrette, and toss to coat.

- sour
- salty
- sweet
- bitter

35 mins
TOTAL TIME

35 mins
ACTIVE TIME

DIFFICULTY

4
PORTIONS

A SWEET
PROSECCO

CALAMARI, WATERMELON & AVOCADO SALAD

Creating this salad marked a milestone in my career: it was one of the first times I threw together ingredients with no long-standing reputation as partners. Calamari, perhaps because it is fairly meek-tasting, is usually coated or sauced with strong flavors. I aimed for a brighter profile by using perfumey watermelon. Avocado, earthy and nutty, keeps the dish from being too ethereal, and adds good textural contrast. The ultimate reward came when Ruth Reichl, then the restaurant critic for *The New York Times*, called the dish "carefully considered exotica."

- 1 egg white, beaten
- 2 teaspoons ground coriander seed
- 1/4 teaspoon salt, plus more as needed
- 2 cranks ground pepper in a mill, plus more as needed
- 2 whole squid (also "calamari"), cleaned and cut into rings and tentacles
- 1 tablespoon corn, grapeseed, canola, or vegetable oil
- 1 tablespoon fresh lemon juice
- 1 tablespoon extra-virgin olive oil
- 2 ounces mesclun or baby salad greens
- Zest of 1 lemon
- 1 shallot, peeled and minced
- 24 thin squares of watermelon, each about 1 inch by 1 inch
- 1 avocado, peeled, pitted, and cut into 8 slices

1. Beat the egg white in a medium bowl until foamy. To the egg white, add coriander, 1/4 teaspoon salt, and 2 cranks pepper; beat to combine. Add the calamari pieces and toss to coat. In a large non-stick sauté pan, heat oil until smoking. Add calamari and actively sauté until just opaque white, about 2 minutes. Remove pan from heat and season calamari with salt and pepper.

2. In a large nonreactive bowl, blend the lemon juice and olive oil by hand. Taste and season. Add salad greens, lemon zest, shallot, and calamari. Toss quickly and blend well.

3. Compose 4 salads by alternating layers of the calamari salad, watermelon squares, and avocado slices. Serve immediately, while calamari are still hot.

- sour
- salty
- sweet
- bitter

CHAPTER 6
ENTREES

QUICK MISO CHICKEN

This is a dish I make all the time in my toaster oven. Since microwaves and countertop convection ovens have largely replaced the toaster oven, I've adapted the recipe for the range.

- ●   4 skinless, boneless chicken breast halves, about 6 ounces each
- ● ●   2 tablespoons medium-colored miso
- ● ○ ●   2 tablespoons orange marmalade
- ● ●   Salt and ground pepper to taste
           1 tablespoon vegetable, canola, or corn oil

1. Place chicken breasts between 2 sheets of plastic wrap or wax paper, and pound thin with a mallet.

2. In a small bowl, whisk together miso and orange marmalade. Sprinkle chicken breasts lightly with salt and pepper and brush all over with marinade. Let stand 30 minutes.

3. Warm a nonstick sauté pan with the oil over medium-high heat. When hot, add the chicken Cook on first side 3 minutes. Flip. Baste tops with any remaining marinade. Cook on second side minutes or until meat is no longer pink. Flip, cook 15 seconds, and transfer to plates.

○   sour

●   salty

●   sweet

○   bitter

50 mins
TOTAL TIME

20 mins
ACTIVE TIME

DIFFICULTY

4
PORTIONS

RIESLING
KABINETT

BUCATINI WITH SUMMER VEGETABLES & A TOMATO-ANISE BROTH

I can't deny my Italian-American heritage: to me, pasta just isn't pasta without a red tomato sauce. Here, I created a bright-tasting, anise-flavored tomato sauce thin enough to run through the holes of the bucatini pasta. If you want to attack this dish the way my family would, skip the knife. Yes, the long, unruly pasta will flail around and lash you in the face, but that's the fun of eating bucatini!

- Salt to taste
- 1/4 cup extra-virgin olive oil
- 1 fennel bulb, trimmed and cut into 1-inch squares
- Ground pepper to taste
- 2 zucchini, cut into 1-inch batons
- Pinch saffron threads
- 1 tablespoon ground anise seed
- 1/4 cup white wine vinegar
- 1 cup white wine
- One 28-ounce can plum tomatoes
- 12 ounces bucatini (spaghetti-length tubes) or spaghetti
- Fresh basil leaves to yield 2 tablespoons when chopped, held whole
- 1/2 cup ricotta cheese, at room temperature

1. Bring a large pot of water to a boil and salt heavily.

2. In a saucepan over medium-low heat, warm 2 tablespoons of the oil. Add fennel, season, stir to coat, cover pan, and cook for 2 minutes. Add zucchini to pan, season, stir, cover, and cook just until no longer crunchy, about 2 minutes. Crumble in saffron and cook 1 minute, stirring. Add anise seed and cook until anise is fragrant, 1 to 2 minutes. Pour in vinegar, increase heat to medium high, and cook until very little liquid is left. Pour in white wine and cook until reduced by half. Add tomatoes with their juices, reduce heat to low, and simmer for about 15 minutes. Use a wooden spoon to help break up the tomatoes while they are cooking.

3. Meanwhile cook pasta to al dente or desired doneness. Drain and set aside.

4. Taste sauce, and season with salt and pepper. Remove pan from heat. Quickly slice basil and stir 2 tablespoons of it into the sauce along with the remaining 2 tablespoons oil. Dump pasta into sauce and toss.

5. Divide pasta among 4 plates and top each serving with some ricotta cheese. Serve hot.

- sour
- salty
- sweet
- bitter

1_{hr}
TOTAL TIME

1_{hr}
ACTIVE TIME

DIFFICULTY

4
PORTIONS

BARBERA

CAULIFLOWER BISTEEYA WITH SPICED EGGPLANT PURÉE

A true Moroccan bisteeya incorporates chicken or pigeon meat. In developing a vegetarian version, I knew I'd have to choose a vegetable filling that was bulky and toothsome. I decided on cauliflower because it acts as a neutral canvas for the spices in the dish. Eggplant, right at home in any Mediterranean dish, is roasted and then turned into a flavorful purée.

- 1/4 cup raisins
- 1/4 cup white wine vinegar
- 2 large Italian eggplants
- 1 1/2 cups olive oil
- Salt and ground pepper to taste
- 10 sheets phyllo dough
- 3 tablespoons unsalted butter, melted
- 2 tablespoons garam masala
- 1/4 cup pine nuts (also "pignoli")
- 1 yellow or Spanish onion, peeled and chopped fine
- 2 tablespoons honey
- 2 heads cauliflower, cut into medium-size florets
- 1/2 cup loosely packed fresh basil leaves

1. Preheat oven to 375°F.

2. Place raisins in a small nonreactive bowl with vinegar. Let stand 30 minutes, or until you're ready to add them to the eggplant purée.

3. Cut eggplants in half from end to end, and score their flat surfaces in a crosshatch pattern. Brush all sides with 2 or 3 tablespoons of the olive oil and sprinkle with salt and pepper. Place eggplant halves cut side down on a baking sheet and roast in oven until shrunken and very tender, about 40 minutes. Remove from oven and let cool.

4. Clear a good-sized work space for the phyllo. Keep phyllo pile covered with a damp tea towel and work quickly to prevent exposed phyllo from drying out. Lay down first sheet of phyllo, brush entire surface with melted butter, and dust 1/4 teaspoon garam masala through a fine mesh sieve over the entire surface. Lay second sheet squarely over first, brush with butter, season with garam masala, and continue stacking this way until the pile has 5 layers. Brush the top layer with butter, but do not spice it with garam masala. Cut 2 large rounds from the phyllo stack with an inverted soufflé dish or bowl as a guide for your knife. Repeat entire process with 5 more phyllo sheets so that you have a total of 4 phyllo "lids." Place lids on a baking sheet and bake until phyllo is golden and crispy, about 12 minutes. Remove from oven.

- sour
- salty
- sweet
- bitter

1 hr 40 mins
TOTAL TIME

1 hr 30 mins
ACTIVE TIME

DIFFICULTY

4
PORTIONS

BEAUJOLAIS
NOUVEAU

5. Place pine nuts in a dry sauté pan over medium heat. Toast until golden and fragrant, shaking pan frequently and monitoring closely so the tiny nuts don't burn.

6. In a large nonstick saucepan over medium heat, warm 2 tablespoons of the olive oil. Add onion, season with salt and pepper, stir to coat with oil, cover pan, and cook for 5 minutes. Add remaining 1 tablespoon garam masala to onions and sauté, stirring continuously, until powder has dissolved and spice fragrance intensifies. Use a fork to scrape eggplant flesh into pan; discard skins. Cook for 10 minutes, using a wooden spoon to break up any eggplant chunks, until you have a thick paste. Season with salt and pepper to taste, and stir in honey. Drain raisins from their vinegar and add raisins and toasted pine nuts to purée. Stir to combine. Remove from heat and cover pan to keep warm.

7. In a sided sauté pan, heat 1 cup of the olive oil until smoking hot. (The oil should be enough to come one-third of the way up the cauliflower, so adjust amount accordingly.) Make sure that cauliflower has no surface moisture. Sprinkle florets with salt and pepper and carefully lower pieces into hot oil. Use long tongs to rotate cauliflower for even frying. Pan-fry until cauliflower is brown and tender, 6 to 8 minutes per batch. Drain on paper towels.

8. Spread some eggplant pureé on each plate and arrange fried cauliflower over purée. Tear the basil leaves by hand and scatter them over the cauliflower and eggplant. Cover each plate with a phyllo lid, leaning it against the cauliflower. Serve hot.

POT AU FEU OF ROOT VEGETABLES

Root vegetables have deep, intense flavors. Most often, the water they are cooked in goes down the drain. I say stop the madness! That water has absorbed so much of the vegetables' essence. In pot au feu, the vegetable cooking water reappears as the broth for the vegetables. Condiments set out on the table with the pot au feu do the balancing: sea salt, cornichons or pickles, mustard, and horseradish.

At first glance, the instructions accompanying this recipe appear complicated. Don't be put off; it's actually an incredibly simple dish to make. I've worked the recipe so that you can use ingredients of your choice.

- 2 1/2 pounds any combination of 3 or more of the following: carrots, celery root, daikon, parsnips, pearl onions, small potatoes (such as baby Red Bliss), rutabagas, or turnips
- 1 tablespoon salt, plus more to taste
- Ground pepper to taste
- Zest and juice of 1 lemon
- Dijon mustard
- Coarse sea salt, preferably gros sel de Guerande, or kosher salt
- Cornichons

1. Start by vigorously scrubbing all vegetables except pearl onions and rutabagas under running water. Peel all vegetables with the exception of potatoes. Cut vegetables into bite-size chunks, reserving peels and scraps. Don't reserve waxed rutabaga peel.

2. Place vegetable peels and scraps in a stockpot and cover with 3 quarts water. Add 1 tablespoon salt. Bring to a boil, lower heat, and simmer for 1 hour. Strain stock twice through a fine mesh sieve lined with a coffee filter. Taste, and season with salt and pepper.

3. Place stock in a large pot and bring to a gentle simmer. Beginning with carrots and parsnips, poach vegetables in pot sequentially, covering pot after each addition. Add ingredients to the pot according the schedule below, which takes into account the cooking times of the various roots and tubers. At 0 minutes: carrots and parsnips. At 5 minutes: celery root, daikon, potatoes, rutabagas, and turnips. At 10 minutes: pearl onions.

Poach until all vegetables have lost their crunch but are firm, about 20 minutes. Add lemon juice and zest to pot. Season pot au feu with salt and pepper.

4. Ladle vegetables and stock into bowls. In keeping with the classic presentation of this rustic French dish, serve small dishes of Dijon mustard, coarse sea salt, and cornichons alongside the bowls of steaming pot au feu.

- sour
- salty
- sweet
- bitter

2 hrs
TOTAL TIME

1 hr
ACTIVE TIME

DIFFICULTY

4
PORTIONS

GRECO
DI TUFO

ORECCHIETTE WITH PESTO ROSSO

When I traveled to Pisa, Italy, I spent time with artisanal pasta makers. Watching them reminded me what an art form hand-shaped pasta is. If you can, buy or make fresh, hand-shaped orecchiette; the chewy texture of each "little ear" is a special treat.

- ● ●   1/2 cup extra-virgin olive oil
- ●   1/4 cup finely chopped fresh garlic
- ● ○   3 cups chopped tomatoes, drained if canned
- ● ○   1/2 cup chopped marinated fresh anchovies (don't use canned) or marinated herring
- ●   1 pound orecchiette, preferably 100 percent semolina
- ● ○   8 jumbo raw shrimp, shelled, deveined, and cut into disks 1/4-inch thick
- ●   1 cup loosely packed fresh basil leaves
- ● ● ●   Salt, ground pepper, and sugar to taste

1. In a saucepan over low heat, warm olive oil. Add garlic and cook until just golden, then add tomatoes. Increase heat to medium-high and cook sauce until thick and chunky, about 15 minutes, crushing tomatoes with a wooden spoon or potato ricer. Stir in anchovies or herring and cook, stirring until fish is cooked through. Cover saucepan and keep over lowest heat while you cook the pasta.

2. Cook pasta in heavily salted boiling water until done, per manufacturer's directions. Drain all but about 3 tablespoons of the cooking water from the orecchiette. Add pasta with reserved cooking water and shrimp pieces to the saucepan over low heat. Stir until shrimp are opaque white. Tear by hand the basil leaves or leave them whole, and add to pasta. Stir once more, season to taste with salt, pepper, and sugar, and serve.

- ○ sour
- ● salty
- ● sweet
- ○ bitter

45 mins
TOTAL TIME

30 mins
ACTIVE TIME

DIFFICULTY

4
PORTIONS

FIANO DI
AVELLINO OR
GRECO DI TUFO

SEARED WILD SALMON WITH SPRING ONIONS & RHUBARB

When you think of foods that feature rhubarb, which come to mind? Rhubarb pie? While I love rhubarb desserts, I parted ways with tradition here by using the unique, tart vegetable in a savory preparation.

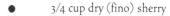

- 3/4 cup dry (fino) sherry
- 1/4 cup sugar, preferably turbinado ("sugar in the raw")
- 1/2 pound rhubarb (about 2 stalks), trimmed and coarsely chopped
- 2 tablespoons kosher salt
- 1 pound fava beans, shelled
- 3 tablespoons unsalted butter
- 1 pound spring onions, thinly sliced
- 1/2 cup chicken stock
- 1 sprig fresh thyme
- 1/8 teaspoon table or sea salt, plus more to taste
- Ground pepper to taste
- 4 skin-on wild salmon fillets, about 6 ounces each
  Vegetable oil
- 1 teaspoon fresh lemon juice

1. In a medium saucepan, combine sherry with sugar and cook over high heat, stirring continuously, until sugar is dissolved. Add rhubarb and cook 2 minutes. Strain, reserving liquid. Boil liquid until reduced by half, add rhubarb and simmer until a thick purée, about 5 minutes.

2. Bring a pan of water to a boil and add 1 tablespoon of the kosher salt. Prepare an ice bath and dissolve into it the other 1 tablespoon kosher salt. Boil fava beans 2 minutes. Transfer them to an ice bath for a few minutes. Drain and peel fava beans.

3. In a medium saucepan, melt butter over low heat. Add onions, cover, and, stirring occasionally, cook until softened, 12 to 15 minutes. Add the stock, thyme, 1/8 teaspoon salt, and pepper. Cover and simmer until the onions are extremely tender, about 8 minutes. Remove from heat. Discard thyme. Gently fold in fava beans.

4. Light a grill or heat a grill pan over medium-high heat. Brush both sides of salmon with oil and sprinkle with salt and pepper. Working in batches if necessary, grill the salmon skin side down until the skin is very crisp, 4 to 5 minutes. Flip the salmon and continue to grill until barely cooked through, 2 to 5 minutes more depending on the thickness of the fish.

5. Before serving, gently reheat both the onion-fava mixture, adding lemon juice, and the rhubarb sauce. For each serving, layer onion-fava mixture, then rhubarb sauce, then salmon fillet.

- sour
- salty
- **sweet**
- bitter

1hr 45mins
TOTAL TIME

1hr 45mins
ACTIVE TIME

DIFFICULTY

4
PORTIONS

PINOT NOIR
FROM OREGON

PRAWNS WITH HANDKERCHIEF PASTA

For all the variety of pasta shapes stocked by the average American grocery store, one type I've never been able to find here is the square-shaped *fazzoletti*, Italian for "handkerchiefs." A simple solution: break lasagna sheets into thirds. What I love about squares is the way they drape over and envelop the other ingredients in the bowl.

- 1/4 cup plus 2 tablespoons olive oil
- Salt and ground pepper to taste
- 12 jumbo raw head-on shrimp (if unavailable, use 15 jumbo shrimp with heads removed), shelled and deveined
- 1 cup sweet white wine, such as Riesling
- 2 tablespoons ground coriander seed
- 1 tablespoon minced fresh garlic
- 1 large onion, peeled and chopped fine
- One 14-ounce can plum tomatoes
- Juice of 1/2 large lime
- 11 sheets lasagna, each sheet broken by hand into 3 squares
- 10 ounces fresh spinach, washed

1. Warm a wide, high-sided sauté pan over medium-high heat with 2 tablespoons of the olive oil. Season both sides of shrimp with salt and pepper. When oil is hot, add as many shrimp to the pan as will fit and cook just until shrimp turn bright pink and opaque. Remove shrimp from pan immediately; do not overcook. Repeat with remaining shrimp. Remove shrimp heads and reserve both bodies and heads. Do not rinse pan.

2. In a blender, combine shrimp heads (substitute 3 shrimp if you've used headless shrimp) with wine. Pass purée through a fine mesh strainer. Discard solids and reserve liquid.

3. Over medium-high heat, warm 1 tablespoon of the oil in the same sauté pan in which you've cooked the shrimp. Add coriander and, stirring continuously to prevent burning, sauté until fragrant, 1 to 2 minutes. Add 1 tablespoon of the oil, garlic, and onions, cover, and cook until translucent and soft, about 5 minutes. Add reserved shrimp-flavored wine, bring to a simmer, and simmer uncovered, for 2 minutes. Add tomatoes with their juices and simmer for 15 minutes, stirring sauce frequently and breaking up tomatoes with a wooden spoon. Stir in lime juice and remaining 2 tablespoons oil. Taste, and season with salt and pepper. Keep over lowest heat.

4. Add lasagna squares to boiling water and cook until al dente, following manufacturer's timing guidelines. Remove pot from heat, add spinach, and steep for 30 seconds. Drain and add to sauté pan along with shrimp. Gently toss all ingredients together and warm through, about 2 minutes.

5. Divide contents of pan among 4 plates; each serving will consist of about 8 handkerchiefs and 3 jumbo shrimp. You may also present everything in a large bowl and let your guests serve themselves.

- sour
- salty
- ● sweet
- bitter

55 mins
TOTAL TIME

55 mins
ACTIVE TIME

DIFFICULTY

4
PORTIONS

ORVIETO OR
SOAVE

BLACK COD WITH CORN & SPINACH

A roadside farm stand kind of recipe! In this late-summer dish, 12 ears of corn become a thick, saffron-laced corn porridge.

- 1/3 cup plus 2 tablespoons sherry or white wine vinegar
- 2 teaspoons honey
- Pinch saffron threads
- 1/2 cup sugar
- 1/2-inch knob fresh ginger, smashed under the blade of a heavy knife
- 1/4 cup soy sauce
- 12 ears corn, husked
- Salt and ground pepper to taste
- 1/4 cup olive oil
- 1 pound spinach, washed
- Pinch cayenne pepper
- 4 skinless black cod, Chilean sea bass, or salmon fillets, about 8 ounces each

1. In a saucepan over medium heat, warm 1/3 cup of vinegar with honey. Crumble saffron into pan. Bring to a simmer, stirring, and remove from heat. Cover pan and let steep for 30 minutes.

2. Place sugar in a small, heavy-bottomed saucepan over medium heat. Stirring continuously, cook until sugar has melted into a smooth, dark caramel. Add ginger to pan and cook 1 minute, stirring. Add remaining 2 tablespoons vinegar, scrape bottom of pan with wooden spoon, and simmer to thicken for 3 minutes. Take pan off heat, discard ginger, and stir in soy sauce. Set aside.

3. Strip corn kernels by running a sharp knife from stem end to tip, rotating each ear to remove all corn. Place kernels in food processor and process until crushed well. Transfer to a saucepan over medium heat, and heat until corn has cooked through, become tender, and released its moisture and cornstarch, about 20 minutes. Aim for a thick, loose corn porridge. Add saffron-vinegar infusion. Stir to combine. Taste sauce, and season with salt and pepper. Cover pan to keep warm.

4. Heat 1 tablespoon of oil in a wide, sided pan over high heat. Add spinach and cayenne pepper, and season with salt and pepper. Sauté until spinach has wilted, about 4 minutes. Keep warm.

5. In a sauté pan, heat the remaining 3 tablespoons oil until very hot. Season one side of fish fillets with salt and pepper. Working in batches if necessary, place fillets seasoned side down in pan and sauté until browned, 3 to 4 minutes. Before flipping, season top of fillets with salt and pepper and dab off any surface moisture. Sauté on second side 3 to 4 minutes. Remove from heat.

6. Spoon corn sauce on 4 plates. Layer a quarter of the spinach over the corn. Center a fish fillet on the spinach, and brush fish generously with glaze. Serve warm.

- sour
- salty
- sweet
- bitter

2 hrs 15 mins
TOTAL TIME

2 hrs 15 mins
ACTIVE TIME

DIFFICULTY

4
PORTIONS

DEMI-SEC
(OFF-DRY)
MONTLOUIS OR
VOUVRAY

SKATE WITH INDIAN LIME PICKLE SWISS CHARD

- sour
- salty
- sweet
- bitter

Skate does not appear on American menus very often. I happen to love its tender, ropy texture. This is my amped-up version of the bistro standby *Raie au Beurre Noisette* (Skate with Brown Butter).

- 1 egg white
- 1/2 cup fine cornmeal
- 2 skate fillets, about 7 ounces each
- Salt and ground pepper to taste
- 2 tablespoons corn oil
- 4 tablespoons (1/2 stick) unsalted butter
- 1/2 cup diced tomato
- Juice of 1/2 lemon
- 1 tablespoon finely chopped fresh chives
- 2 cups Indian Lime Pickle Swiss Chard (page 232)
- 1/2 cup Onion Soubise (page 228)

1. In a shallow bowl, lightly whip egg white. Spread cornmeal over a plate. Brush skate fillets all over with egg white and dredge in cornmeal. Shake off excess cornmeal. Sprinkle bony side of fish with salt and pepper.

2. Heat a sauté pan with 1 tablespoon of the oil until hot. Place a skate fillet in pan bony side down and sauté until underside is deep brown and crisped, 3 minutes. Just before flipping, season top side of skate with salt and pepper. Flip and cook on second side until interior is completely opaque, about 2 minutes. Transfer to paper towel and cover to keep warm. Add remaining 1 tablespoon of to pan, and, when hot, sauté second skate fillet. Transfer to paper towel and keep warm.

3. Drain oil from sauté pan and dab with a paper towel to remove any black bits. Set pan over medium high heat and add butter. When the butter's milk solids have browned, add tomato and sauté minute. Stir in lemon juice and chives. Season to taste with salt and pepper.

4. Dollop some Swiss chard on each plate. Center a skate fillet over the chard and spoon som onion soubise on the fish. Finish by spooning brown butter–tomato sauce over the dish.

30 mins
TOTAL TIME*

30 mins
ACTIVE TIME*

DIFFICULTY

4
PORTIONS

RIESLING
SPÄTLESE

*not including
accompani-
ments

BREADED COD WITH SPICY ROASTED TOMATO PURÉE

If this dish looks familiar, it's because the Aromatic Tomato and Kimchee Soup on page 116 was its predecessor. I simply made the soup a bit thicker and used it to sauce fish. Soups often make great sauces for fish, meat, and vegetables, so keep your mind and options open!

- 4 large beefsteak tomatoes, 2 halved along the equator and seeded and 2 chopped in large dice
- Salt and ground pepper to taste
- 3 cloves garlic, peeled and minced
- 1/4 cup plus 1 tablespoon extra-virgin olive oil
- 1 onion, peeled and cut into large dice
- 1 tablespoon tomato paste
- 3 tablespoons chopped prepared cabbage kimchee
- 4 tablespoons (1/2 stick) unsalted butter plus enough to grease baking sheet and 1 tablespoon melted butter
- 1 cup fresh bread crumbs (white sandwich bread and brioche are good choices)
- 1/4 cup chopped fresh cilantro leaves
- 1 cup chopped fresh Thai basil or regular basil
- 4 boneless, skinless cod or hake fillets, about 6 ounces each
- Juice of 1/2 lime

1. Preheat oven to 375°F.

2. Season tomato halves with salt and pepper and place hollow side up on a baking sheet. Fill each cavity with about 1/4 teaspoon garlic and drizzle the 1 tablespoon olive oil over the 4 halves. Roast in oven for 20 minutes. Drain excess liquid from tomatoes and tent with aluminum foil to keep warm. Keep oven at 375°F.

3. In a saucepan over medium heat, warm remaining 1/4 cup olive oil. Add remaining garlic and all but 1/4 cup of the chopped onions, sprinkle with salt, and cover pan. Reduce heat and sweat 2 minutes or until onions and garlic are translucent but not yet colored. Add tomato paste, stir to coat, and sauté uncovered until tomato paste is dry, thick, and starting to darken. Add kimchee and diced tomatoes, reduce heat to medium-low, and simmer for 10 minutes.

4. Lightly grease a baking sheet with butter and scatter reserved 1/4 cup chopped onions over sheet. In a small bowl, mix together bread crumbs, 1 tablespoon melted butter, 1 tablespoon cilantro, and 1 tablespoon basil. Season fillets liberally with salt and pepper, then coat the top side of each with bread crumb mixture. Lay fillets in a single layer over onions with coated side facing up. Bake

- sour
- salty
- sweet
- bitter

1 hr 10 mins

TOTAL TIME

1 hr 10 mins

ACTIVE TIME

DIFFICULTY

4

PORTIONS

DRY CHENIN
BLANC

oven until bread crumb topping is slightly brown and fish is cooked through and firm, bout 8 minutes.

5. After it has simmered 10 minutes, transfer half the tomato-kimchee sauce to a blender or food rocessor and purée until smooth, then recombine with unprocessed sauce. Alternatively, use an nmersion blender to purée sauce just a bit: I like this sauce chunky, with pieces of tomato and kim-hee evident. Return sauce to a pan over lowest possible heat. Add 4 tablespoons butter, a piece at a ime, swirling pan to dissolve. Add lime juice and remaining cilantro and Thai basil, and stir to com-ine. Season to taste. Cover pan to keep warm.

6. Place an upturned tomato half on each plate, and fill with sauce. Use a spatula to lay one bread-d fish fillet with its onions over each half. Drizzle fish with more sauce and serve hot.

FRICASSÉE OF SCALLOPS WITH PICKLED CABBAGE

Who's ever heard of a white curry? Well, to me a curry can be any soupy combination of strong flavors. I love the way the honeycomb texture of the savoy cabbage contrasts with the squishy softness of the scallops.

- 1/4 cup olive oil
- 1/2 inch knob fresh ginger, peeled, sliced, and slices smashed under the blade of a heavy knife
- 3 cloves garlic, peeled and minced
- Salt and ground pepper to taste
- 1 large onion, peeled and diced
- 1 head savoy cabbage, thick ribs removed and leaves torn into smaller pieces
- 2 cups chopped tomatoes
- 1/4 cup white wine vinegar
- 2 stalks lemongrass, lightly crushed under the blade of a heavy knife and cut in half
- 1/2 cup coconut milk
- 1 1/2 pounds sea scallops
- 3/4 cup fresh cilantro leaves

1. In a large stockpot over medium-high heat, warm 3 tablespoons of the oil. Add ginger and garlic, season with salt and pepper, cover pot, and cook 1 minute. Add onions, cover, and cook 3 to 4 minutes until soft. Add cabbage and cook until it shows signs of wilting. Add tomatoes and sauté until much of tomatoes' moisture has evaporated. Add vinegar, lemongrass, and coconut milk. Simmer until sauce is a thickened stew, about 15 minutes. Discard lemongrass and ginger. Cover to keep warm.

2. Heat a sauté pan with remaining 1 tablespoon oil until hot. Decide how many scallops will fit in the pan, and season that number of scallops on one side only with salt and pepper. Pat dry: any surface moisture will prevent browning and caramelization. Immediately place scallops seasoned side down in pan and cook until well browned, 1 to 2 minutes. Season top side with salt and pepper, pat dry again, and flip. Cook until second surface is browned and scallops' centers are opaque white, 1 to 2 minutes more. Remove to a bowl and tent with aluminum foil to keep warm. Repeat process with remaining scallops.

3. Stir cilantro into fricassée of vegetables, and season with salt and pepper according to your preference. Spoon some fricassée onto each of 4 plates. Arrange scallops over each bed of fricassée and serve.

- sour
- salty
- ● sweet
- bitter

1 hr 30 mins
TOTAL TIME

1 hr
ACTIVE TIME

DIFFICULTY

4
PORTIONS

VIOGNIER

SCALLOP
CLASSIFICATIONS

There are four classifications of scallops that you should know: bay, sea, dry, and wet. Bay scallops come from (surprise!) bays in the North Atlantic and are small, sweet, and expensive. Sea scallops range in size from medium to colossal. Calico scallops, which have a tough texture, are tiny sea scallops often passed off as bays (don't be swindled!). The ultimate treat is scallops sold live in their shells. But if you can't get live, the first thing to know about shucked scallops is that they deteriorate rapidly. For this reason, most of the scallops marketed as "fresh" are soaked in chemical preservatives. Rinse these "wet" scallops thoroughly before cooking. When shopping for scallops to eat raw, stay away from "wet" scallops. Though the preservative won't harm you, you'll definitely notice its flavor. Better fishmongers carry just-shucked, sashimi-grade "dry" scallops.

Sea Scallops

Bay Scallops

Wet Scallops

SEA BASS WITH A SALTY DRIED PLUM GLAZE

Chilean sea bass, a luxuriously rich fish, begs for a sweet-salty treatment. What I appreciate about prune juice is its viscosity. Once reduced, it is a sauce all on its own; it needs no butter, cream, or syrup to give it body. Pear juice has the same ability.

- 2 grapefruits
- 1/4 cup sugar
- 1/4 cup sherry vinegar
- 3/4 cup prune juice
- 1/2 tablespoon soy sauce
- Salt and ground pepper to taste
  Corn oil
- 4 boneless, skinless Chilean sea bass fillets, about 8 ounces each, brought to room temperature
- Wondra flour
- Asian Mustard Greens (page 230) (optional)

1. Segment grapefruits: begin by removing peel and white pith with a sharp knife. Cut a bit off both ends of the grapefruits so that you can see the membranes dividing the segments. Free segments by slipping a knife along the side of each membrane, letting segments and juice fall into a bowl. Drain and reserve fruit and juice separately. Squeeze the juice from the grapefruit skins into the bowl with the juice.

2. Place the sugar in a heavy-bottomed saucepan over medium-high heat. Stirring continuously, cook until the sugar has become a smooth, light-colored caramel. Add vinegar and stir until the caramel has redissolved—it will harden upon contact with the room-temperature vinegar. Add prune juice and grapefruit juice, stir mixture, and increase heat to high. Cook until mixture has reduced to 1/2 cup of a fairly thick glaze, lowering heat as the liquid approaches this stage, 15 to 20 minutes. Remove pan from heat and stir in soy sauce. Season to taste with salt and pepper. The glaze should have a nice sweet-salty character.

3. Preheat oven to lowest setting.

4. Pour 1/2 inch of corn oil into a wide sauté pan and heat until very hot. (You will probably be able to fit only 2 fillets in the pan at a time. If you want to speed things up, heat 2 sauté pans simultaneously. Otherwise, work in batches.) Meanwhile, season one side of each fillet with salt and pepper, and sprinkle with a thin dusting of Wondra flour. To avoid contact with spattering oil, tilt pan away from you so that the oil runs to the far side, and place the fillets seasoned side down on the

sour
salty
sweet
bitter

1 hr 10 mins
TOTAL TIME

55 mins
ACTIVE TIME

DIFFICULTY

4
PORTIONS

GEWÜRZ-
TRAMINER

near side of the pan. Pan-fry until golden brown on bottom, about 2 minutes. Blot dry tops of fillets, quickly sprinkle with salt, pepper, and flour. Tilt pan away from you again and carefully flip fillets. Cook until same color on second side, then remove fish to paper towels. If working in batches, keep cooked fillets hot in a low oven while you pan-fry remaining fish.

5. Because the glaze is sweet, you'll want to serve this fish with a bitter green, such as the Asian Mustard Greens on page 230, spinach, escarole, or Brussels sprouts. Form a small mound of greens on each plate. Center a fish fillet over the greens. Drizzle a few spoons of prune glaze over each fillet so that the glaze runs over the sides of the fish. Distribute grapefruit segments around the plate and serve.

JOHN DORY WITH A RAGOUT OF DILL & LITTLENECK CLAMS

Some herbs go especially well with briny, salty clams. Parsley and dill are two of them. The potatoes at the bottom of the heap of this dish sponge up the sauce. John Dory, a delicate-tasting, firm-fleshed fish, is the only fish I know of that splits into three parts when you fillet it.

- 4 pounds littleneck, Manila, or other small clams or cockles
- 2 tablespoons cornmeal
- 1/4 cup kosher salt for blanching, plus more to taste
- 1/2 cup picked fresh flat-leaf parsley
- 1/2 bunch fresh dill
- 1 cup white wine
- 2 tablespoons chopped shallots
- 2 tablespoons corn oil
- 3 tablespoons unsalted butter
- 4 skinless John Dory (also called "St. Pierre"), cod, grouper, or red snapper fillets, about 6 ounces each
- Ground pepper to taste
- Wondra flour
- Luxurious Potato Purée (page 236)

- sour
- salty
- sweet
- bitter

1. Chip clams for 1 hour. (See Cleaning Clams on page 50.) Remove from water and hold in refrigerator.

2. Bring a saucepan of water to a boil and add 2 tablespoons of the salt. While water comes to a boil, prepare an ice bath with 2 tablespoons salt dissolved into water. Blanch parsley in boiling water for 30 seconds and immediately submerge in ice bath. Let sit for 1 minute, then remove with a slotted spoon (don't drain ice bath). When hot water has returned to a rolling boil, add dill and blanch 5 seconds. Shock dill in same ice bath for 1 minute. Pack blanched parsley and dill in a blender with 1/3 cup cold water. Purée herbs, pouring in more water as needed through the blender's feed hole until blade turns freely. Purée until smooth. Hold aside.

3. Choose a wide-bottomed pan with a tight-fitting lid (a see-through glass cover will let you watch the clams opening). Place pan over medium-high heat and add wine and shallots. When mixture comes to a boil, arrange clams in a single layer so that all have contact with the bottom of the pan, work in batches if necessary. Cover pan and steam clams, pulling each from the pan as soon as its shell is opened wide. All clams should open within 10 minutes. Discard any clams that haven't opened. Shake liquid out of clams into the steaming broth, spread clams on a baking sheet, and let cool to room temperature. Strain steaming broth through a fine mesh sieve into a clean pan.

2 hrs

TOTAL TIME

1 hr 30 mins

ACTIVE TIME

DIFFICULTY

4

PORTIONS

MEDIUM-
BODIED
CHARDONNAY

4. Once clams are cool enough to handle, you may remove them from their shells. However, a simpler and charmingly rustic approach is to serve them in their shells; the choice is yours.

5. Heat oil and 2 tablespoons of the butter over high heat in a wide sauté pan. Season fillets with salt and pepper on one side only, and dust same side with Wondra flour. When butter starts to foam and smoke, place fish dusted side down in pan and cook until well colored, 1 to 2 minutes. Blot moisture from tops of fillets, repeat seasoning (salt, pepper, Wondra flour), and flip. Cook on second side 1 to 2 minutes. Transfer fillets to paper towels to drain. Cover with pan lid or aluminum foil to keep warm.

6. Turn heat to medium-low under pan containing strained clam cooking liquid. Add parsley-dill purée, stir, and heat until sauce is warmed through, about 3 minutes. Add remaining 1 tablespoon butter and swirl pan to incorporate butter. Season to taste with salt and pepper. Remove pan from heat. Add clams, in their shells or shelled, to sauce and swirl pan to coat.

7. Shape a round of Luxurious Potato Purée on each plate and center a fillet on potatoes. Ladle clam sauce over entire dish. Serve hot.

HAKE WITH A SWEET POTATO BEURRE BLANC

Hake is not commonly fished for directly, but rather obtained as a by-catch of cod fishing in the Atlantic. With its springy texture, hake takes well to poaching and other long cooking methods. Substitute cod if you can't find hake.

- 2 medium sweet potatoes (1 pound total)
- 2 tablespoons extra-virgin olive oil, plus more to coat sweet potatoes
- Salt and ground black pepper to taste
- 4 tablespoons (1/2 stick) unsalted butter, cut into small pieces
- 4 sprigs fresh thyme or 1 teaspoon dried thyme
- 1 chunk smoked ham hock, about 3-inch square or 2-inch cube
- 1/2 garlic head (split garlic head horizontally)
- 1 tablespoon fresh lemon juice, plus more as needed
- 4 skinless, boneless hake, merluza, or cod fillets, about 6 ounces each
- Sugar as needed
- 1 hard-boiled egg, diced small
- 1 tablespoon chopped capers
- 1 tablespoon chopped shallots
- 1 tablespoon chopped fresh chives
- 2 teaspoons finely grated lemon zest

1. Preheat oven to 400°F.

2. Rub sweet potatoes with a thin film of olive oil, sprinkle with salt and pepper, and wrap eac separately in aluminum foil. Roast in oven until very soft, 45 minutes to 1 hour. When cool enoug to handle, peel. Place flesh in a blender with 2 1/2 cups water and purée until smooth.

3. Transfer sweet potato liquid to a wide sauté pan over medium heat. When warm, add butt pieces gradually while swirling pan to melt the butter. Season to taste. Add thyme, ham hock, garli and lemon juice, and bring to a gentle simmer. Lower fillets into liquid and cover pan. Poach fis until opaque throughout, about 6 minutes, basting occasionally. Remove fillets with a spatula an keep warm. Strain poaching liquid into a saucepan over high heat. Cook until reduced to a fair thick sauce, about 10 minutes. Taste and adjust seasoning with salt, pepper, sugar, or lemon juice.

4. In a small saucepan, combine diced egg, capers, shallots, chives, lemon zest, and 2 tablespoo olive oil. Place pan over low heat and, stirring gently, cook just until warmed through. Seaso gribiche with salt and pepper.

5. Center a hake fillet on each plate and sauce with the sweet potato beurre fondue. Top with a fe spoons of gribiche and serve.

- sour
- salty
- sweet
- bitter

CHAR WITH PEA SPROUTS &
FOREST MUSHROOMS

sour
salty
sweet
bitter

People either love or hate mushrooms. Personally, I can't figure out what there is to hate about them. But somehow, adding vinegar to mushrooms tempers that woodsi ness that turns people off. Vinegar also contributes to that all-important tension.

- 5 tablespoons plus 1 teaspoon olive oil
- 12 ounces mixed fresh flavorful mushrooms (black trumpet, chanterelle, cremini, hedgehog, mousseron, oyster, and portobello), chopped into bite-size pieces
- Salt and ground pepper to taste
- 2 tablespoons chopped shallots
- 1/2 tablespoon minced fresh garlic
  3 tablespoons all-purpose flour
- 1/4 cup champagne or white wine vinegar
- 3 cups chicken or vegetable stock
- Fresh tarragon to yield 1 tablespoon chopped, held whole
- 4 skin-on Arctic char fillets, about 6 ounces each (cod will work as substitute)
- 6 cups (about 10 ounces) pea sprouts (if unavailable, substitute chopped spinach or escarole)

1. In a sauté pan over medium-low heat, warm 3 tablespoons of the oil. Add mushrooms, season cover pan, and cook 10 minutes. Push mushrooms into a ring around sides of pan and add shallot and garlic to center of pan. Season. Cook, covered, until shallots are translucent, about 4 minutes Sprinkle pan with flour and stir to coat ingredients. When flour has dissolved, stir in vinegar Increase heat to high and cook, uncovered, until very little liquid is visible. Add stock and cook unt reduced to a medium-bodied sauce, 14 to 17 minutes. Chop 1 tablespoon tarragon, add to mushroor sauce, and simmer 1 minute. Season sauce with salt and pepper and keep warm.

2. Heat 2 tablespoons of the oil in a sauté pan over high heat until very hot. Sprinkle skin side o fillets with salt and pepper. Lay fillets skin side down in oil and sauté until skin is brown and crisp about 3 minutes. Pat dry the top sides of fillets, season, and flip. Cook on second side 2 to 3 min utes. Remove to plate and keep warm. Pour off oil from pan and clean with a bunched paper towel Return pan to high heat.

3. Add remaining 1 teaspoon oil to pan. While oil heats, place sprouts or other greens in a larg bowl and toss with a sprinkling of salt and pepper. Add seasoned shoots to very hot oil and sauté to 2 minutes, until shoots are wilted and slightly charred.

4. Spoon mushroom sauce over each dish. Lay a char fillet on the sauce and scatter pea shoots ove entire dish. Serve hot.

1hr
TOTAL TIME

1hr
ACTIVE TIME

DIFFICULTY

4
PORTIONS

CHIANTI OR
OTHER
SANGIOVESE-
BASED WINE

BLACK SEA BASS WITH CHESTNUTS & BLOOD ORANGES

I'll never forget the first time I ordered a glass of orange juice in Italy. The café server disappeared behind a corner, turned on a machine, and came out bearing a glass of dark red juice. I was horrified; too young to know better, I thought the bartender had cut himself on the machine and bled into my juice. My uncle set me straight. Blood oranges are a beautiful, tart winter treat, though you can find bottled juice year-round.

- 1 teaspoon plus a few dashes Pernod or other anise-flavored liqueur
- 8 blood oranges (if unavailable, use navel oranges)
- 9 tablespoons (1 1/8 sticks) unsalted butter
- 1 medium sweet onion, peeled and diced medium
- 1 teaspoon fennel seeds
- 2 tablespoons sugar
- 2 tablespoons vermouth
- 1 to 4 tablespoons champagne vinegar
- 2 cups unsweetened chestnut purée (15.5-ounce can)
- 3 tablespoons salt, plus more to taste
- Ground pepper to taste
- 20 scallions, dark green tops only
- 3 tablespoons corn oil
- 1/2 cup Wondra flour
- 4 skin-on black sea bass fillets, 6 to 8 ounces each

1. Place Pernod in a bowl. Segment 2 oranges: begin by removing peel and white pith with a sharp knife. Cut a bit off both ends of the oranges so that you can see the membranes dividing the segments. Free segments by slipping a knife along the side of each membrane, letting segments and juice fall into a bowl. Transfer segments to the bowl containing the Pernod. Into the bowl containing the orange juice, squeeze the juice from the empty orange skins and juice the remaining oranges (you should have about 2 cups juice).

2. In a large saucepan, melt 2 tablespoons of the butter over medium-low heat. Add onion and fennel seeds and cook slowly, allowing the onion to brown only slightly. Sprinkle in sugar and stir while it melts. Increase heat to medium and cook for 5 minutes. Add vermouth and stir. Add vinegar, using 1 tablespoon for blood oranges or 4 tablespoons for sweeter navel oranges, and continue to cook until very little liquid is visible. Pour in orange juice and simmer for 20 minutes or until reduced by half. Pour through a fine mesh strainer and set aside.

3. Combine chestnut purée with 3 tablespoons of the butter in a saucepan over medium heat and

- sour
- salty
- sweet
- bitter

1 hr 40 mins
TOTAL TIME

1 hr 15 mins
ACTIVE TIME

DIFFICULTY

4
PORTIONS

MEDIUM-
BODIED
CHARDONNAY
WITH NO OAK

whisk until butter has melted. Whisk in up to 1 cup of water, or until purée is relatively smooth and the consistency of whipped mashed potatoes. Season well with salt and pepper and set aside.

4. Bring a large pot of water to a boil and add salt until water tastes salty, about 3 tablespoons. Cook scallions in water until tender, about 7 minutes, then drain and blot dry with paper towels. Hold aside.

5. Heat a large sauté pan, preferably cast-iron, until very hot. Add oil and heat until almost smoking. Put the Wondra in a shallow plate, lightly dredge only the skin side of the fish fillets in the flour and season both sides well with salt and pepper. Carefully add the fish skin side down to the pan and cook, pressing with a spatula to prevent fillet from curling, for about 30 seconds. When the fish has "relaxed," remove spatula and cook an additional 2 to 3 minutes, until the edges of the fish turn opaque. Just before flipping, dab the tops of the fillets to remove moisture and season with salt and pepper. Flip and add 2 tablespoons butter to the pan. While the butter foams and then begins to brown, tilt the pan toward you so the butter pools at the edge of the pan and use a large spoon to baste the flesh side of the fish. When the flesh side is opaque, flip fillets so they're skin side up, baste quickly, remove from pan, and blot pan with a paper towel. Add the scallions to the same sauté pan and sauté about 30 seconds, until warm. Season with salt and pepper and remove from heat.

6. Place the sauce over low heat and fold in the orange segments. Perfume the sauce with a few dashes of Pernod and quickly whisk in remaining 2 tablespoons butter. Spoon chestnut purée on platter or 4 individual dinner plates. Ladle the sauce over the purée and scatter scallions over entire dish. Top with the fish fillets and serve.

○ sour
○ salty
● sweet
○ bitter

STRIPED BASS WITH LEMON ZEST

Once the TV Food Network invited me, an hour before airtime, to be on the program *In Food Today*. "Sure," I said, "no problem." The producer asked me to demonstrate a dish that was uncomplicated, easy-to-prepare, and seasonal. It was the height of striped bass season, so by the time my cab reached their studio, I had decided that striped bass would be the focus of my ad-libbed recipe. Inside, I grabbed three of the first foods I saw: a lemon, a red onion, and a bunch of chives. My dish was done.

- 2 red onions, peeled and halved along their equators
- 1/4 teaspoon coarse sea salt
- 4 skinless, boneless striped bass fillets, about 6 ounces each
- Salt and ground pepper to taste
- 1/2 pound unsalted butter (2 sticks), cut into small pieces
- Zest of 2 lemons
- Twelve 4-inch chive points (cut off the tip ends of 12 chives)

1. Preheat oven to 350°F.

2. Place onions cut side up on baking sheet. Sprinkle with sea salt. Bake for 20 to 25 minutes or until onions collapse. Remove from oven when done and set aside.

3. Season fish fillets on both sides with salt and pepper. Wrap each fillet tightly in three layers of plastic wrap. Fill a 5-quart saucepan two-thirds of the way with hot water and bring to 160°F. (At 160°F, the water will be very steamy and small bubbles will appear near the sides of the pan.) Remove pot from heat and carefully lower fish into water. Let fish poach off heat for 20 minutes. Fish should be opaque throughout but moist.

4. Meanwhile, prepare the lemon sauce: in a small saucepan over medium heat, bring 2 tablespoons water to a boil. Make a beurre fondue by introducing butter pieces gradually, whisking continuously to create a creamy emulsification. Remove pan from heat. Add lemon zest and swirl pan to combine. Season with salt and pepper to taste.

5. Center an onion half on each of 4 plates. Unwrap fish and place 1 fillet on each onion. Spoon lemon butter on top of fish. Garnish each plate with 3 chive points. If desired, serve any remaining sauce in a separate dish.

- sour
- salty
- sweet
- bitter

1hr20mins
TOTAL TIME

40mins
ACTIVE TIME

DIFFICULTY

4
PORTIONS

MEDIUM-
BODIED
CHARDONNAY

COD SANDWICH
WITH CURRY AIOLI

I won't claim any lofty inspiration for this sandwich: it's the evolution of my child-hood passion for Mrs. Paul's fish sticks and my later discovery of British fish and chips. I started getting creative with fried fish condiments in college, when I worked part-time in a cafeteria at Harvard (not just any cafeteria, mind you!). The aioli here has some great flavors, including curry, garlic, and lime.

- 1 head garlic, top 1/4 cut off
- 1 cup plus 1 tablespoon extra-virgin olive oil
- 1 1/2 tablespoons curry powder
- 1 tablespoon sugar
- 2 tablespoons fresh lime juice (about 1 lime)
- 1 tablespoon white wine vinegar
- 1 egg
- 1/2 teaspoon salt, plus more to taste
- Ground pepper to taste
- 1/2 cup corn oil
- 2 boneless cod fillets, 6 to 8 ounces each, cut in half lengthwise
- 1 cup Wondra or all-purpose flour
- 12 scallions, dark green tops only, sliced lengthwise into ribbons 1-inch thick
- 8 slices brioche, challah, Pullman loaf, or other good-quality white bread
- 1/4 cup butter (1/2 stick), at room temperature

1. Preheat oven to 375°F.

2. Wrap the garlic in foil and roast in oven until cloves are completely soft, about 40 minutes. Remove from oven and, when cool enough to handle, squeeze garlic paste from individual cloves.

3. Heat a small sauté pan over low heat with 1 tablespoon of the olive oil. Add garlic paste and curry powder, and lightly sauté for 3 minutes, stirring. Remove pan from heat and stir in sugar, lime juice, and vinegar. Stir until sugar is completely dissolved. Transfer paste to a food processor and purée until smooth. Add egg and 1/2 teaspoon salt through the feed tube, and continue to purée until smooth. Slowly pour the remaining 1 cup olive oil through the feed tube, adding it drop by drop until an emulsification is created, then adding the rest in a steady stream. Transfer aioli to small bowl and season to taste with salt and pepper. Hold aside.

4. Heat a large skillet or sauté pan, preferably cast-iron, over medium-high heat. Add the corn oil and heat until very hot. Season cod fillets with salt and pepper and dredge in flour. Shake to remove excess.

- sour
- salty
- sweet
- bitter

2 hrs
TOTAL TIME

1 hr 15 mins
ACTIVE TIME

DIFFICULTY

4
PORTIONS

VOUVRAY

Carefully slip fillets into the skillet and cook until golden brown and crisp on both sides, about [   ] minutes per side. Transfer fillets to paper towels to drain.

5. To the same pan, add scallion greens and sauté until wilted and tender, about 3 minutes. Remov[   ] the greens and wipe pan with a bunch of paper towels.

6. For each slice of bread, butter 1 side and spread the other with aioli. Assemble sandwiches by lay[   ] ering cod and scallions inside bread slices with the aioli sides facing in.

7. Reheat same pan over medium heat. To cook all 4 sandwiches at once, heat a second skillet c[   ] sauté pan over medium heat. Place buttered sandwiches in pan(s) and sauté, turning once and press[   ] ing with a spatula to flatten, until golden brown on outside. Remove sandwiches from pan and cu[   ] in half along the diagonal. Serve with more curry aioli on the side, if desired.

○ sour
○ salty
● sweet
○ bitter

ROASTED MISO SALMON
WITH CUBANELLE PEPPERS

What do you imagine chefs keep in their refrigerators? Well, the inside of mine is no centerfold for a decorating magazine; it's usually pretty empty because I rarely cook at home. But one food I can count on to be in there is miso. Miso never goes bad, and one bag has a seemingly infinite life.

- 6 cubanelle peppers (also "Italian frying peppers")
- 1/4 cup plus 2 tablespoons olive oil
- 1/4 cup rice wine vinegar
- 1/8 teaspoon salt, plus more to taste
- Ground pepper to taste
- 3 tablespoons unsalted butter
- 2 large sweet onions, such as Maui or Vidalia, peeled and cut into rings 1-inch wide
- 1/2 cup light-colored miso
- 1 teaspoon Japanese mustard paste, preferably S&B brand, or other prepared mustard
- 4 skinless salmon fillets, about 6 ounces each

1. Light a gas burner or flame grill. Hold a pepper with tongs directly over the flame and roast unt blackened, rotating for even blistering. Place pepper in a paper bag and loosely fold bag. Repeat wit remaining peppers. When cool, peel and seed. Cut 4 peppers into 1-inch squares. Reserve scrap (Or, if you have only an electric oven, roast peppers in a baking pan for 45 minutes at 350°F, rota ing them every 15 minutes.)

2. Chop remaining 2 peeled peppers and place in blender along with reserved scraps. Add 1/4 cu of the oil and 2 tablespoons of the vinegar. Purée until smooth. Season with salt and pepper.

3. Preheat oven to 325°F.

4. In a shallow pan over low heat, combine butter, onion rings, 1/4 cup water, and a sprinkle eac of salt and pepper. Cover pot and cook until onions are tender, about 20 minutes. Drain. Add pe per purée and stir to bind onions with purée.

5. In a bowl, whisk together miso, remaining 2 tablespoons vinegar, and 2 tablespoons oil, mus tard, 1/8 teaspoon salt, and several twists of ground pepper. Arrange fillets on a lightly oiled bakin sheet. Brush a generous amount of miso dressing on the top sides of the fillets. Bake 8 to 10 min utes for medium-rare. Transfer fillets to a broiler and broil until tops are lightly browned, about minutes.

6. To serve, dollop some onion-pepper mixture on each of 4 plates. Lay a salmon fillet on the sau and garnish servings with roasted cubanelle pepper squares. Serve immediately.

- ○ sour
- ◐ salty
- ● sweet
- ○ bitter

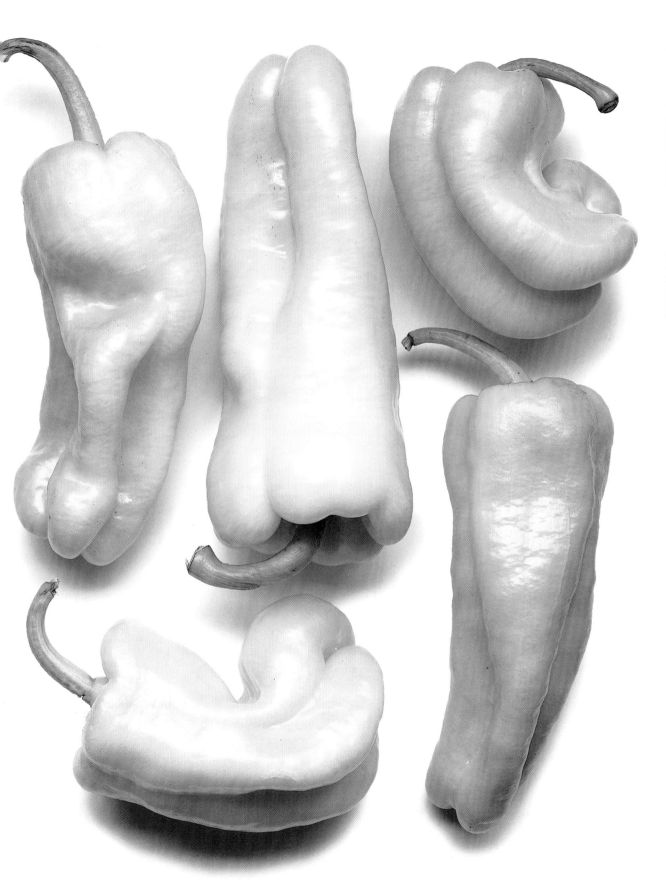

55 mins
TOTAL TIME

55 mins
ACTIVE TIME

DIFFICULTY

4
PORTIONS

CHARDONNAY
WITH NO OAK

CHICKEN WITH EGGPLANT CARPACCIO & TURMERIC MARMALADE

Turmeric is the unsung hero of the global spice rack. Fresh turmeric is a deep yellow rhizome with a slightly bitter taste and complex aroma. Ground dried turmeric turns acrid with age, so buy it in small quantities and store it no longer than 6 months.

- 4 boneless skin-on chicken breasts
- 1/4 cup olive oil
- 1 tablespoon ground turmeric
- 2 sweet onions, such as Vidalia, Maui, or Mayan Sweet, peeled and coarsely chopped
- 1 teaspoon honey
- Salt and ground pepper to taste
- 2 eggplants, sliced crosswise into rounds as thin as possible
- 1 tablespoon unsalted butter

1. Preheat oven to 200°F. Wrap each chicken breast tightly in several layers of plastic wrap. Place wrapped breasts on a sheet pan and put into oven for 10 minutes to seal plastic.

2. In a large saucepan, heat water until 160°F (small bubbles will form at bottom of pan and the water will be steamy). Lower wrapped chicken into water and cook for about 45 minutes, or until flesh is firm to the touch.

3. While the chicken cooks, heat a large sauté pan over medium heat. Add 1 tablespoon of the oil and turmeric and cook 1 minute. Add onions, stir to coat, and cook for 10 minutes, stirring frequently. Pour in 1/4 cup water, cover, reduce heat to low, and cook another 10 minutes until onions are very soft, stirring occasionally and adding a few spoons of water if onions stick to the pan. Off heat, stir in honey. Transfer contents of pan to a food processor and purée until smooth. Taste, and season with salt and pepper. Keep marmalade warm until ready to serve.

4. Heat grill pan over high heat. Brush eggplant slices on both sides with 2 tablespoons oil. Season. Working in batches, grill eggplant on both sides until tender and browned, 3 minutes per side.

5. Heat large sauté pan over high heat. Add butter and oil to pan. Unwrap chicken breasts and season them on both sides with salt and pepper. Sauté skin side down until skin is golden brown and crispy, about 10 minutes.

6. To serve, fan several eggplant slices on each plate. Form a round of onion marmalade on top of the eggplant. Place a chicken breast on top of the marmalade and serve.

- sour
- salty
- sweet
- bitter

1 hr 35 mins
TOTAL TIME

1 hr 5 mins
ACTIVE TIME

DIFFICULTY

4
PORTIONS

🍷
PINOT NOIR

TECHNIQUE SOUS VIDE

The inspiration for this indispensable culinary technique came to us straight from the grocery store meat aisle. Vacuum-sealed packaging inspired chefs to tinker with cooking things in airtight plastic packages, and with astounding results. Sous vide cooking entails sealing a protein or vegetable in plastic (using an industrial cryovac machine in some restaurant kitchens), then poaching in simmering water for a long time. Pressure exerted on the covered food encourages any additional ingredients wrapped in the package—diced vegetables, for example, or a spice rub—to deeply penetrate the food. Shielded from direct contact with hot water, food loses none of its flavor and gives up none of its mass, and proteins cooked this way gelatinize and yield buttery-soft textures. Heat is distributed evenly throughout the encased food, and a sous vide fish will be cooked to a uniform doneness and texture from skin to spine. Sous vide cooking can be easily replicated at home by oven-sealing food wrapped tightly in several layers of good-quality plastic wrap. Note that sous vide cooking adds zero fat to your food.

BRAISED BEEF SHORT RIBS WITH TRUFFLED TARO ROOT

Hearty and rich, this middle-of-a-snowstorm-by-a-roaring-fire dish warms you by its sheer heft. When braised for hours, short ribs become irresistibly tender and completely saturated with the essences of the other winter ingredients in the braising liquid. Before braising, season the short ribs generously and brown them completely. These preliminary steps will really contribute to the flavor of the final dish.

- 4 pounds beef short ribs, trimmed to 4 inches
- Salt and ground pepper to taste
  2 tablespoons corn oil
  Braising vegetables and aromatics*
- 1/2 cup cognac or brandy
- 1 cup red wine
- 3 cups chicken stock
  Finishing herbs and spices†
- Truffled Taro Root (page 234)

* For braising vegetables and aromatics, choose 4 ingredients from this list:
- 7 shallots, peeled and sliced
- 6 tomatoes, chopped
- 2 large carrots, peeled and chopped
- 2 leeks, washed well, white and pale green sections chopped
- 1 sweet potato, peeled and cubed
- 1 stalk celery, chopped
- 1 stalk lemongrass, lower third of inner stalk chopped
- 1 head garlic, peeled and chopped
- 2 teaspoons minced fresh ginger

† For finishing herbs and spices, choose 2 ingredients from this list:
- 3 sprigs fresh parsley
- 3 sprigs fresh tarragon
- 3 sprigs fresh thyme
- 2 whole star anise
- 3 whole cloves
- 1 teaspoon whole cumin seed

- sour
- salty
- sweet
- bitter

1. Season short ribs with salt and pepper on all sides. In a large heavy-bottomed pot over medium heat, warm corn oil. When hot, add short ribs in batches and brown well on all sides, about 15 minutes per batch. Remove and hold aside.

2. To the same pot add the braising vegetables and aromatics. Increase heat to high and cook veg-

4 hrs
TOTAL TIME

1 hr 45 mins
ACTIVE TIME

DIFFICULTY

4
PORTIONS

CINSAULT
FROM
CALIFORNIA

etables for 10 minutes, stirring frequently. Return short ribs to pot and bury under vegetables. Ad
cognac or brandy and red wine; continue cooking, uncovered, for 10 minutes, until liquid ha
reduced. Add chicken stock and simmer for 5 minutes.

3. Tie finishing herbs and spices in a piece of cheesecloth and add to pot. Reduce heat to low s
that liquid is just under a simmer, cover, and cook until ribs are tender, about 2 hours 15 minutes.

4. When ribs are done, strain 2 cups of the braising liquid into a small pan over high heat. Hol
pot with ribs over very low heat. Reduce braising liquid until a thick sauce, about 10 minutes. Tast
and season with salt and pepper.

5. Sprinkle short ribs with salt and pepper if desired. Form a mound of Truffled Taro Root on eac
of 4 plates, top with short ribs and braised vegetables, and smother ribs and taro with sauce.

TECHNIQUE BRAISING

Braising works wonders on tough cuts of meat and root vegetables. To braise anything, you first brown it well on the stovetop in a high-sided, ovenproof pan with a tight-fitting lid. Add liquid and aromatic ingredients to the pan, cover, and transfer to a preheated oven. Cook for a long time: the goal is for all the pan's contents to be perfectly tender. Beef requires a braising time of several hours. The technique melts collagen and creates a gelatinous, tender texture. Almost always, the highly flavorful braising liquid becomes the basis of a final sauce. Pot roasting, by the way, is simply shallow braising.

POMEGRANATE & CINNAMON LACQUERED DUCK

As a kid, I was entranced by the pomegranates we'd bring home from produce stands in Queens. I'd break one open and gawk at the rows of tightly packed, ruby-hued seeds. Each time I ate one, I tried to discover the approach that would spill the least amount of juice on my clothes. Now what I appreciate most about this winter fruit is its blended sweet-sour taste. In this dish, pomegranate's tartness is a perfect foil for the richness of duck.

Zest of 2 oranges

Zest of 2 lemons

2 teaspoons minced fresh tarragon

1 sprig fresh thyme

5 cloves garlic, peeled and minced or pressed

1 teaspoon salt, plus more to taste

4 skin-on duck (preferably Pekin) breasts, about 8 ounces each, fat trimmed

2 tablespoons sugar

1 tablespoon champagne vinegar or white wine vinegar

1 cinnamon stick, 2 1/2 to 3 inches long

1 cup pomegranate or cranberry juice

Ground black pepper to taste

1 tablespoon canola oil

1. In a small bowl, combine 2 tablespoons orange zest, 1 tablespoon lemon zest, tarragon, thyme, garlic, and 1 teaspoon salt. Mash with a fork.

2. Score skin of duck breasts in a grid pattern and arrange in a shallow baking dish. Coat duck with marinade on both sides. Cover and refrigerate for at least 5 hours, or overnight. Just before cooking remove duck from refrigerator and use a butter knife to gently scrape off visible marinade bits.

3. Combine sugar and vinegar in a small saucepan and cook over medium-high heat until thick, bubbly, and reduced by half, 2 to 3 minutes. Add the remaining orange and lemon zests, cinnamon stick, and pomegranate or cranberry juice. Cook and reduce by half. Strain and discard solids. Transfer liquid to a clean saucepan and reduce until a syrupy glaze, 12 to 15 minutes. Taste and season with salt and pepper.

4. In a large cast-iron skillet, heat oil over medium-high heat. Working in batches if necessary, lay duck breasts skin side down on the skillet and sauté until skin is dark brown and crispy, about 7 minutes. Flip and continue to sauté duck 3 to 5 minutes. The internal temperature should be about 140°F. If working in batches, keep duck warm while cooking remaining breasts. Transfer duck to a cutting board and, using a kitchen brush, coat skin side with glaze. Slice against the grain and serve.

- sour
- salty
- sweet
- bitter

6 hrs
TOTAL TIME*

1 hr
ACTIVE TIME

DIFFICULTY

4
PORTIONS

PINOT NOIR
FROM OREGON

*5 hours
marinating

Pictured with Chinese Long Beans & Caramelized Plantains (see page 240).

ROAST LOIN OF PORK WITH CINNAMON-GLAZED TART APPLES

When *Reader's Digest* asked me for a pork dish, I looked to the American classics for inspiration. What, as the cliché goes, is more American than apple pie? This pork roast is supposed to taste like a collision between an apple pie—green apples, sugar, and cinnamon—and a pork loin. Try it as the centerpiece of a holiday meal.

3 tablespoons corn oil

● 2 pounds boneless loin of pork, untrimmed

● 1/4 teaspoon salt, plus more to season pork

● Ground pepper to season pork

● 2 tablespoons unsalted butter

● 1/4 cup sugar

● ● 2 cinnamon sticks, 2 1/2 to 3 inches each

● 1/4 cup white vinegar

● 3/4 cup apple juice

● ● 2 Granny Smith or other tart apples, peeled, cored, and sliced into rings 1/4-inch thick

1. Preheat oven to 375°F.

2. Heat a sauté pan or roasting pan large enough to accommodate the roast, then add the corn oil and heat until hot but not smoking. Season the pork loin with salt and pepper. Brown the roast on all sides, then transfer to a roasting pan fitted with a rack. Roast in the oven for 30 to 45 minutes until the internal temperature of the pork reaches 160°F.

3. In a saucepan over medium heat, melt 1 tablespoon of the butter and add the sugar and cinnamon sticks. Stir over very low heat until the sugar has cooked into a smooth, light brown caramel. Gradually stir in the vinegar and 1/2 cup of the apple juice. (As you do, the caramel may harden and clump. Don't be alarmed; any solids that form will redissolve.) Discard cinnamon sticks. Raise the heat to medium-high and boil the mixture until it has reduced to a glaze consistency. Remove pan from heat.

4. Melt the remaining 1 tablespoon butter in a sauté pan over medium heat. When the foaming subsides, add the apples and sauté until golden brown, 12 to 15 minutes. Add the remaining 1/4 cup apple juice and heat until there is no visible juice in the pan. Remove pan from heat. If cinnamon glaze has stiffened and doesn't run, briefly rewarm it over low heat just to soften. Pour the glaze over the apples and gently toss to coat.

5. When the pork is done, remove from oven and let rest 10 minutes. Carve into 1-inch-thick slices. Arrange several slices on each plate and smother with glazed apples. Serve hot.

○ sour

● salty

● sweet

○ bitter

1 hr
TOTAL TIME

1 hr
ACTIVE TIME

DIFFICULTY

4
PORTIONS

RIESLING
SPÄTLESE

HANGER STEAK WITH MUSTARD JUS

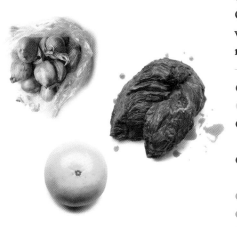

One of my first cooking jobs was at the New Hyde Park Inn, a restaurant with a German chef who taught me the importance of discipline. His kitchen turned out a wonderful *Wiener Rostbrauten*, or strip steak cooked in the Viennese style. I couldn't resist the urge to reinterpret this vintage European dish.

- 1/2 cup grapefruit juice
- 1/4 cup red wine vinegar
- 5 shallots, peeled, 2 coarsely chopped for marinade and 3 cut into long, thin slivers for pan sauce
- 3 hanger steaks, about 7 ounces each (sirloin or top butt may be substituted)
- 1/2 cup all-purpose flour
- 1/2 cup corn oil
- Salt and ground pepper to taste
- 1 cup chicken stock
- 1 cup red wine
- 2 tablespoons rice wine vinegar
- 2 tablespoons Japanese mustard paste (I like S&B brand) or strong Dijon mustard
- Sugar, as needed

TECHNIQUE

PAN-FRYING

Unlike with deep frying, pan-fried food is not fully submerged in fat. The fat should come a third to halfway up the sides of the food being cooked—any less than this and it's a sauté. Larger cuts of protein, such as chicken, are often pan-fried, but the technique also works for smaller cuts of food. Pan-frying requires frequent flipping.

- sour
- salty
- sweet
- bitter

1. One day in advance, marinate the steak: in a glass baking dish, blend together grapefruit juice, red wine vinegar, and the chopped shallots. Place steaks in dish and turn them several times to coat them with marinade. Cover dish and refrigerate for 24 hours.

2. Remove steaks from marinade, brush off shallots, and pat dry with paper towels. Carve steak on the bias into slices about 1 inch thick. Put flour in a shallow bowl, and dredge steak slices in flour shaking off excess.

3. Heat a high-sided sauté pan over high heat. Add the corn oil. (You will be pan-frying the steak here, as opposed to merely sautéing it; therefore, it is important that the oil be hot enough for frying.) When oil is smoking hot, add the steak slices all at once and flash-fry by cooking 1 minute per side for rare meat or 2 minutes for well-done. Transfer slices to paper towels and sprinkle with salt and pepper. Tent with aluminum foil to keep hot.

4. Drain all but 1 tablespoon oil from the sauté pan and lower heat to medium. Add slivered shallots and sauté for 2 minutes. Pour in chicken stock, red wine, and rice wine vinegar, and use a wooden spoon to release any flavorful steak bits from bottom of pan. Increase heat to medium-high and cook until sauce has reduced by half. Whisk in mustard. Taste, and season with salt, pepper, and sugar if needed.

5. Transfer pan-fried steak to individual plates or a single large platter. Spoon pan sauce with shallots over steak. Serve hot.

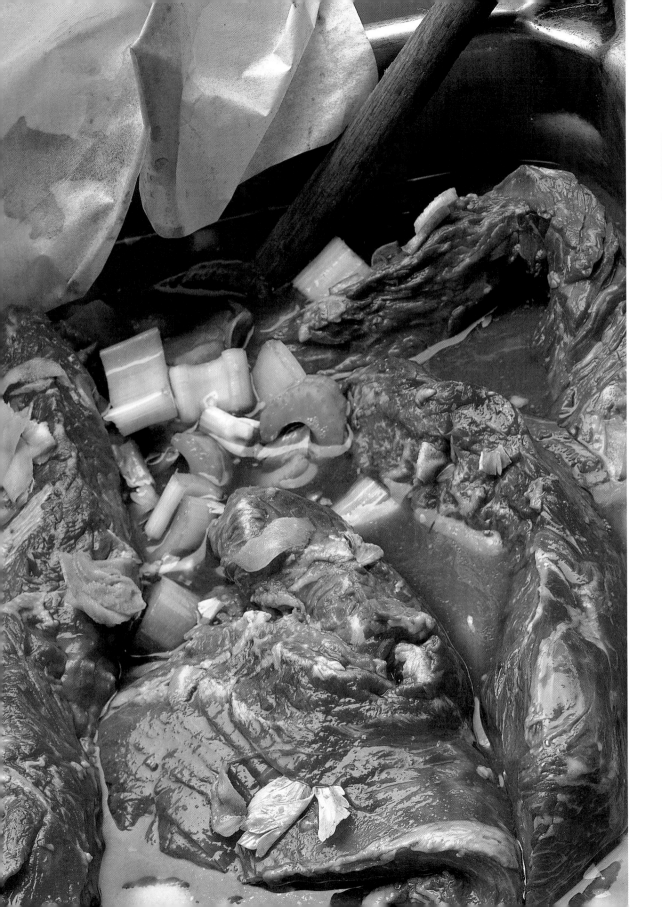

24hrs35mins
TOTAL TIME

35mins
ACTIVE TIME

DIFFICULTY

4
PORTIONS

CÔTES DU
RHÔNE

SZECHUAN PEPPERCORN-RUBBED FILLET OF BEEF

A few Decembers back, I was asked to create a centerpiece dish that was interesting and yet rooted in traditional holiday fare. This beef dish is my riff off the classic steak au poivre. Szechuan peppercorns, which aren't actually peppercorns at all, lend their delicate perfume and eye appeal but no heat. A great example, I think, of how a single unexpected ingredient can transform an entire meal.

- 1 cup Szechuan peppercorns (called "red peppercorns" in many Asian markets)
- 1/4 cup sweet paprika
- 1 tablespoon brown sugar
- 1 tablespoon freshly ground black pepper, plus more to taste
- 1 tablespoon salt, plus more to taste
- 1/4 cup plus 2 tablespoons olive oil
- One 3- to 4-pound fillet of beef, trimmed, cleaned, and trussed, scraps reserved
- 3 tablespoons corn oil
- 4 carrots, peeled and cut into large dice
- 2 large onions, peeled and cut into large dice
- 1 clove garlic, peeled and chopped
- 6 sprigs fresh thyme
- 1/2 cup red wine
- 1 cup chicken stock

1. Lightly crush peppercorns by either pounding them on a cutting board with a heavy sauté pan or crushing them in a mortar with pestle. Place in a small bowl with paprika, brown sugar, 1 tablespoon black pepper, 1 tablespoon salt, and 1/4 cup of the olive oil; mix together with your hands. Rub spice mixture over all sides of the fillet. Place in a baking dish, cover, and refrigerate 2 hours.

2. After 2 hours, place a flameproof roasting pan in the oven and preheat to 425°F. When oven has reached 425°F, add corn oil, carrots, onions, garlic, thyme, and beef scraps to pan, stirring to combine. Roast until vegetables soften and beef scraps brown, about 20 minutes.

3. While vegetables roast, heat a large sauté pan over medium-high heat with remaining 2 tablespoons olive oil. Generously sprinkle all sides of fillet with salt. Add beef to pan and sear thoroughly on all sides, about 20 minutes total.

4. When vegetables are roasted, push vegetables to the sides of the roasting pan, place the fillet in the center, and return pan to the oven. Cook for 30 to 40 minutes, or until the internal temperature of the beef reads 125°F.

sour
salty
sweet
bitter

3 hrs 30 mins
TOTAL TIME

1 hr 10 mins
ACTIVE TIME

DIFFICULTY

4
PORTIONS

SAGRANTINO
DE
MONTEFALCO

5. Remove roasting pan from oven and transfer fillet to a dish. Tent with foil to keep warm.

6. On stovetop, heat roasting pan with vegetables over medium-high heat. Add red wine and deglaze the pan by scraping the bottom with a wooden spoon to loosen any caramelized bits. Simmer until there is almost no wine left, about 10 minutes. Pour in chicken stock and bring to a boil. Cook until stock has reduced by half, about 10 minutes. Strain contents of pan through a fine mesh strainer into a bowl. Taste jus and adjust seasoning with salt and freshly ground pepper.

7. Slice fillet into 1/2-inch medallions and pour jus over meat, or serve jus separately as you would gravy. My favorite accompaniment for this dish is the Yam Purée on page 242.

OPEN-FACED LAMB SANDWICH WITH CUCUMBER RAITA

For this creation, I owe a "thanks" to my friend Gabrielle Hamilton, the chef of Prune in the East Village. She does a capon-on-a-crouton thing with a light jus that's out of this world. I borrowed the crouton idea, swapped lamb for capon, and gave my dish a Mediterranean accent with raita and preserved lemon.

- 1/2 cup extra-virgin olive oil
- 1 cup plus 2 tablespoons chopped fresh mint
- 1/4 cup chopped fresh rosemary
- 5 cloves garlic, peeled and chopped
- 1 tablespoon salt, plus more to taste
- 5 cranks ground pepper in a mill, plus more to taste
- 1 boneless half leg of lamb, about 3 pounds, rolled and tied by your butcher
- 3/4 cup sliced cucumber
- 3/4 cup plain yogurt
- 1 tablespoon finely chopped preserved lemon or 2 teaspoons fresh lemon juice
- 4 slices country bread
- 1 small bunch watercress, tough stems removed

1. In a casserole or baking dish large enough to hold the lamb, stir together olive oil, 1 cup of the mint, rosemary, garlic, 1 tablespoon salt, and 5 cranks ground pepper. Add the half leg of lamb to the dish and use a spoon to coat meat evenly with the marinade. Cover with plastic wrap and refrigerate at least 8 hours or overnight.

2. Place a roasting pan in the oven and preheat to 375°F.

3. Scrape marinade off lamb, season with salt and pepper, and place in preheated roasting pan. Roast for 1 hour, at which time the lamb should be medium rare, with an internal temperature of 145°F. Reserve pan juices. Let lamb sit at room temperature for 30 minutes, then refrigerate at least 1 hour. Carve into thin slices.

4. In a small bowl, blend cucumber, yogurt, the remaining 2 tablespoons mint, preserved lemon or lemon juice, and salt and pepper to taste.

5. Toast the bread on a grill pan or in a toaster oven. Make open-faced sandwiches by spreading some cucumber raita over each slice of bread, then piling slices of lamb on the raita. Drizzle lamb with some of the pan juices and top sandwiches with watercress. Serve at room temperature.

- sour
- salty
- sweet
- bitter

11 hrs
TOTAL TIME

35 mins
ACTIVE TIME

DIFFICULTY

4
PORTIONS

MISO STEAK WITH CLUSTER MUSHROOMS

In the restaurant, we use Japanese mushrooms with names like *shimeji* and *mai-itake*. They're pretty special—they have an acidic, almost lemony bite. If you can find Japanese cluster mushrooms to use in this dish, go for it. Oyster mushrooms, widely available in supermarkets, are similar enough.

- 2 heads garlic, cloves separated
- 1 cup olive oil
- Salt and ground pepper to taste
- 1/3 cup miso, preferably light-colored
- 3 tablespoons honey
- One 40-ounce New York strip steak, ribeye steak, or other steak or roast, trimmed of excess fat
- 1 pound oyster mushrooms in clusters, broken into small clusters, or other mushrooms
- 1 onion, peeled and cut into large dice
- 1/4 cup red wine vinegar
- 3 tablespoons light (low-sodium) soy sauce
- 1 1/2 cups chicken stock

1. Preheat oven to 325°F.

2. Soak garlic cloves in warm water for 10 minutes. Peel and dry. Transfer to a small saucepan with the olive oil. Set pan over very low heat, and let cook until garlic is golden and soft when pierced with a knife, about 20 minutes. Increase heat to high and fry just until garlic becomes brown, about 4 minutes. Remove pan from heat and transfer garlic cloves to paper towels to drain. Season with salt and pepper, and tent loosely with aluminum foil to keep warm (put in the oven before serving to warm up a bit). Reserve garlic-infused oil.

3. Whisk together miso and 1 tablespoon of the honey. Pat dry the steak or roast and season one side of the steak liberally with salt and pepper. Heat a large sauté pan over high heat. Add 2 tablespoons of garlic-infused olive oil to the pan. When oil is very hot, place beef seasoned side down in pan and sear until well browned on bottom, about 4 minutes. Season top side with salt and pepper, then flip to sear second side to same color. Transfer beef to a cutting board and brush generously on all sides with miso-honey mixture. Place on a rack set over a roasting pan and roast in oven for 55 minutes (internal temperature should reach 125°F). Remove from oven and let rest for 10 minutes. Reserve pan drippings.

4. Prepare the sauce while the beef roasts: drain the sauté pan used to brown the meat of all but about 2 tablespoons of oil and return to medium heat. Add mushroom clusters, season with salt and

- sour
- salty
- sweet
- bitter

1hr 30mins
TOTAL TIME

1hr
ACTIVE TIME

DIFFICULTY

4
PORTIONS

SHIRAZ FROM
AUSTRALIA

pepper, and sauté until mushrooms are soft and colored, scraping pan to release any beef bits. Add onions, season, and sauté until translucent. Add remaining 2 tablespoons honey to vegetables, stirring to coat. Cook until mushrooms and onions appear glazed, then add vinegar and soy sauce. Reduce by half. Add chicken stock and cook until reduced to a viscous, molasses consistency. If desired, incorporate roasting pan drippings into this sauce.

5. Carve steak or roast against the grain into 8 slices. Spoon sauce with its mushrooms on individual dishes or a serving platter, and arrange beef slices over sauce. Top with fried garlic cloves. Season dish with salt and pepper and serve immediately.

TECHNIQUE CLEANING
FRESH MUSHROOMS

The popular wisdom on how to clean mushrooms includes "Don't wipe them!"; "You can't wash them!"; and "You gotta use a special brush." Really it's easy, though choosing the best cleaning method will depend on variety:

Delicate mushrooms such as chanterelle, black trumpet, mousseron, yellowfoot, shiitake: dip quickly in cold water and spin in a salad spinner. Let dry on paper towels.

Firm, dense varieties such as button, oyster, porcini, cremini, portobello: trim stems and wipe with a damp cloth or peel top layer off cap.

Morels: do nothing.

- sour
- salty
- sweet
- bitter

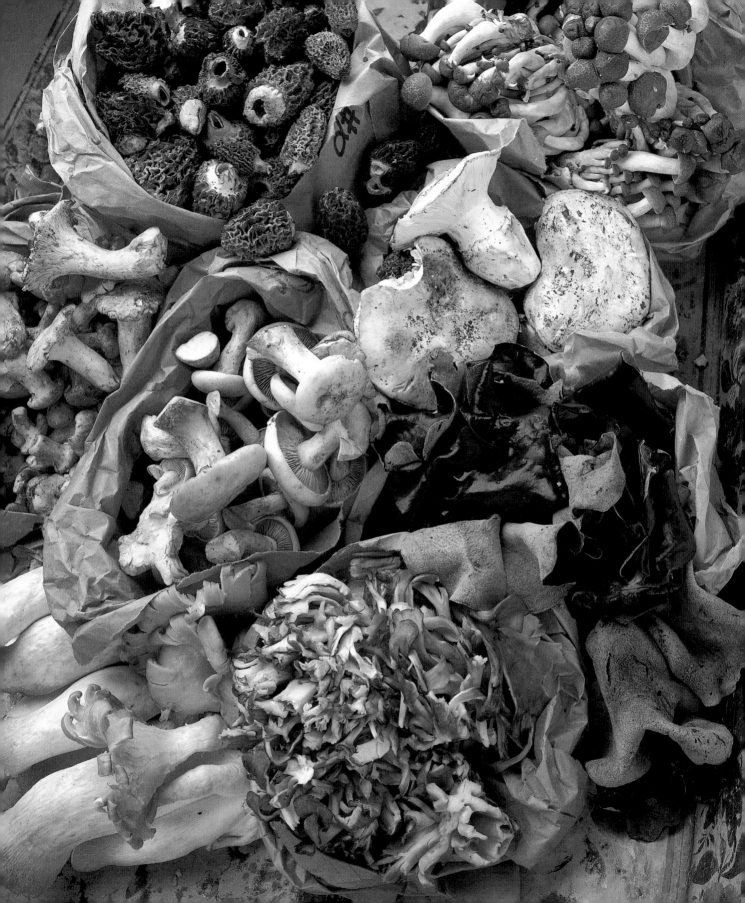

VEAL CHOPS À LA BARIGOULE

You're saying, "Bari-what?" It was Tom Colicchio, now chef of New York's ultrasuccessful Gramercy Tavern, who clued me in years ago. Barigoule is a stock or sauce made from artichokes, bacon, and mushrooms. I made it part of my repertoire, and you'll want to, too; it works wonders for any meat, fish, or vegetable.

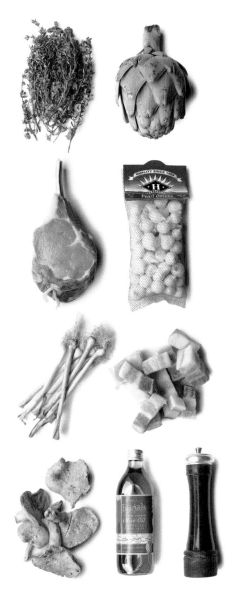

- 2 cups dry white wine
- 6 artichokes
- 10 ounces pearl onions
- 1/2 cup lardons or 24 strips bacon, cut crosswise into 1-inch pieces
- 6 cloves garlic, smashed under the blade of a heavy knife
- 2 cups whole chanterelles or halved cremini mushrooms
- 1/2 bunch fresh parsley and 1/2 bunch fresh thyme bundled together with kitchen string
- Salt and ground pepper to taste
- 4 veal chops, about 8 ounces each
- 1/4 cup olive oil
- Crushed Potatoes with Parsley and Thyme (page 244) (optional)

1. Place wine in a large bowl. Trim artichokes down to the heart and cut each heart into 6 pieces, dropping pieces into wine immediately (the wine's acid will retard discoloration).

2. Bring a large pot of salted water to a boil, and blanch pearl onions for 30 seconds. Run under cold water. Peel onions.

3. Heat a saucepan over medium heat and add lardons or bacon. Cook just until most of the fat has been rendered; the bacon should be soft, not crispy. Add garlic cloves, cover pan, and sweat 10 minutes. Add mushrooms, season, cover pan, and cook, stirring every few minutes, until mushrooms are soft, about 12 minutes. Pour wine with artichokes into pan, add bundled herbs, and bring to simmer. Add pearl onions. Simmer barigoule until artichokes and onions are tender and sauce has thickened, 8 to 10 minutes. Discard herbs and garlic.

4. Preheat oven to 350°F.

5. Pat dry the veal chops and season all sides liberally with salt and pepper. Heat a large sauté pan over high heat. Add oil to the pan. When oil is very hot, place the chops in the pan and brown on first side, allowing the meat to stay undisturbed in one position until well colored. Flip and color second side. Transfer chops to a roasting pan and roast in oven for 18 minutes. Remove from oven and let rest for 15 minutes.

6. Gently reheat the barigoule. Dollop some Crushed Potatoes with Parsley and Thyme on each plate, arrange a veal chop over the potatoes, and smother with the artichoke barigoule. Serve warm.

- sour
- salty
- sweet
- bitter

1 hr 45 mins

TOTAL TIME

1 hr 25 mins

ACTIVE TIME

DIFFICULTY

4

PORTIONS

RIOJA RISERVE

RACK OF LAMB WITH SOUR CHERRY GLAZE

I'm crazy about the flavor combinations in this dish. If you're skimming through this book's recipes for the first time, dog-ear this page and put Rack of Lamb with Sour Cherry Glaze at the very top of your "Must Try" list.

- 1/4 cup red wine vinegar
- 1/2 cup dried sour cherries
- 1/2 cup sugar
- 2 cups chicken stock (14 1/2-ounce can)
- 1 teaspoon Japanese mustard paste or other strong prepared mustard
- 1 full, 8-bone rack of lamb, split into 2 half-racks and frenched by your butcher
- Salt and ground pepper to taste

1. In a small nonreactive bowl, combine red wine vinegar, 1/2 cup water, and sour cherries. Let stand overnight. Strain cherries and reserve liquid. Pulse cherries in a food processor or chop fine.

2. Preheat the oven to 375°F.

3. Place sugar in a saucepan over medium heat and, stirring frequently, cook until sugar turns into a smooth caramel. Add cherry soaking liquid to pan. Stir constantly until caramel, which will harden when the room-temperature liquid comes in contact with it, has completely redissolved. Add cherries and chicken stock to pan, bring to a low boil, and cook until reduced to a light-bodied glaze (it will thicken further upon standing), 25 to 30 minutes. Stir in mustard and season to taste with salt and pepper.

4. Liberally sprinkle lamb with salt and pepper. Place bone side down in a roasting pan and roast in oven for 15 minutes. Increase heat to 425°F, flip meat so that the bones curve upward, and roast 5 minutes more. Remove pan from oven and let lamb rest 10 minutes before carving.

5. Cut lamb racks into separate chops, and arrange on a serving platter or divide among 4 plates. Spoon cherry glaze with its cherries over lamb. I recommend that you serve this dish with Baby Carrots, Thai Eggplant, and Pearl Onions (page 246).

- sour
- salty
- sweet
- bitter

13 hrs 20 mins
TOTAL TIME*

45 mins
ACTIVE TIME

DIFFICULTY

4
PORTIONS

ZINFANDEL

*12 hours
for marinating

ORGANIC CHICKEN WITH BEANS & CRUSHED RED BEETS

Want to do something interesting with chicken? This is the dish. Take it to an even higher level of tastiness by seeking out heirloom beans and lemon thyme—both are late summer/early fall farmers' market staples. The recipe can also be made with skinless chicken breasts: skip the skin-crisping step if you do go skinless.

- 2 large or 3 medium beets, trimmed
- Salt and ground pepper to taste
- Olive oil
- 1/4 cup kosher salt for blanching
- 1 cup green beans, ends trimmed and cut on the bias into 2 or 3 pieces each
- 1 cup yellow wax beans, ends trimmed and cut on the bias into 2 or 3 pieces each
- 4 organic skin-on chicken breasts, preferably with the wing attached
- 3 tablespoons unsalted butter
- 1 tablespoon chopped shallots
- 1/3 cup corn or vegetable oil
- 1/2 bunch fresh lemon thyme or thyme, leaves stripped and leaves and stems held separately
- 1 teaspoon honey
- 1/4 cup red wine vinegar

1. Preheat oven to 400°F.

2. Sprinkle beets with salt and pepper and smear each with a thin film of olive oil. Wrap beets individually in aluminum foil and bake on oven rack 1 hour or until very soft—a skewer inserted should meet no resistance. Lower oven to 200°F. When cool enough to handle, remove beet skins and chop flesh coarsely.

3. While beets are roasting, blanch the beans: bring a large pot of water to boil and add 2 tablespoons of the kosher salt. Prepare an ice bath and stir in remaining 2 tablespoons kosher salt. Immerse green and yellow wax beans in boiling water and blanch for 2 1/2 minutes, until crisp-tender. Transfer immediately to ice bath and let stand 2 minutes. Drain and set aside.

4. Tightly wrap each chicken breast in 3 layers of plastic wrap. Place on a baking sheet and keep in 200°F oven for 10 minutes to seal plastic wrap. Remove from oven.

5. Bring a large pot of water to 160°F. Lower wrapped chicken breasts into water and simmer for 15 minutes, or until juices from joint where wing meets breastbone run clear.

- sour
- salty
- **sweet**
- bitter

2 hrs 30 mins
TOTAL TIME

1 hr
ACTIVE TIME

DIFFICULTY

4
PORTIONS

LIGHT-BODIED MERLOT

6. Make beet sauce while chicken cooks: in a wide sauté pan over medium heat, melt 1 1/2 table-spoons of the butter. Add shallots and beets; season with salt and pepper. Cook, crushing beets with the back of a fork, until mixture is a chunky beet-shallot compote, about 5 minutes. Season with salt and pepper to taste. Cover to keep warm.

7. In a large, sided sauté pan over high heat, heat corn oil until very hot. Unwrap chicken breasts and dry completely. Season with salt and pepper all over. Place breasts in sauté pan skin side down and add to the pan 1 tablespoon butter and thyme stems. Basting frequently, sauté chicken until skin is crispy and deep golden brown. Do not flip. Remove chicken breasts to a plate. Drain pan of all fat and use a bunched paper towel to dab off any burnt bits. Add honey to pan, return to medium heat and, when honey bubbles, add vinegar, 1/2 cup water, and thyme leaves. Simmer until thickened about 5 minutes. Add remaining 1/2 tablespoon butter, swirl pan to incorporate, and season with salt and pepper. Fold in beans and cook just until sauce is warmed through.

8. On each of 4 plates, spread some beet-shallot mixture. Center a chicken breast on the beets, and spoon the pan sauce with beans over the entire dish. Serve hot.

sour
salty
sweet
bitter

 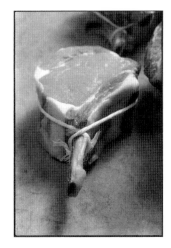 

BROWNING (SEARING)

Browning and searing are roughly synonymous: both imply quick conversion of a meat's or a fish's concentrated surface proteins into sugar. Proteins are cooked in a pan over high heat with a small amount of fat, and a pinch of sugar may be thrown in to coax the transformation. Browning intensifies sweetness and contributes a rich depth of flavor. As the name indicates, this method is all about color change: when you brown something, go for dark. There is a widely held misconception that browning meats "seals" in moisture. As food scientist Harold McGee thoroughly dispels in *The Curious Cook*, this just isn't so. Browning contributes a great deal of flavor but does not magically create an impenetrable crust.

VENISON WITH CHESTNUTS & A PORT REDUCTION

For this recipe, you'll need a large, flameproof roasting pan or casserole dish.

- 1 pound chestnuts or 13 ounces shelled chestnuts from a jar
- 3 tablespoons olive oil
- 2 pounds any cut of venison, such as medallions, saddle, rack, chops, or top round roast
- Salt and ground pepper to taste
- 1/2 cup port
- 1 cup chicken stock
- 1/4 cup red wine vinegar
- Sprig fresh thyme
- 12 ounces Brussels sprouts, sliced thin from top to bottom
- Finely grated zest of 1 large or 2 small lemons

1. Bring a large pot of water to a boil. Score flat sides of chestnuts with a small *X* and drop into boiling water. When water returns to a boil, drain pot and wrap chestnuts in a kitchen towel: chestnuts will steam themselves open. Peel when cool enough to handle. Slice into 2 or 3 chunks.

2. Preheat oven to 375°F.

3. Heat 2 burners. Warm 2 tablespoons of the oil in a large flameproof roasting pan over high heat. Season venison on all surfaces with salt and pepper. When oil is hot, brown meat in pan on all sides until well colored. Move pan to oven and roast venison. For rare meat, roast medallions 3 minutes on each side; a rack or chops 12 minutes; and a thick roast 1 hour. Transfer meat to a cutting board, tent with foil, and let stand for 10 minutes before serving. Do not drain or wash pan.

4. Use a bunched paper towel to swab excess grease off roasting pan. Place pan over medium-high heat (again, use 2 burners) and add port. Reduce until syrupy, about 5 minutes. Pour in chicken stock and reduce until thick, about 7 minutes. Pour in vinegar and reduce until thick. Remove pan from heat, add thyme sprig, let stand 5 minutes, then discard thyme. Season to taste with salt and pepper.

5. In a sauté pan, heat remaining 1 tablespoon oil until smoking. Add Brussels sprouts, season, and sauté until lightly browned, about 6 minutes, being careful not to overcook. Add chestnuts and lemon zest, stir to combine, and remove pan from heat. Season to taste.

6. If serving a roast, carve into slices about 1/2-inch thick. If serving a rack, carve into individual chops. Lay venison on plates and spoon some port-vinegar sauce over meat. Mound some Brussels sprouts–chestnut mixture directly on the meat and finish each plate with a ring of more sauce. Serve warm.

- sour
- salty
- sweet
- bitter

1-2 hrs
TOTAL TIME*

50 mins
ACTIVE TIME

DIFFICULTY

4
PORTIONS

SYRAH FROM
WASHINGTON
STATE

*depending on
cut of meat

BRAISED VEAL ROULADE WITH ROOT VEGETABLES

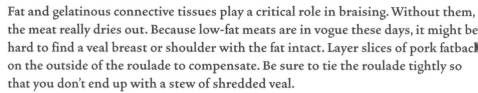

Fat and gelatinous connective tissues play a critical role in braising. Without them, the meat really dries out. Because low-fat meats are in vogue these days, it might be hard to find a veal breast or shoulder with the fat intact. Layer slices of pork fatback on the outside of the roulade to compensate. Be sure to tie the roulade tightly so that you don't end up with a stew of shredded veal.

- One 2-pound boneless veal shoulder or breast, pounded thin
- Salt and ground pepper to taste
- 7 ounces pork fatback, cut into slices about 1/4-inch thick
- 1/4 cup vegetable or canola oil
- 2 large carrots, peeled and cut into 2-inch pieces
- 1 turnip, peeled and cut into 2-inch pieces
- 8 cippoline or 16 pearl onions, peeled
- 3 sprigs fresh thyme
- 4 tomatoes, peeled, seeded, and diced
- 1/2 cup white wine
- 6 to 8 cups chicken or veal stock
- 1 tablespoon minced fresh parsley

1. Preheat oven to 350°F.

2. Sprinkle both sides of the veal with salt and pepper. Lay fatback slices in a single layer on one side of veal, flip, and roll into a roulade so fatback is on the outside of the roll. Tie off at 1-inch intervals with kitchen string. Place oil in a large flameproof Dutch oven (a heavy-bottomed pot with tight-fitting lid) and heat over medium-high heat. When hot, add veal roulade and sear on all sides until well browned. Remove veal from pot. Add carrots, turnips, onions, and thyme, and sauté until vegetables are nicely colored. Add tomatoes and sauté until they begin to collapse and release their juice, 2 to 3 minutes. Strain contents of pan through a colander, reserving vegetables and discarding grease. Add wine to same pot, increase heat, and stir to loosen flavorful browned bits. Cook until wine has reduced by half. Return vegetables to pot and place roulade on vegetables. Pour in enough stock so that only the top of the roulade is exposed. Bring to a bare simmer, cover, and place in oven. Braise for 3 hours or until meat is extremely tender.

3. About 20 minutes before the veal is done, remove 3 cups of liquid from the pan and strain it into a smaller saucepan. Degrease. Simmer over high heat until reduced by half. Taste and adjust seasoning with salt and pepper.

4. Cut and discard kitchen string. Carve roulade into 1-inch slices and place a slice on each plate. Serve vegetables on top of and alongside the meat. Sauce each plate with the reduced braising liquid and garnish with parsley.

- sour
- salty
- sweet
- bitter

5 hrs
TOTAL TIME

2 hrs
ACTIVE TIME

DIFFICULTY

4
PORTIONS

SYRAH

PORK CHOPS WITH A CHICORY GLAZE

Glazing just might be my favorite cooking term. To me, the very word *glaze* implies endless possibilities, because any flavor can be captured in a sugar syrup— or fruit juice—based glaze. The chicory glaze for these pork chops is also super with ham, especially fresh (not cured or brined) ham. Use glazes to add luster, texture, flavor, or all three.

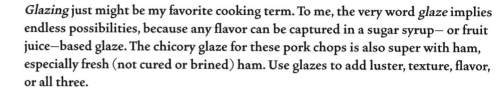

- 1/4 cup sugar
- 2 shallots, peeled and minced
- 1/3 cup unsweetened apple juice
- 1/4 cup plus 1 tablespoon red wine, malt, or cider vinegar
- 1 cup chicken stock
- Salt and ground pepper to taste
- 1/4 cup ground roasted chicory
- 1 tablespoon unsalted butter
- 4 pork chops, about 6 ounces each
- Extra-virgin olive oil

1. Place sugar in a heavy-bottomed saucepan over medium heat. Cook until sugar has become smooth caramel. Add shallots, apple juice, and vinegar. (Caramel will redissolve within a few minutes.) Simmer, stirring, until mixture is thick enough to coat the back of a spoon. Add chicken stock, return to a simmer, and reduce until a thick glaze. Season with salt and pepper to taste. Strain. Stir in chicory.

2. Heat a wide sauté pan with butter over medium-high heat. Rub pork chops with a generous coating of olive oil and season liberally. When butter is melted, place chops in pan and cook until bottoms are well browned, about 5 minutes. Flip and sauté 5 minutes more, or until pork is fully cooked. Transfer pork chops to a plate and let rest 10 minutes. Brush pork chops all over with chicory glaze and serve right away.

- sour
- salty
- sweet
- bitter

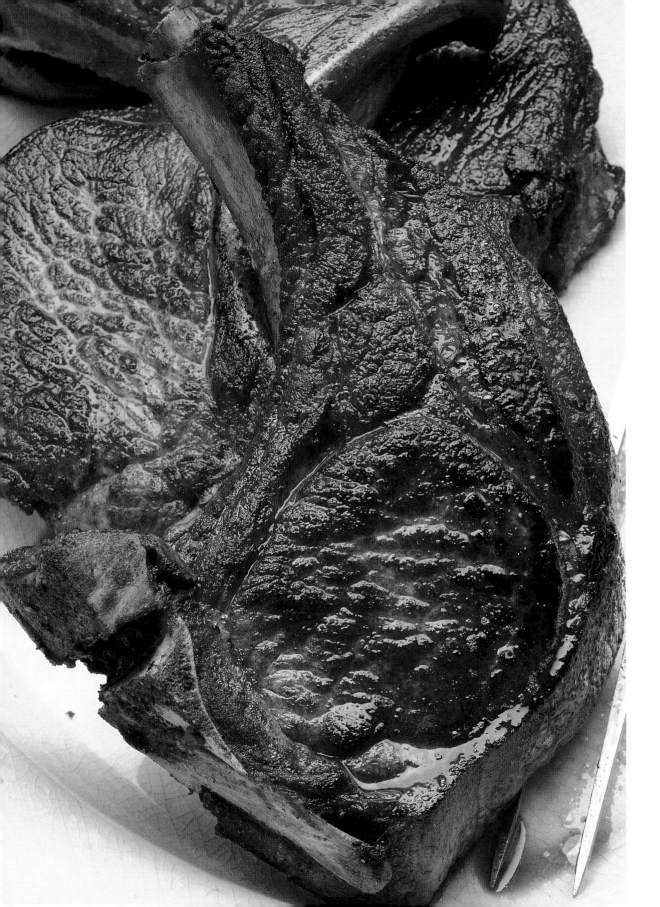

30 mins
TOTAL TIME

30 mins
ACTIVE TIME

DIFFICULTY

4
PORTIONS

FRUITY
CALIFORNIA
PINOT NOIR

PUFFY DUCK WITH GREEN CURRY

"Rocco, make us something faaaah-bulous and divine," once begged a TV producer. I knew this duck preparation was the answer. When you drop rice noodles into hot oil, they expand instantly, making for some pretty groovy visuals. And with Sean "Puffy" Combs dominating the TV headlines at the time, I couldn't resist paying tribute to him.

1 tablespoon corn oil

1 pound mixed Asian greens, such as baby bok choy, Chinese broccoli, or Chinese watercress, coarsely chopped

1-inch knob ginger, peeled and smashed under the blade of a heavy knife

1 long red chile pepper, preferably Thai, split, seeded, and chopped

1 tablespoon Thai green curry paste

2 cans unsweetened coconut milk

1 Gala apple, grated against the largest holes of a box grater

6 cups canola oil

4 ounces rice stick noodles

4 skinless duck breasts, each cut into 3 pieces and pieces pounded to 1/4-inch thick

Salt and ground pepper to taste

3 egg whites, beaten until foamy

1. In a wide pot, heat the corn oil over medium heat. Add the greens, ginger, and chile pepper, an sauté for 5 minutes. When greens are bright and ginger is fragrant, add the curry paste and continu to sauté for 2 minutes. Add the coconut milk and apple, and simmer uncovered for 5 minutes. Cove pot to keep warm.

2. Meanwhile, pour the canola oil into a 4-quart, high-sided stockpot. Place pot over medium-high heat and heat oil to 425°F. At 425°F the oil will be smoking hot; to test it, drop a noodle in the oil— it should sizzle and puff up immediately.

3. While the oil heats, prepare the duck breasts. Cut the rice sticks into 1 1/2-inch lengths and plac on a shallow plate. You will need 2 cups of cut noodles. Season the duck pieces with salt and peppe and coat lightly with egg white. Roll the duck in the rice stick pieces and press down until meat i well coated. Immediately transfer the duck into the hot oil; the noodles should puff up right away Do not crowd the pot; fry in batches if necessary. Fry for 45 seconds for medium rare duck and trans fer right away to a plate lined with a paper towel. Season again with salt and pepper.

4. To serve, pour equal amounts of the green curry into 4 shallow bowls. Top each with 3 pieces o duck and serve hot.

sour

salty

sweet

bitter

1 hr
TOTAL TIME

1 hr
ACTIVE TIME

DIFFICULTY

4
PORTIONS

GEWÜRZ-
TRAMINER

ROAST LEG OF LAMB WITH SUMMER SAVORY & BEANS

As with many of the dishes in this book and served at Union Pacific, this one is based on a centuries-old French recipe: leg of lamb with tiny white beans. My contribution is the summer savory. In 1991, I was riffling through some things in the walk-in cooler at Lespinasse when a pungent, camphorlike smell hit me square in the nose. It turned out to be a bunch of fresh summer savory. The herb has been a regular in my lineup ever since.

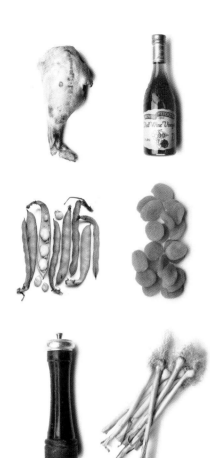

- 2 heads garlic, 1 kept whole and 1 with cloves separated, peeled, and coarsely chopped
- 1 bunch fresh summer savory, leaves and stems coarsely chopped
- 1/2 cup plus 1/4 teaspoon olive oil
- 1 boneless leg of lamb, about 4 pounds
- 1 cup red wine
- 1/2 cup red wine vinegar
- Salt and ground pepper to taste
- 2 cups chicken stock
- 2 tablespoons kosher salt for blanching
- 1 pound fava beans, shelled
- 1 pound yellow wax beans, strings removed, trimmed, and cut on the bias into 1-inch sections
- 1 cup diced dried apricots
- 2 tablespoons unsalted butter

1. Marinate the lamb 1 day in advance: combine chopped garlic, about 1/2 of the summer savory and 1/2 cup of the oil in a deep roasting pan or casserole dish. Place the leg of lamb in the dish and rotate to coat with marinade. Cover and refrigerate at least 24 hours. On the same day, place remaining savory in a bowl with wine and vinegar and let stand.

2. The next day, preheat oven to 325°F.

3. Slice the top off the whole garlic head, set on a square of aluminum foil, and douse garlic with remaining 1/4 teaspoon olive oil. Wrap tightly and roast in oven for 1 hour. When cool enough to handle, squeeze paste from individual cloves and mash paste until smooth.

4. Scrape marinade off lamb, sprinkle all over with salt and pepper, and transfer to a rack set in flameproof roasting pan. Pour chicken stock in pan. Roast 20 minutes per pound for rare (135°F internal temperature), 22 minutes per pound for medium rare (145°F internal temperature), and 2 minutes per pound for medium (155°F internal temperature).

- sour
- salty
- sweet
- bitter

26 hrs 20 mins
TOTAL TIME*

45 mins
ACTIVE TIME*

DIFFICULTY

4
PORTIONS

MEDIUM-
BODIED
BORDEAUX

*24 hours for
marinating,
plus 2 hours 20
minutes

5. While garlic and lamb are in the oven, blanch the beans: bring a large pot of water to a boil and add 1 tablespoon of the kosher salt. Prepare an ice bath and stir into it remaining 1 tablespoon kosher salt. Immerse fava beans in boiling water and blanch 2 minutes. Use a slotted spoon to transfer favas to ice bath. Blanch yellow wax beans in the same boiling water for 2 1/2 minutes; shock in ice bath. Drain beans. Peel favas.

6. When lamb has roasted to desired doneness, reduce oven temperature to lowest setting, remove pan from oven, tent the lamb with foil, and let stand 10 minutes. After 10 minutes, return the lamb, still loosely covered with foil, to the very low oven.

7. Place roasting pan with juices on stovetop over medium-high heat. (If your roasting pan isn't flameproof, scrape bottom of pan to loosen any solids, then transfer liquid to a saucepan over medium-high heat.) Add apricots and 2/3 of the roasted garlic paste, then strain savory-infused vinegar mixture into pan. Simmer until reduced by half, degreasing sauce periodically.

8. Melt butter in a shallow pan. Whisk in remaining roasted garlic paste with a pinch of salt and a crank or 2 of pepper in a mill. Add fava and wax beans and heat through, stirring to coat with butter sauce. Season to taste.

9. Carve lamb on the diagonal. Arrange slices of lamb and beans on individual plates or a single platter and cover with sauce. Serve warm.

sour

salty

sweet

bitter

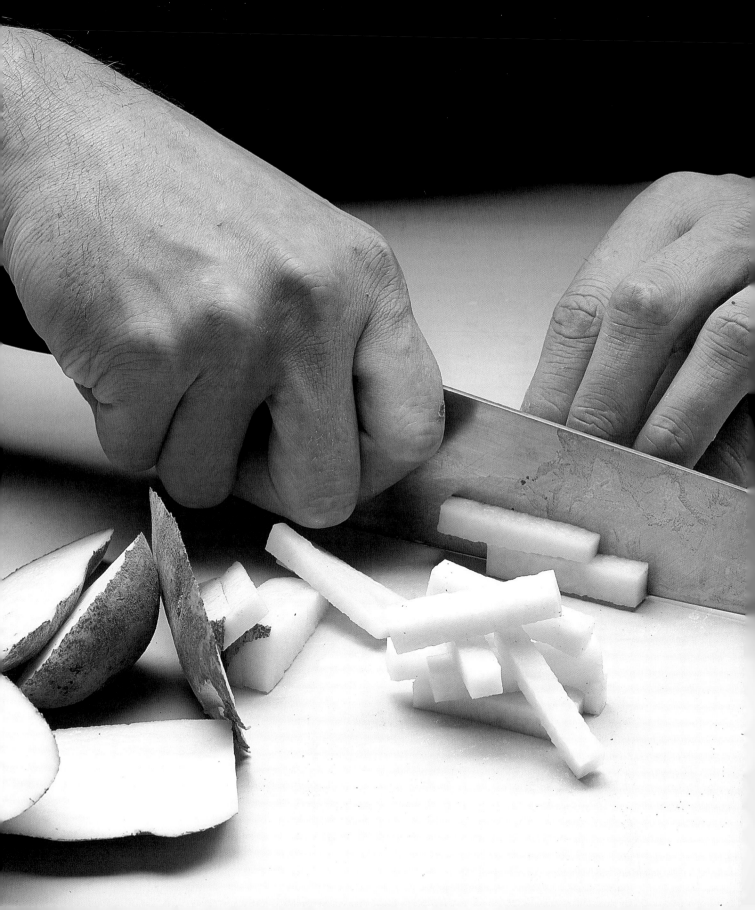

CHAPTER 7
SIDE DISHES

ONION SOUBISE

Onion soubise is a *My Fair Lady* of cooking. Long, gentle cooking mellows brash onions into an unrecognizably suave, sweet side dish. The onions swelter in their own juices for a half hour. You will love this dish ... even if you're a lifelong onion hater. It goes with anything and everything, and complements bitter greens especially well. Onion soubise is a dish you'll find yourself making again and again.

- 3 tablespoons unsalted butter
- 1 pound sweet (such as Vidalia or Maui) or spring onions, peeled and thinly sliced
- Salt to taste
- 1 tablespoon chopped fresh chives
- Ground pepper to taste

In a wide sauté pan or saucepan over low heat, melt butter. Add onions, season with salt, and stir to coat with butter. Cover pan and, stirring occasionally, cook until softened, 20 to 25 minutes. Uncover and cook just until most of the liquid has evaporated. Look for the viscous texture of a marmalade. Stir in chives and season with salt and pepper to taste.

- sour
- salty
- ● sweet
- bitter

50 mins
TOTAL TIME

30 mins
ACTIVE TIME

DIFFICULTY

4
PORTIONS

ASIAN MUSTARD GREENS

Asian mustard greens, *gai choy*, come in two sizes (look for the small—*su gai choy*) in Chinese markets. This preparation does wonderful things for just about any strong-flavored, bitter green. This might be the recipe that gets kids to eat their spinach!

- 1 slice bacon, halved
- 24 ounces Chinese mustard greens (*gai choy*) or other mustard greens, all tough stems and central spines removed, dried well
- 3/4 teaspoon sugar
- 1/4 teaspoon salt
- 2 cranks ground pepper in a mill
- 1 large clove garlic, peeled and smashed
- 1 knob fresh ginger, peeled and smashed with the blade of a heavy knife

1. In a large pot over medium heat, cook bacon until all fat has been rendered, 4–6 minutes. Remove bacon and discard or eat.

2. While bacon is cooking, place greens in a large bowl. Sprinkle with sugar, salt, and pepper, and toss.

3. To the pot with the bacon fat, add garlic and ginger; sauté 4 minutes. Increase heat to high. When bacon fat is sizzling hot, add about a third of the seasoned mustard greens to pot and stir-fry, using tongs to circulate greens, until wilted and bright green, 1 to 2 minutes. Use tongs to transfer greens to serving bowl or individual dishes, leaving garlic and ginger in pot. Repeat with remaining greens. Serve hot.

- sour
- salty
- sweet
- bitter

INDIAN LIME PICKLE
SWISS CHARD

Indian lime pickle—a pungently acidic, spicy condiment—transforms simple Swiss chard into an explosion of flavor. This dish goes especially well with fish, such as the skate recipe on page 158.

- 1/2 cup (about 3 ounces) mild Indian lime pickle
- 3 tablespoons fresh lemon juice
- 2 tablespoons extra-virgin olive oil
- 2 tablespoons kosher salt for blanching, plus more to taste
- 2 bunches Swiss chard, stems and tough central spines removed
- 1 tablespoon unsalted butter
- 1 small shallot, peeled and minced
- Ground pepper to taste
- 1 teaspoon finely grated lemon zest

1. In a blender, combine lime pickle, lemon juice, and olive oil and purée until smooth, adding water as necessary to coax a purée. Set aside.

2. Bring a pot of water to a boil and add 1 tablespoon salt. Prepare an ice bath and dissolve into it remaining 1 tablespoon salt. Add Swiss chard and boil until bright green and very tender. Transfer to ice bath to shock, remove from water, and squeeze chard to release most of the water. Set aside.

3. Heat a large stockpot over medium heat until hot. Add butter. When melted, add shallot, sprinkle with salt and pepper, cover pot, and sweat until shallots are translucent, about 4 minutes. Add the Swiss chard (stuff it in there!), lime pickle purée, and lemon zest. Use tongs to break up the clumps of Swiss chard and mix together the ingredients. Sprinkle with salt and pepper and serve.

- sour
- salty
- sweet
- bitter

30 mins
TOTAL TIME

30 mins
ACTIVE TIME

DIFFICULTY

4
PORTIONS

TRUFFLED TARO ROOT

In my mind, truffles and taro root are a preordained pairing. One is a fungus and the other a root, but both exhibit the same earthiness. This purée works as a side dish (for example, with Braised Beef Short Ribs on page 186), or as the foundation of a main dish.

- 2 pounds taro root, peeled and cut into chunks
- 3 tablespoons truffle butter, or 2 tablespoons unsalted butter plus 2 tablespoons truffle oil
- 1/4 cup (1/2 stick) unsalted butter
- 1 teaspoon minced fresh chives
- 1 teaspoon minced fresh parsley
- 1 teaspoon minced fresh tarragon
- Salt and ground pepper to taste

Place taro root in a large pot and cover with water. Bring to a boil and cook until fork-tender, 25 to 30 minutes. Drain and transfer to a large serving bowl. Add truffle butter (or butter and truffle oil) and unsalted butter, and mash as you would mashed potatoes. Mix in chives, parsley, and tarragon. Taste and season with salt and pepper. Serve hot.

- sour
- salty
- sweet
- bitter

50 mins
TOTAL TIME

20 mins
ACTIVE TIME

DIFFICULTY

4
PORTIONS

LUXURIOUS POTATO PURÉE

Mashed potatoes are elevated from merely tasty to divine when you include a generous amount of butter. Indulge yourself! In my kitchen, we like the ultrasmooth texture of boiled potatoes that have been forced through a mesh sieve. It takes some elbow grease, but we find it's worth the effort! Use waxy, not starchy, varieties of potatoes for any mashed potato recipe: fingerlings, Yukon golds, and French rattes are all good bets.

- 4 pounds waxy potatoes, such as Yukon golds or fingerlings, peeled and cut into 1/2-inch rounds
- 3 tablespoons salt, plus more to taste
- 6 ounces unsalted butter (1 1/2 sticks)
- 1/2 cup whole milk
- Ground pepper to taste
- Ground nutmeg to taste

1. Place potatoes in a large stockpot and fill with water to cover potatoes by 2 inches. Add salt. Bring to a boil and lower heat immediately so water is at a brisk simmer: the potatoes will break if they're boiled, resulting in smaller pieces of potato that cook too fast, absorb too much water, and become mushy. Simmer for about 20 minutes, or until a knife inserted into a piece of potato meets no resistance. Drain potatoes and pass them right away through the fine disk of a food mill or through a potato ricer, letting potatoes fall into a clean stockpot. You can also mash the potatoes with a mallet-like masher, but the final texture of the purée won't be as refined.

2. Place pot with mashed potatoes over low heat. Add butter 2 tablespoons at a time, mixing vigorously with a rubber spatula. When all the butter has been incorporated, add the milk and stir to combine; the milk and the butter will emulsify. Taste, and season with pepper, grated nutmeg, and more salt if desired; mix to combine. Serve, or proceed to next step.

3. Optional: immediately transfer potatoes into a mesh strainer and use the back of a small ladle to push the potatoes through. This step takes some real effort, but I promise that your effort will be rewarded with a luxuriously smooth purée! Serve hot or warm.

- sour
- salty
- sweet
- bitter

50 mins
TOTAL TIME

25 mins
ACTIVE TIME

DIFFICULTY

4
PORTIONS

PROCESS
POTATO PURÉE

CHINESE LONG BEANS
& CARAMELIZED PLANTAINS

I developed this dish to go with the Pomegranate & Cinnamon Lacquered Duck on page 190, but it is a fine accompaniment to any protein looking for a sweet sidekick. The beans take on some smoke flavor from the bacon, which should be slab bacon if possible. Chinese long beans are sold in Asian markets. If you can't find them, okra is the best stand-in; the two vegetables both have a slightly mucilaginous texture. Green beans are quite different.

1 tablespoon corn oil

1 pound Chinese long beans (also "yard-long beans"),
   trimmed and cut on the bias into 1-inch pieces

4 ounces applewood smoked slab bacon or other bacon, slivered

1 shallot, peeled and finely chopped

2 tablespoons unsalted butter

3 very ripe plantains, cut into 1/2-inch cubes

1 teaspoon salt, plus more to taste

4 cranks ground pepper in a mill, plus more to taste

1 to 2 tablespoons sugar, as necessary

1. Heat a large sauté pan with corn oil over high heat. Add long beans to the pan and toss to coat with oil. Sauté for 5 minutes. Add the bacon and shallots and continue to sauté until beans are tender and bacon is cooked through but not crispy, 5 to 10 minutes. Cover pan and hold off heat.

2. Heat a second large sauté pan over high heat with the butter. When butter has turned a light brown, add plantains and stir to coat. Reduce heat to medium-high. Sprinkle plantains with 1 teaspoon salt and 4 cranks pepper. Taste plantains, and sweeten by sprinkling with sugar if necessary—they should taste as sweet as ripe bananas. Continue to cook, stirring frequently, until the plantains are golden brown, about 15 minutes.

3. Add the caramelized plantains to the pan with the long beans and stir everything together. Warm over low heat if necessary. Taste; season with salt and pepper. Serve immediately.

sour

salty

sweet

bitter

40 mins
TOTAL TIME

40 mins
ACTIVE TIME

DIFFICULTY

4
PORTIONS

YAM PURÉE

I don't know how to improve upon traditional mashed sweet potatoes, so I haven't tried. This is an unadulterated classic—you might recognize it as one of the side dishes in grandma's Thanksgiving lineup. It goes especially well with the Szechuan Peppercorn–Rubbed Fillet of Beef on page 196.

- 2 pounds yams or sweet potatoes
- 2 tablespoons olive oil
- Salt and ground pepper to taste
- 1/2 cup honey, preferably clover honey
- 1/2 cup (1 stick) unsalted butter

1. Preheat oven to 375°F. Rub yams or sweet potatoes with oil, then sprinkle with salt and pepper. Wrap each separately in aluminum foil and roast in oven for 1 1/2 hours. Transfer to a plate and let rest just until cool enough to handle.

2. Peel skin off yams and place yams in a bowl. Add honey and butter and mash with a fork; butter should melt completely. Yams can be reheated in an oven or microwave if necessary. Taste and season with salt and pepper. Serve immediately.

- sour
- salty
- sweet
- bitter

1hr 40mins
TOTAL TIME

10mins
ACTIVE TIME

DIFFICULTY

4
PORTIONS

CRUSHED POTATOES WITH PARSLEY & THYME

An über—side dish! Not only does this simple, neutral potato dish go with just about any entrée, it's very easy to make—you don't even have to peel the potatoes. Fork-crushing the potatoes instead of ricing or mashing them is another time-saver.

- 2 pounds small waxy potatoes, such as fingerling or baby Yukon gold, scrubbed vigorously to smooth skins
- 2 tablespoons salt for boiling, plus more to taste
- 3 tablespoons extra-virgin olive oil
- 2 tablespoons unsalted butter
- 2 cups chopped fresh parsley
- 1 tablespoon fresh thyme leaves
- Ground pepper to taste

Place potatoes in a large pot and cover by 3 times with water. Add 2 tablespoons salt. Bring water to a gentle boil and cook potatoes until they offer no resistance when pierced with a skewer, 15 to 20 minutes, depending on size of potatoes. Drain and place in large bowl. Stir in olive oil, butter, parsley, and thyme. Crush with the back of a fork or wooden spoon. Season to taste with salt and pepper.

○ sour
● salty
● sweet
● bitter

45 mins
TOTAL TIME

20 mins
ACTIVE TIME

DIFFICULTY

4
PORTIONS

BABY CARROTS, THAI EGGPLANT & PEARL ONIONS

sour

salty

sweet

bitter

Though the eggplant of my childhood was always large and purple, I've since come to know the whole eggplant universe. Different varieties range dramatically in bitterness and water content. With creamy white eggplant, you'll never be tempted to pre-salt slices, because white eggplant is quite sweet. Slender Japanese eggplants have very few seeds and cook quickly. And then there's the tiny, round Thai eggplant it's one of the firmest eggplants out there, with a taste that's medium sweet.

- 4 cloves garlic, peeled
- 2 tablespoons kosher salt, for blanching
- 20 pearl onions
- one 10-ounce bag baby-cut carrots
- 1 1/2 cups mixed picked herbs, a combination of any of the following: Thai or regular basil, chervil, chives, cilantro, parsley, or tarragon
- 1/4 teaspoon sugar
- Salt and ground pepper to taste
- 2 tablespoons olive oil
- 8 Thai eggplants or 3 Japanese eggplants, cut into large dice

1. In saucepan, bring 1 1/2 cups water to a boil. Immerse garlic in water and boil 15 minutes.

2. While the garlic is boiling, bring a saucepan of water to a boil and add 1 tablespoon of the kosher salt. Prepare an ice bath and stir into it remaining 1 tablespoon kosher salt. Drop pearl onions in boiling water, boil 3 minutes, and transfer immediately with a slotted spoon to the ice bath. In the same water, blanch carrots for 1 minute. Shock carrots in ice bath. Drain ice bath. Peel onions. Cut larger onions in half across the equator.

3. After garlic has boiled 15 minutes and is soft, add herbs to water with garlic and remove pan from heat as soon as water has returned to a boil. Stir in sugar. Purée contents of pan in a blender or with an immersion blender. The purée should be fairly smooth but with flecks of herbs evident. Season to taste with salt and pepper.

4. Heat olive oil in a wide nonstick sauté pan over medium heat. When oil is hot, add onions, season with salt and pepper, cover, and cook 8 minutes, stirring occasionally, until onions no longer taste raw. Add carrots to pan, season, cover, and cook 4 minutes. Push vegetables to the sides of the pan and add eggplant to the center. Season, cover, and cook 8 minutes, stirring frequently, until eggplant is very tender and translucent. Pour herb purée over vegetables, remove pan from heat, and stir to coat. Check and adjust seasoning once more before serving.

40mins
TOTAL TIME

40mins
ACTIVE TIME

DIFFICULTY

4
PORTIONS

CRUNCHY PICKLED VEGETABLES

What is it that you should love about pickling? Yes, it's a practical way to extend the life of summer produce. Yes, colorful Ball jars of pickled vegetables make great gifts, and yes, thank God your aunt with no job has something to keep busy with all day. These are all fringe benefits, though. The big deal is that pickling zaps sweet-sour-salty-bitter right into foods—and the number and variety of foods you can try are limitless.

For a really different taste experience, serve pickled foods with their unpickled counterpart; for example, pickled beet wedges with sliced cooked beets.

- 5 cups vegetables, such as gherkin cucumbers, radishes, baby-cut or small carrots, pearl onions, sliced bell peppers, beets, celery, sliced fennel, or baby turnips
- 2 cups cider vinegar
- 1/3 cup sugar
- 1 tablespoon kosher or sea salt (table salt should not be used)
- 2 tablespoons coriander seeds
- 1 tablespoon black peppercorns
- 1 tablespoon whole allspice
- 1 tablespoon juniper berries
- 5 bay leaves
- 1 cup chopped fresh dill

1. Cook and peel any vegetables that you wouldn't normally eat raw. Pearl onions and beets should be boiled until tender, 12 minutes for onions and 30 minutes for beets.

2. Place vegetables in glass canning jars or other nonreactive, heatproof containers. If you use beets, I recommend giving them their own jar; otherwise, all your pickles will be fuchsia!

3. In a large stainless steel saucepan, combine vinegar, 3 cups water, sugar, salt, coriander seeds, peppercorns, allspice, juniper berries, bay leaves, and dill. Place over high heat. When mixture reaches a boil, remove pan from heat and ladle pickling liquid with its spices over the vegetables. Allow jars to come to room temperature, cover, and refrigerate 12 to 24 hours. These pickles should be consumed within 3 days.

- sour
- salty
- sweet
- bitter

12hrs
10-40 mins

TOTAL TIME*

10-40mins

ACTIVE TIME†

DIFFICULTY

5cups

PORTIONS††

* 12 hours
for pickling,
plus 10 to
40 minutes,
depending on
vegetables used

†depending on
vegetables used

††5 cups (about
2 medium jars)
pickles

FENNEL PURÉE

Use this purée to thicken other sauces and vinaigrettes. For me, it's like Worcestershire sauce: a dollop of it enhances just about anything and is barely detectable. On its own, fennel purée goes great over fish and vegetables.

- 1 fennel bulb
- 2 tablespoons fresh lemon juice
- Salt and ground pepper to taste
- Honey to taste

1. Trim the fennel of its outer layer, then cut in half. Cut each half into quarters, remove the tough inner core, and chop into roughly equal-sized pieces.

2. Bring 1/3 cup water to simmer in a large saucepan. Reduce heat to low. Add lemon juice and fennel, season with salt and pepper, cover, and simmer until completely tender, about 10 minutes. Drain the fennel, reserving the cooking liquid, and purée in a blender. Add just enough cooking liquid to get the blade moving. Taste, and season with honey, salt, and pepper.

- sour
- salty
- sweet
- bitter

20 mins
TOTAL TIME

20 mins
ACTIVE TIME

DIFFICULTY

4
PORTIONS*

*2 cups purée

CHAPTER 8
DESSERTS

CHILLED WATERMELON COCKTAIL WITH YUZU

- 3 tablespoons sugar
- 5 stalks lemongrass, cut into smaller lengths and smashed
- 2 tablespoons yuzu juice, or 1 tablespoon lime juice plus 1 tablespoon grapefruit juice
- 3 pounds ripe watermelon, seeded and cubed, plus 1/2 cup small watermelon balls
- Pinch salt

1. In a small saucepan, bring 1 cup water and sugar to a boil. Add lemongrass and yuzu juice, remove pan from heat, cover, and allow to steep for 2 hours. Strain and discard solids. (Lemongrass syrup may be made up to 2 days in advance.)

2. In a blender, purée cubed watermelon until a smooth liquid. Pass through a fine sieve. Add lemongrass syrup to the watermelon purée in increments, tasting after every addition of syrup and stopping when the cocktail is as sweet as you would like it to be. Stir in salt. Garnish with watermelon balls. Serve chilled in cocktail glasses.

- sour
- salty
- **sweet**
- bitter

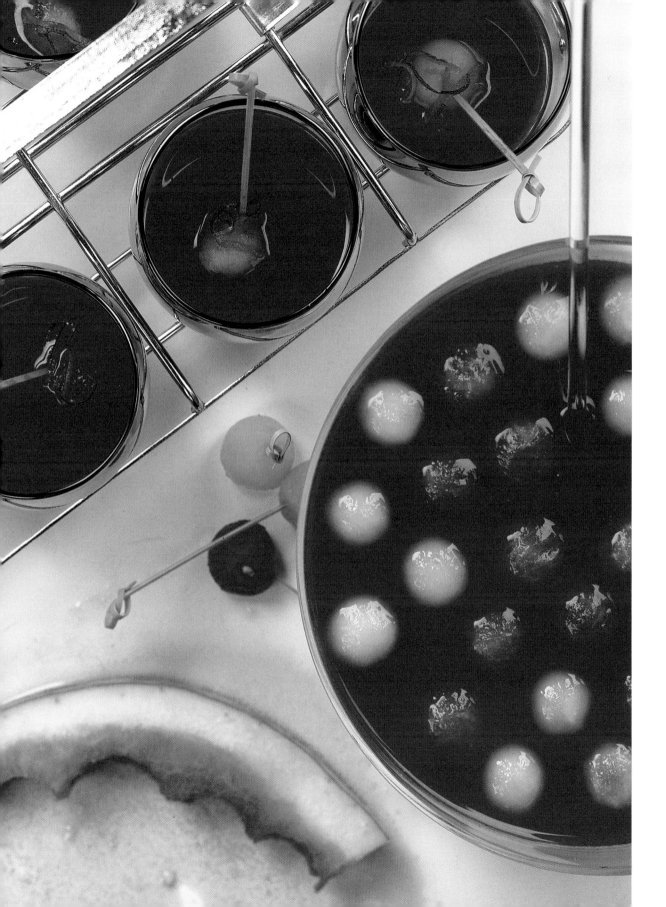

2 hrs 15 mins

TOTAL TIME

25 mins

ACTIVE TIME

DIFFICULTY

4

PORTIONS

WARM CHOCOLATE CAKE

By now, certainly everyone has tried a version of this popular chocolate cake in a restaurant. The exterior is solid yet the interior is molten: "How *do* they do that?" You will be amazed by how easy it really is! A tip: this is a single-flavor dessert, so use the very best chocolate you can find.

- 4 ounces good-quality semisweet chocolate
- 1/2 cup (1 stick) unsalted butter, plus more for ramekins
- 2 eggs
- 2 egg yolks
- 1/4 cup all-purpose flour, plus more for ramekins
- 1/4 cup plus 1 tablespoon sugar
- 1/4 teaspoon salt

1. Preheat oven to 375°F.

2. In a double boiler over medium heat, melt the chocolate and butter together, whisking to blend. When fully melted, remove from stove and allow to cool.

3. In a large mixing bowl, whisk the eggs and the yolks together. Add in the flour and sugar and mix just until well blended; you want to beat in as little air as possible. When chocolate mixture has cooled, add it to the egg mixture with a whisk, again being careful not to overmix or incorporate excess air. Stir in salt.

4. Butter and flour 4 individual 1/2-cup ramekins, tapping afterward to remove excess flour. Pour the chocolate batter into the ramekins.

5. Place ramekins in the middle rack of the oven and set timer for 9 minutes. At 9 minutes, test for doneness: cakes are perfectly cooked when surface appears set, cakes jiggle when shaken, and a toothpick inserted in the middle comes out coated with thick liquid. Cook 1 to 2 minutes longer if necessary. Remove ramekins from the oven and let stand 1 minute. To unmold, run a knife along the inner wall of each ramekin, cover with a small plate, quickly invert, and tap the bottom of the ramekin several times with the blade of a heavy knife. Serve with a spoon.

sour
salty
sweet
bitter

30 mins
TOTAL TIME

20 mins
ACTIVE TIME

DIFFICULTY

4
PORTIONS

BANYULS

SUMMER BERRIES
IN SPICED PHYLLO

The first sheets of phyllo always tear. Accept it and be grateful phyllo's cheap. Brush those scraps with butter, sprinkle them with sugar, and bake them alongside your berry tarts. Use the scraps, crumbled, as a garnish. Or, if you can't resist, enjoy them as a cook's snack!

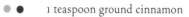

- 1 teaspoon ground cinnamon
- 1/2 teaspoon ground cloves
- 1/2 teaspoon ground star anise
- 3 cups wild or cultivated mixed berries, such as currants, raspberries, blackberries, and strawberries
- 1/4 cup honey
- Finely grated zest of 1 lime
- 4 sheets phyllo dough
- 1/4 cup (1/2 stick) unsalted butter, melted
- 1/4 cup plus 2 tablespoons confectioners' sugar
- 1/4 cup shelled almonds, coarsely ground in a food processor
- 1 cup crème fraîche

1. Mix together cinnamon, cloves, and star anise. Place berries in a separate bowl, sprinkle with 1 teaspoon spice mixture, and fold gently to coat. Fold in honey and lime zest. Set aside.

2. Preheat oven to 350°F.

3. On a countertop, unroll the phyllo sheets. Cover with a damp tea towel to prevent drying out. Using a pastry brush and working quickly, brush the first phyllo sheet with melted butter and sprinkle evenly with half of the remaining spice mixture and 2 tablespoons sugar. Place the second sheet squarely on top of the first, brush with butter, and sprinkle the almonds evenly over the surface. Place the third sheet on the second, brush with butter, and sprinkle with the remaining spice mixture and 2 tablespoons sugar. Cover with the fourth sheet. Prick the phyllo all over with a fork. With a circular cookie cutter or inverted mold, cut 6 disks from the phyllo stack and mold each disk to fit the cups of a nonstick muffin tin or 6 individual nonstick molds. Bake at 350°F for 10 minutes, or until the shells are crisp and golden brown on sides and bottom. Remove from oven and allow to cool completely in molds.

4. Use a whisk to whip crème fraîche with 2 tablespoons confectioners' sugar. Crème fraîche should look airy and a little like homemade whipped cream.

5. To assemble, remove phyllo cups from molds and fill each with 3/4 cup berries. Top with a dollop of whipped crème fraîche. Serve at room temperature.

- sour
- salty
- **sweet**
- bitter

1 hr
TOTAL TIME

40 mins
ACTIVE TIME

DIFFICULTY

6
PORTIONS

ARMAGNAC ICE CREAM

Ice cream is so versatile. This flavor is very adult, and though we tend to link frozen desserts with summer, Armagnac ice cream is best suited to cool weather. It is magnificent with desserts made with fall fruits like plums, prunes, pears, and figs. The Armagnac is added after the crème anglaise has been cooked, which gives the final ice cream a punch of raw alcohol and the warm, woodsy note of Armagnac. Feel free to use either cognac or brandy if that's what you have on hand.

- 1 quart half & half
- 1 cup plus 2 tablespoons sugar
- 9 egg yolks
- 3 tablespoons Armagnac

1. Fill a large bowl or sink with ice. (The ice bath will need to accommodate the saucepan that yo will use to cook the ice cream base.)

2. In a large saucepan over medium heat, heat the half & half. When it comes to a boil, remove pa from heat.

3. Place sugar and egg yolks in a mixing bowl. Beat with an electric mixer until smooth and pal yellow, about 3 minutes. Whisking constantly, slowly pour the sugar and egg yolk mixture into th saucepan containing the half & half; return pan to stove over very low heat. Stir continuously wit a wooden spoon until the foam disappears and the mixture is thick enough that the moving spoo leaves a "track" that fills in slowly. Set pan in the ice bath to stop the cooking process; stir a fev times. Add the Armagnac. Cool to room temperature. Transfer batter to an ice cream machine an freeze according to manufacturer's instructions.

- sour
- salty
- sweet
- bitter

40 mins
TOTAL TIME

20 mins
ACTIVE TIME

DIFFICULTY

1 quart
YIELD

LAVENDER CRÈME BRÛLÉE

This one's for my sister, whose favorite dessert has always been crème brûlée. I don't know whether it's the crackly crust or warm, creamy interior that she loves most. Creme brûlée, like ice cream, will happily take on any flavor you propose.

- 1 cup whole milk
- 1 cup heavy cream, preferably not ultrapasteurized
- 1/2 stalk fresh lavender or 3 tablespoons dried lavender intended for cooking
- 6 large egg yolks
- 1/4 cup granulated sugar
- 1/4 cup plus 2 tablespoons turbinado sugar ("sugar in the raw")

1. In a small saucepan, bring milk and cream to a boil, monitoring it closely so it doesn't boil over. Remove from the heat. Add lavender, and allow lavender to infuse the cream for 1 hour at room temperature. Strain mixture into a clean saucepan. Bring to a boil again and remove from heat.

2. Preheat oven to 275°F.

3. In a mixing bowl, whisk the yolks and granulated sugar until just combined. Temper the egg mixture by very slowly whisking a small amount of warm lavender cream into the eggs. Take your time with this step so that the yolks don't scramble. Once the egg mixture and cream are roughly the same temperature, whisk the remaining egg mixture into the cream.

4. Divide custard among four 4-ounce ramekins. Place ramekins in a baking dish or roasting pan. Fill dish or pan with water so that water comes halfway up the sides of the ramekins and transfer to the oven rack. Bake for 25 to 35 minutes. During the last 10 minutes, check frequently for doneness; when fully baked, the crème brûlées will be firm and will wiggle just slightly when shaken. Remove ramekins from water bath and refrigerate until chilled, at least 2 hours.

5. Before serving, sprinkle each dessert with 1 1/2 tablespoons turbinado sugar. If you own a propane torch, hold the torch about 8 inches from the custard's surface and flame the sugar into a golden brown, brittle crust. Alternatively, place ramekins under a preheated broiler and broil until sugar has caramelized, 1 to 3 minutes. Watch carefully: sugar turns from light brown to black quickly. Serve immediately.

TECHNIQUE INFUSING

Whenever you soak an ingredient in liquid with the intent of flavoring the liquid, you're infusing. A lot of kitchen terms masquerade as distinct processes but are really just types of infusions: we talk about "steeping" tea leaves, for example, and "brewing" coffee. Both tea and coffee are water-based infusions. An important thing to know about infusing is that all foods are either hydrophilic (literally, "water-loving") or lipophilic ("fat-loving"). It has to do with molecular chemistry and ion charges and a lot of other scientific babble. A good illustration: a bunch of chopped cilantro submerged in warm water won't do a thing to the water, because cilantro molecules are decidedly lipophilic. Put the same cilantro in heated oil or heavy cream, and the cilantro infuses effortlessly.

- ○ sour
- ◐ salty
- ● sweet
- ◑ bitter

4 hrs
TOTAL TIME

35 mins
ACTIVE TIME

DIFFICULTY

4
PORTIONS

Y
TOKAJI OR
OTHER DESSERT
WINE

NUTELLA SANDWICHES

On visits to Rome, my family usually stayed with my father's sister Elena, a nun. Breakfast at the convent was almost always day-old bread and Nutella, and the memory remains one of my fondest of Italy. Those breakfasts were truly a religious experience.

- 1 baguette or other long loaf, about 1 1/2 feet long
- 2 bananas, peeled and sliced into thin rounds
- 2 tablespoons unsalted butter, melted
- 3 tablespoons sugar
- 1/2 cup Nutella or other chocolate-hazelnut spread
- 1/4 cup shelled hazelnuts, toasted and coarsely chopped
- Several pinches fleur de sel

1. Preheat broiler to 350°F.

2. Slice bread into 4 mini baguettes and each mini baguette in half lengthwise, yielding 4 top and 4 bottom pieces. Place all 8 pieces flat side up on a baking sheet. Layer banana rounds on 4 of the pieces of bread, overlapping if necessary. Brush the bananas with half the butter and sprinkle with half the sugar. Brush the remaining butter and sprinkle the remaining sugar on the 4 pieces of bread with no banana. Broil for 10 minutes or until the bread is toasted and the bananas appear lightly caramelized. Remove baking sheet from broiler and let stand until bread is no longer hot.

3. Spread Nutella on the 4 pieces of bread with no banana and sprinkle each with 2 tablespoons of hazelnuts and a pinch of fleur de sel. Make 4 sandwiches by topping banana-covered bread pieces with Nutella-covered pieces. Eat while still warm.

- sour
- salty
- sweet
- bitter

20 mins
TOTAL TIME

10 mins
ACTIVE TIME

DIFFICULTY

4
PORTIONS

PEACH-PHYLLO STRUDEL WITH GOAT CHEESE CREAM

Goat cheese in a dessert? OK, I'll admit it: the idea seems a little strange. But once you taste this strudel, you'll see that the tang of goat cheese perfectly balances the luscious sweetness of ripe summer peaches.

A real Austrian strudel gets wrapped in paper-thin sheets of handmade pastry dough. My version, however, uses phyllo dough—a product that works simple magic in a cook's oven. You just brush on plenty of melted butter, pile it up, stick it in the oven, and—poof!—your flat stack of phyllo has turned into an inflated, flaky wonder.

- 4 fresh peaches, halved and pitted
- 8 tablespoons (1 stick) unsalted butter
- 1/2 cup sugar
- 3/4 cup milk
  1 1/4 tablespoons cornstarch
- 1 egg
- 1/4 cup plain yogurt
- 1 ounce fresh (not aged) goat cheese, at room temperature
  1 teaspoon vanilla extract
- Juice of 1/2 lemon
- 10 sheets phyllo dough

1. Preheat oven to 400°F.

2. Place peaches hollow side up on a baking sheet. Cut 1 tablespoon of the butter into 8 pieces and drop 1 piece into each peach cavity. Sprinkle 1 tablespoon of the sugar over all halves. Place sheet in oven and roast peaches until thoroughly soft and a bit browned where fruit contacts the sheet, 25 to 30 minutes. Keeping oven at 400°F, remove peaches and cut each half into 4 or 5 slices.

3. Make pastry cream while peaches roast: in a small saucepan, whisk together milk, 2 tablespoons of the sugar, and 1 tablespoon of the butter. Place pan over medium heat, and remove from heat when mixture comes to a boil. In a mixing bowl, combine 1/4 cup of the sugar, cornstarch, and egg and whisk to blend. To temper the egg, slowly pour about half of the hot milk mixture into the egg mixture while whisking continuously. Return tempered mixture to same saucepan and return pan to medium heat. When cream comes to a boil, pull from heat and stir in yogurt, goat cheese, vanilla, and lemon juice. Hold at room temperature.

4. Melt the remaining 6 tablespoons butter. Keep melted butter and remaining 1 tablespoon sugar

1hr 30mins
TOTAL TIME

1hr 10mins
ACTIVE TIME

DIFFICULTY

4
PORTIONS

to the side of the baking sheet. Roll out first phyllo sheet onto the baking sheet and, keeping the stack of phyllo covered by a damp tea towel and working as quickly as possible so the phyllo doesn't dry out, brush to cover with melted butter and sprinkle with sugar. Lay second phyllo sheet squarely over first, and again brush with butter and sprinkle with sugar. Repeat with remaining 8 sheets, reserving a bit of butter for the top of the strudel. Once all 10 sheets have been stacked, arrange peach slices side-by-side in a single layer over phyllo, leaving a 1-inch clear border between peaches and the edge of the phyllo. Spoon goat cheese pastry cream over the peaches, observing same border. Use enough pastry cream to generously coat all peaches. Starting from a long side of the rectangle, roll phyllo in a jelly roll fashion. Brush top with reserved melted butter. Bake in 400° oven until phyllo is golden brown, about 20 minutes.

5. Slice strudel into sections. Serve while warm, with ice cream, if desired.

- sour
- salty
- ● sweet
- bitter

STRAWBERRY SHORTCAKE

This dessert is something of a misfit in this book. It's not my recipe at all, but a straightforward replica of a charming American classic. Strawberry shortcake is delicious and unpretentiously perfect; that's why you'll see it on Union Pacific's dessert menu whenever the summer yields knockout berries.

- 1 pint fresh strawberries
- 1/4 cup plus 1 tablespoon granulated sugar
- 2 cups all-purpose flour
- 1 tablespoon baking powder
- 1/8 teaspoon cinnamon
- 1/8 teaspoon salt
- 1/4 cup (1/2 stick) chilled unsalted butter, cut into small pieces
- 1 egg
- 1/2 cup plus 2 tablespoons milk
- 1 cup chilled whipping cream
- Confectioners' sugar to taste

1. Wash, hull, and drain the strawberries. In a large bowl, crush 2 or 3 berries with a fork. Slice the remaining berries and add them to the crushed berries. Sprinkle all with 1 tablespoon of the granulated sugar. Cover bowl and refrigerate for about 1 hour.

2. Preheat oven to 400°F.

3. In a mixing bowl, combine flour, remaining 1/4 cup granulated sugar, baking powder, cinnamon, and salt. With a pastry blender or 2 knives, cut in butter pieces until mixture contains particles the size of small peas. In a small bowl, beat egg, divide in half, and add one half to the dough. Add milk and stir until dough is homogeneous.

4. Divide dough into 4 equal-sized balls. On a lightly floured surface, pat balls into four 4-inch rounds. Place on a greased baking sheet and bake until well risen and golden brown, 15 to 17 minutes.

5. While shortcakes bake, beat cream to stiff peaks. One teaspoon at a time, add confectioners' sugar to taste.

6. Let shortcakes stand until warm (not hot) to the touch. Using gentle pressure, split shortcakes in half with a serrated knife. Spoon strawberries over bottom halves, close with top shortcake halves, and spoon more strawberries on top. Finish each serving with a generous dollop of whipped cream. Serve while shortcake is still warm.

- sour
- salty
- sweet
- bitter

1 hr 10 mins
TOTAL TIME

40 mins
ACTIVE TIME

DIFFICULTY

4
PORTIONS

MANGO & PAPAYA CARPACCIO WITH CILANTRO CANDY

A simple but elegant tropical fruit dessert. The balancing act that you orchestrate among tastes in a meal should extend through dessert. Here, lemon zest stirred into the mango gelée keeps things from getting sickeningly sweet. We borrowed the word *carpaccio* in describing the thin slices of this dessert.

- 12 fresh cilantro leaves
- 2 tablespoons superfine sugar
- 1 egg white
- 2 firm mangoes, peeled (look for the ripest fruit that will still hold its shape when cut)
- 1 ripe papaya, peeled
  Two 1/4-ounce packages unflavored powdered gelatin (about 15 grams total)
- 1/4 cup granulated sugar
- Zest of 1 lemon
- Ground white pepper to taste
- Pineapple Sorbet (page 274) (optional)

1. Wash the cilantro leaves and dry them completely between paper towels. Spread cilantro leaves flat over a work space and have the superfine sugar nearby. Beat the egg white until foamy. Using a small pastry brush, coat the top side of each leaf with just enough egg white to cover, then sprinkle a pinch of sugar over each. Flip leaves and repeat. Arrange leaves in a single layer on a grid baking rack and place rack in a dry environment 115°F to 125°F warm, such as in a toaster oven on lowest setting or gas oven heated only by its pilot flame. Dry this way, checking frequently, just until sugared leaves are brittle, 10 to 18 minutes depending on temperature. Immediately remove leaves from baking rack and hold aside. Stored in an airtight container, candied cilantro leaves will keep for several weeks.

2. Use a mandoline or very sharp knife to slice mangoes and papaya as thinly as possible. Transfer slices to a plate and refrigerate. Save scraps of mango.

3. Add gelatin to 1/4 cup warm water and stir until dissolved.

4. In a saucepan over high heat, combine 3/4 cup water, 1/2 cup mango scraps, 1/4 cup granulated sugar, and lemon zest. When the mixture comes to a boil, transfer it to a blender and purée until smooth. Pour into a bowl and add the dissolved gelatin; whisk to combine. Pour through a fine mesh strainer into a clean bowl. Season with a bit of white pepper.

5. Overlap alternating slices of mango and papaya in a circle on 4 dinner plates. Brush fruit with an even coating of mango gelée. Refrigerate until gelée is firm, about 30 minutes. Top each dessert with a scoop of Pineapple Sorbet, if using, and garnish each with 3 candied cilantro leaves.

- sour
- salty
- sweet
- bitter

1hr 45mins
TOTAL TIME

1hr
ACTIVE TIME

DIFFICULTY

4
PORTIONS

COTEAUX
DE SAUMER*

* or other
late-harvest
Chenin Blanc

PINEAPPLE SORBET

A good-quality pineapple sorbet should be white or barely ecru. Don't tamper with its pureness by adding yellow food coloring!

- 3/4 cup sugar
- 2 cups pineapple purée (from 1 medium pineapple), strained
- 2 tablespoons fresh lime juice
- Pinch salt

1. In a small, heavy-bottomed saucepan over medium heat, warm sugar with 1 cup water, stirring until sugar is completely dissolved. Let simple syrup cool to room temperature.

2. In a nonreactive mixing bowl, whisk together pineapple purée, lime juice, simple syrup, and salt. Freeze in an ice cream machine according to manufacturer's instructions. If you don't own an ice cream machine, try making a pineapple granita instead: pour sorbet base into a baking dish, cover with plastic wrap, and place in the freezer. Stir every 30 minutes until base is completely frozen. Stirring frequently creates ice crystals.

- sour
- salty
- **sweet**
- bitter

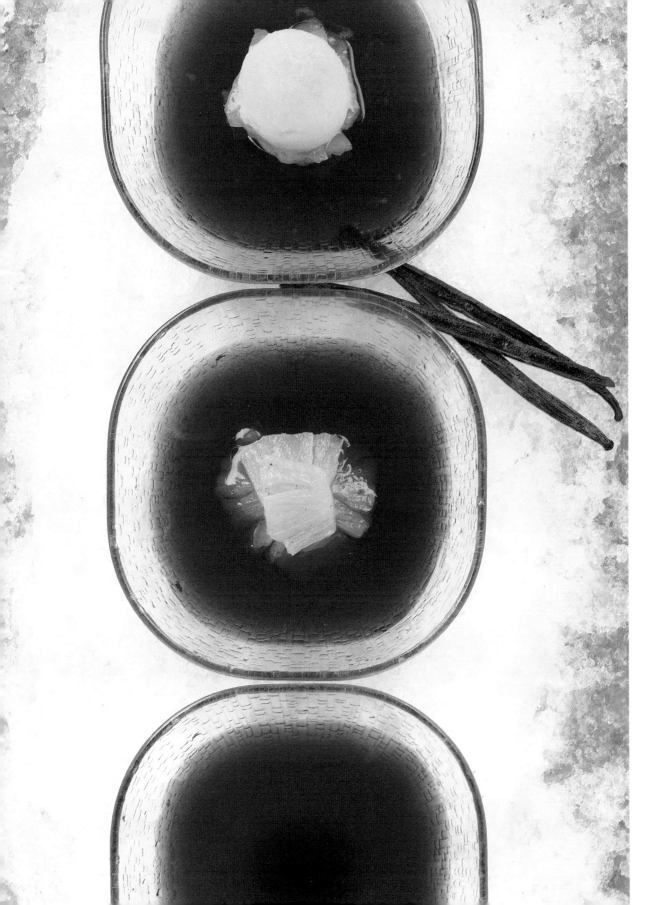

55 mins
TOTAL TIME

25 mins
ACTIVE TIME

DIFFICULTY

1 quart
YIELD

PLUM TARTLETTES

Buy the sweetest plums available for these tarts. I recommend you shop at a farmers market, where sampling is rarely discouraged. Almonds are related to and partner effortlessly with stone fruits like peaches, apricots, and plums.

- 1/4 cup confectioners' sugar
- 1 cup all-purpose flour, plus more for dusting
- 3/4 cup (1 1/2 sticks) unsalted butter, 1/2 stick cold and cut into chunks and 1 stick at room temperature
- 3 eggs
  1/2 teaspoon vanilla extract
- 1/2 cup granulated sugar
- 1 1/2 cups almond flour, purchased or made by finely grinding blanched almonds in food processor
- 4 1/2 cups pitted plums cut into sixths (from about 8 medium black plums)

1. In a mixing bowl or bowl of a stand mixer, combine confectioners' sugar and 1 cup all-purpose flour. Using a manual pastry cutter or stand mixer, work in cold butter pieces. Process until mixture resembles sand. If using a stand mixer, change beater to dough hook. Add 1 egg and vanilla, and continue to mix just until the dough is cohesive, adding cold water a tablespoon at a time if dough is dry. Shape into a ball, wrap in wax paper or plastic wrap, and refrigerate at least 1 hour.

2. In a mixing bowl or bowl of a stand mixer, beat together 1 stick room temperature butter and granulated sugar. Beat in 3/4 cup almond flour, then the 2 remaining eggs, one at a time. Add remaining 3/4 cup almond flour and stir until the filling comes together.

3. Preheat oven to 325°F.

4. Butter six 4-inch tart molds and dust with flour.

5. On a lightly floured surface, roll out chilled dough into a circle about 1/8-inch thick. Use a 5-inch cookie cutter or ring mold to make 6 dough rounds. If you come up short, wad the scraps into a ball and reroll. Place a dough round in each tart mold and gently press so that the lip of the dough just meets the top of each mold. Fill each shell with enough almond filling to come two-thirds of the way up the sides—about 1/4 cup filling per tart. Arrange plum slices over filling to completely cover. Bake for 35 to 40 minutes, or until dough is golden and firm.

6. Unmold tartlettes and serve warm with Fromage Blanc Sorbet (page 278).

sour
salty
sweet
bitter

2 hrs 20 mins
TOTAL TIME

50 mins
ACTIVE TIME

DIFFICULTY

6
PORTIONS

FROMAGE BLANC SORBET

This tangy, snow white sorbet is a perfect foil for sweeter desserts. Any pie would be happy for a scoop of Fromage Blanc Sorbet as its "à la mode"!

- 1 1/3 cups sugar
- Zest of 1 lemon
- 8 ounces (1 small container) fromage blanc
- 8 ounces (1 small container) plain yogurt, not low-fat
- 1 1/3 cups sour cream

1. Place 1 cup water and the sugar in a small, heavy-bottomed saucepan over medium heat. Stir while mixture comes to a low simmer. When the sugar has dissolved completely and the liquid is transparent, remove pan from heat. Add the lemon zest, stir, and let syrup infuse for at least 30 minutes.

2. In a large bowl, whisk together the fromage blanc, yogurt, and sour cream. Add the syrup with its zest and whisk until mixture is smooth and homogeneous. Freeze in an ice cream machine according to manufacturer's instructions. Because of its high acidity, this ice cream takes longer than most to freeze completely. If you have a model of ice cream machine that begins to thaw after a set period of time, you may find that the sorbet does not thicken enough in the machine. If this happens, simply transfer the bowl to the freezer for about 4 hours or overnight.

- sour
- salty
- sweet
- bitter

45 mins
TOTAL TIME

15 mins
ACTIVE TIME

DIFFICULTY

1 quart
YIELD

FROZEN DESSERTS

How many varieties of ice cream exist around the world? I'd honestly like to know. Here are brief descriptions of the frozen confections we encounter most often in the U.S.:

FROZEN YOGURT: Like regular yogurt, frozen yogurt is enriched by cultures.

GELATO: A soft-textured ice cream made with a high proportion of egg yolks.

ICE CREAM: Strictly speaking, the base of an ice cream is always a crème anglaise (cream or milk, sugar, and eggs). The amount of air forced into an ice cream has a lot to do with its final texture.

ICE MILK: An American invention. Ice milk is a low-cost, eggless, milk-only ice cream.

FROZEN ICE: Flavored, colored, sweetened water can be found in many forms. Italian ice, granitas, shaved ice, popsicles, and convenience store slushes all qualify.

SHERBET: Similar to sorbet, but usually stiffened by egg whites or gelatin.

SORBET: An eggless ice cream. Can be made with or without dairy products.

- sour
- salty
- ● sweet
- bitter

WHITE CHOCOLATE RISOTTO

Here's a loose rice pudding sweetened by white chocolate. Just as traditional rice pudding becomes more complex with cinnamon, nutmeg, or raisins, this risotto really soars when you go one step further on your own. Try blending in some not-so-sweet fruit just after the white chocolate has melted. Huckleberries, chopped persimmon, and pomegranate seeds would all be great additions.

- 4 ounces white chocolate (chips or chopped from a block)
- 2 ounces heavy cream
- 1 tablespoon unsalted butter
- 3/4 cup arborio rice
- 2 1/2 to 3 cups whole milk
- 1/3 cup sugar
  1 vanilla bean, split and scraped

1. Place white chocolate in a heavy mixing bowl. In a small saucepan, bring cream to a boil and pour over chocolate. Let sit for a minute and then stir until chocolate has melted and mixture is homogeneous. Add butter; stir. Refrigerate 30 minutes, until firm.

2. Combine rice, milk, sugar, and vanilla bean in a heavy-bottomed saucepan over medium heat. Stir frequently until rice is tender and most liquid has been absorbed. Add in white chocolate ganache a little at a time, stopping when risotto is as sweet as you'd like. Serve warm.

○ sour
● salty
● sweet
● bitter

1hr
TOTAL TIME

20mins
ACTIVE TIME

DIFFICULTY

4
PORTIONS

BRANDY

CHAPTER 9
RESERVE LIST

The recipes I call the "Reserve List" will ask a bit more of you than the others in the book, generally speaking. Some involve tricky techniques; some have long preparation times; others just require that you be able to keep your cool while multitasking like crazy. These are no-holds-barred dishes designed to challenge advanced cooks.

HAVE FUN!

HEIRLOOM TOMATOES WITH THAI BASIL & SUPERSWEET CORN

"Foods that grow together taste good together" is a little culinary mantra of mine. Tomatoes, basil, and corn coexist in warm, sunny landscapes at the very end of the summer. Any way you throw them together, they work as a dish. If you've never given much thought to where cornstarch comes from, boiling the cobs for this salad will be an eye-opener.

- 2 heads garlic, cloves separated
- 2 cups extra-virgin olive oil
- 4 large heirloom beefsteak tomatoes, such as Brandywine, German Stripe, Cherokee Purple, or Dixie Gold
- 1/2 teaspoon salt, plus more to taste
- Ground black pepper to taste
- 1 1/2 bunches Thai basil, 1 bunch chopped
- 3 ears supersweet corn
- Sugar, as needed
- 1/4 cup red wine vinegar
- 4 ounces fresh goat cheese (optional)

1. To make peeling the garlic easier, soak cloves in hot tap water for 10 minutes. Peel with a paring knife; the skins should slip off easily. Place garlic in a 2-quart saucepan and cover with cold water by 4 inches. Bring to a boil and drain immediately. Quickly rinse and thoroughly dry the pan, return garlic to it, and add olive oil. Bring to a bare simmer and cook until garlic is soft throughout, about 30 minutes. Be careful not to let garlic turn brown; lower the heat as necessary. Strain garlic-infused oil and let it cool to room temperature. Reserve cloves for another use.

2. To peel tomatoes, roast each over an open flame until their skins are blistered all over. Peel with a paring knife and slice each along its equator into five 3/4-inch-thick slices. Season slices with salt and pepper. In a glass baking or casserole dish, combine garlic oil and the chopped Thai basil and immerse tomato slices in marinade. Allow the tomatoes to marinate at room temperature for at least 1 hour or, ideally, overnight. Remove tomatoes and reserve marinade.

3. Make the corn syrup. Husk corn and cut ears in half. Grate on a box grater to strip off all kernels. Reserve cobs. Place corn and cobs in a saucepan and add water to cover. Bring to a boil, reduce heat, and simmer until corn flavor is well developed and starches have converted to sugar, at least 10 minutes. Taste the syrup for sweetness: the syrup should be very sweet, so add a pinch or two of sugar if you need to. Stir to dissolve. Strain syrup through a fine mesh sieve, and season to taste with salt and pepper.

- sour
- salty
- sweet
- bitter

4. While corn syrup simmers, pluck 8 nice sprigs from the half bunch of basil; set aside as a garnish. From the remaining basil, separate stems, cut stems into 1/2-inch lengths, and place basil stems, red wine vinegar, and 1/2 teaspoon salt in a small nonreactive bowl. Let the mixture stand at room temperature for 30 minutes.

5. Make a sauce by mixing some of the marinade with some of the corn syrup, letting your taste buds determine the best proportion. Chop remaining basil leaves and add them to the sauce.

6. Arrange tomato slices attractively in the center of each of 4 plates and season with salt and pepper. Spoon corn syrup sauce over the tomatoes. Splash some basil vinegar (minus the stems) over each dish and garnish plates with 2 sprigs of Thai basil each. Optional: crumble 2 tablespoons of fresh goat cheese over tomatoes. Serve immediately.

SAUTÉED FOIE GRAS WITH GLAZED PEACHES

If you're shelling out for foie gras, I'll bet the hoity-toity market you're shopping in also carries excellent sel de Guerande, a coarse, hand-harvested sea salt from Normandy. A few crunchy grains of the stuff scattered over perfectly seared foie gras is heavenly. Be sure to spend a lot of money on it because, hey, it's salt, after all.

- 2 tablespoons kosher salt for blanching, plus more to taste
- 2 cups celery leaves
- 1 tablespoon olive oil
- Ground pepper to taste
- 2 small ripe peaches, preferably donut-shaped
- 2 tablespoons plus 1 teaspoon sugar
- 1 1/2 tablespoons unsalted butter, cut into small pieces
- 1/4 cup sherry vinegar
- 12 ounces Grade A or B foie gras, cut into 4 slices
- Coarse sea salt for garnish, preferably sel de Guerande

1. Preheat oven to 375°F.

2. Boil a pan of water with one tablespoon salt. Prepare an ice bath with one tablespoon salt. Blanch celery leaves for 30 seconds and transfer to ice bath. Remove leaves from bath and wring out. Chop fine. In a food processor, crush celery leaves into a paste. Stir in oil. Season to taste.

3. Cut the peaches in half by deeply scoring them around their equators—then gently twisting the halves. Discard pits. Place peach halves cut side down in a roasting pan. Sprinkle with 1 teaspoon of the sugar and dot with butter pieces. Roast in oven until softened and slightly browned on cut side, 8 to 15 minutes depending on fruit's ripeness. Remove pan from oven and lower heat to 100°F. Strain pan's peach juice. Peel peaches, return to pan, and hold in oven to keep warm.

4. Heat a small saucepan over medium heat with remaining 2 tablespoons sugar. Cook, stirring frequently, until sugar has transformed into a light-colored caramel. Add vinegar and stir with a wooden spoon until sugar has redissolved. Add reserved peach juice and cook mixture until reduced to a syrup. Taste and season with salt. Cover pan to keep warm.

5. Choose a cast-iron skillet large enough to accommodate all 4 foie gras slices, and heat over high heat until very hot. Season both sides of foie gras slices with salt and pepper. Lay on skillet and cook, draining off fat as it renders, until foie gras is deep golden brown on both sides, 2 to 3 minutes per side. Keep warm in oven with peaches.

6. Spread some celery leaf paste on each plate. Place a peach half hollow side up on the purée, followed by a foie gras slice on each peach. Spoon glaze over the entire dish—over the foie gras, peach, and plate itself. Sprinkle with fleur de sel and serve while foie gras is still warm.

- sour
- salty
- sweet
- bitter

45 mins
TOTAL TIME

45 mins
ACTIVE TIME

DIFFICULTY

4
PORTIONS

COTEAUX DU
LAYON

WHITE TRUFFLE RISOTTO WITH A GULF SHRIMP FONDUE

For me, risotto, with its creamy, 15-ply cashmere luxuriousness, is the ultimate blank canvas. Use it as a neutral platform for your favorite flavors. White truffles are hard to come by, and expensive. But this dish is forgiving: the risotto will be redolent of truffles even if you skip the truffle shavings and rely on truffle butter alone. Truffle oil, however, is not a good substitute.

- 1/4 cup extra-virgin olive oil
- 2/3 pound uncooked, head-on Gulf shrimp, shelled and deveined, heads severed and heads and shells reserved
- 1/4 cup plus 1 tablespoon chopped shallots (about 4 shallot lobes)
- 2 stalks lemongrass, chopped into shorter lengths and crushed
- 1/2 teaspoon fennel seeds
- 1/4 cup sherry
- 1/4 cup dry vermouth
- 5 medium tomatoes, 4 coarsely chopped and 1 peeled, seeded, and cut into large dice
- Pinch cayenne pepper
- 6 sprigs fresh thyme
- Salt and ground pepper to taste
- 2 teaspoons minced fresh garlic
- 4 cups chicken stock
- 1/4 cup (1/2 stick) unsalted butter
- 1 1/2 cups arborio rice
- 1/4 cup dry white wine
- 2/3 cup truffle butter, preferably white truffle butter
- 1/4 cup chopped fresh chervil or parsley
- 2 tablespoons fines herbes (a blend of chervil, parsley, tarragon, and chives)
- 3 grams white truffles, shaved

1. Start by making a shrimp stock: in a saucepan over high heat, heat 2 tablespoons of the olive oil until smoking. Add shrimp heads and shells, and sauté actively until they turn coral. Add 2 tablespoons of the shallots, lemongrass, and fennel seeds, and stir until highly aromatic, about 3 minutes. Add sherry and reduce until pan is almost dry. Repeat with vermouth. Add the coarsely chopped tomatoes, cayenne pepper, and 2 sprigs of thyme, and lower heat to medium. Simmer ingredients in the released tomato juice for 25 minutes.

2. Use an immersion blender to crush the ingredients to a lumpy purée. Strain through a fine mesh sieve into a small saucepan over medium heat. Cook stock until consistency is thick and viscous. Taste, and season with salt and pepper according to your preference. Set aside.

- sour
- salty
- sweet
- bitter

45 mins

TOTAL TIME

45 mins

ACTIVE TIME

DIFFICULTY

4

PORTIONS

GRAND CRU
WHITE
BURGUNDY

3. Prepare the tomato fondue: in a saucepan over low heat, warm 1 tablespoon of the olive oil. Add tablespoons shallots and 1 teaspoon garlic. Sauté until translucent, about 5 minutes, and add diced tomatoes to pan. Cook over low heat until the tomatoes have "melted" into a fondue: the tomatoes' juice will have evaporated, and the tomato pieces should be very tender but still have some form. (Do not cook them so long that they resemble a pasta sauce!)

4. Begin the risotto: warm chicken stock over low heat in a saucepan. Keep at a simmer.

5. In a saucepan over medium-low heat, melt 1 tablespoon of the butter in 1 tablespoon of the olive oil. Add remaining 1 tablespoon shallots and 1 teaspoon garlic, and sauté until translucent, about 5 minutes. Add rice and toast in oil until just golden. Add 4 remaining sprigs of thyme and white wine, and allow liquid to come to a boil. Ladle chicken stock into rice one ladle at a time, allowing the rice to fully absorb each batch before adding more. Test rice frequently for doneness, and stop cooking when the texture of the risotto is tender yet toothsome. Discard thyme. Stir in truffle butter and chervil or parsley. Taste and season with salt and pepper. Cover to keep warm.

6. Finish the sauce: in a saucepan over medium-high heat, melt 1 tablespoon of the butter. Add shrimp and cook on one side only, until opaque and pink, 2 to 4 minutes. Remove shrimp from pan and keep warm. Add shrimp stock and tomato fondue to the same pan. Reduce heat to low and simmer just until warmed through and thick. Off the heat, add the remaining 2 tablespoons butter in pieces to sauce and swirl pan to incorporate. Cut shrimp into bite-size pieces and drop in sauce. Stir in fines herbes.

7. To serve, divide risotto among 4 large or 6 small plates. Shave truffles over each serving of risotto. Spoon shrimp fondue alongside the risotto or serve separately in small soup bowls.

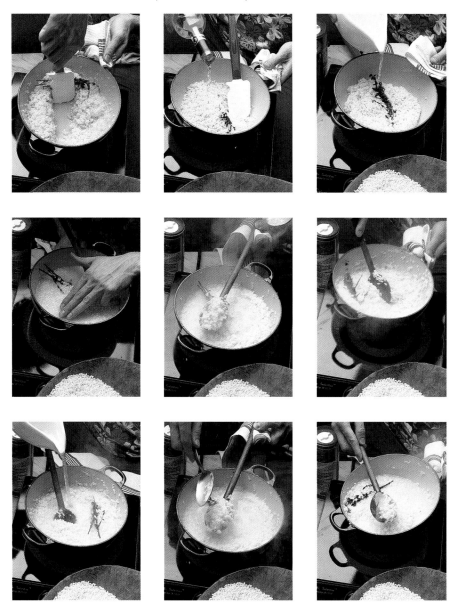

HALIBUT WITH YOUNG GINGER & SHALLOT CRACKLING

I love ginger, but its flavor is a challenge to work into my dishes. Ginger is hydrophilic (meaning its molecules bind with water), so we'd need a high-tech emulsification machine to force a ginger oil. Young ginger, however, is mild-tasting and tender enough to use in pieces in this halibut preparation. Look for cream-colored young ginger with pink shoots in Asian markets during the spring and summer. The crispy shallots provide a textural counterpoint to the velvety, goose fat–poached halibut. In the restaurant, we use a combination of shallot cracklings and pig's feet. If you want to try the pig's feet at home, give me a call.

- 8 ounces young ginger, peeled, sliced very thin on a mandoline, and rough-chopped into smaller pieces
- 1/4 cup sugar
- 4 whole allspice
- 1 1/2 pounds Swiss chard (about 3 bunches), lower stems and thicker interior spines removed
- Duck or goose fat to cover halibut, about 1 1/2 quarts
- 24 ounces halibut, cut into 4 squares
- 2 tablespoons unsalted butter
- 3 ounces bacon, preferably slab, diced small
- Salt and ground pepper to taste
- 1/2 cup diced shallots
- Zest of 1 lemon
- 1/2 teaspoon chopped fresh chervil or parsley

1. Bring a medium saucepan of water to a boil. Immerse ginger and cook 2 minutes. Drain ginge and empty pan. Repeat process 2 more times, cooking ginger in boiling water for 2 minutes each time. (Blanching helps tame the ginger's assertive bite.) After third blanching, combine ginger, 2 1/: cups water, sugar, and allspice in original pan. Simmer until ginger is completely tender, about : hour. Set aside. (Ginger can be candied up to a week in advance and preserved in its cooking liquid.

2. Bring a large pot of salted water to a boil. Immerse as much Swiss chard as will fit in pan, anc cook 30 seconds. Remove chard from hot water, run under cold water briefly, and wring dry. Repea with any remaining chard. Set aside.

3. In a large, deep saucepan, melt the duck or goose fat and heat to 110°F. If you don't have a ther mometer, use your finger: at 110°F, you'll be able to hold your finger in the fat for 1 or 2 seconds comfortably, but not much longer. Carefully slip halibut into the fat. Poach until fish is cooked throughout but still translucent in the center, about 10 minutes. Remove from pan and let rest.

- sour
- salty
- **sweet**
- bitter

3 hrs
TOTAL TIME

3 hrs
ACTIVE TIME

DIFFICULTY

4
PORTIONS

RIESLING
KABINETT

4. While fish is being poached, finish the Swiss chard: in a high-sided saucepan, melt 1 tablespoon of the butter. When foaming subsides, add bacon and sweat just to the point where most of its fat has been rendered but bacon is not yet crisp, 4 to 5 minutes. Add the Swiss chard and stir vigorously to coat; it's OK if chard breaks. Season generously with salt and pepper. Keep warm.

5. Melt remaining tablespoon of butter in a sauté pan over medium heat. Add shallots and sauté until golden brown and crispy. Drain through a strainer and combine with lemon zest and chervil or parsley. Taste, and season with salt and pepper.

6. Overlap ginger slices in a ring on each plate. Mound some Swiss chard in the center of each ring, and top each mound with a halibut square. Sprinkle with crispy shallots. Serve immediately.

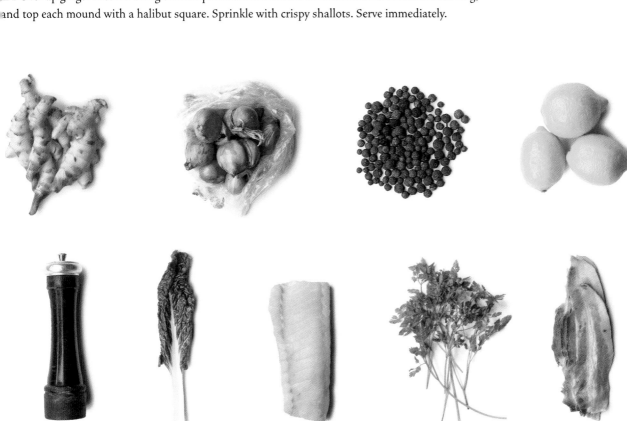

SLOW-COOKED SALT-CRUST SALMON WITH ENDIVE

From steadying oyster shells to breaking in new cast-iron pans, salt has an almost endless number of uses in the kitchen. Baking foods in salt is an old, old tradition. By hermetically sealing a protein like salmon in salt, the fish keeps all its juices, and the collagen in the fish becomes luxuriously gelatinous. Use a thick center cut of salmon for this dish, with skin on both sides: the skin will prevent the fish from becoming salty. By the way, the same dough can be shaped with cookie cutters and baked in the oven to make ornaments!

- 4 heads Belgian endive
  3 tablespoons corn oil
- Salt and ground pepper to taste
- 3 tablespoons plus 1 teaspoon sugar
- 3 tablespoons plus 2 teaspoons fresh lemon juice (from about 2 lemons), plus more if desired
- 1/2 cup white wine
- 1 cup kosher salt
- 4 cups all-purpose flour
- 3 egg whites
- 1 thick, 2-pound salmon cross section, with skin on both sides
- 6 fresh tarragon leaves
- 1 teaspoon extra-virgin olive oil

1. Coarsely chop 2 heads of the Belgian endive. Heat a sauté pan over high heat with 2 tablespoons of the corn oil until very hot but not smoking. Add chopped endive, season with salt and pepper, and sauté until the endive is dark brown all over but not burnt, 7 to 10 minutes. Lower the heat to medium and sprinkle endive with 1 teaspoon of the sugar and 2 teaspoons of the lemon juice. Continue to cook until endive is completely soft, then transfer to a blender and purée. Check seasoning and add salt and pepper to taste. Pass purée through a fine mesh sieve, using a rubber spatula to push it through. (This endive purée can be used as the basis of a quick sauce.)

2. Preheat oven to 350°F.

3. Heat remaining tablespoon of corn oil in a large ovenproof sauté pan over medium-high heat. Cut remaining 2 heads of endive in half lengthwise, and sprinkle with salt, pepper, and 1 tablespoon of the sugar. Place endive halves in pan cut side down and cook until nicely caramelized on flat side, about 2 minutes, then flip and lightly brown rounded side, about 2 minutes more. Reduce heat to medium and transfer endive to a plate. To the same pan, add remaining 2 tablespoons sugar, stirring to incorporate pan juices. When sugar granules have browned slightly, add white wine and

- sour
- salty
- ● sweet
- bitter

2 hrs 15 mins
TOTAL TIME

2 hrs 15 mins
ACTIVE TIME

DIFFICULTY

4
PORTIONS

PINOT NOIR
OR LIGHT
BURGUNDY

emaining 3 tablespoons lemon juice. Stir to dissolve sugar. Return endive halves to the pan cut side down, and add water to come a third of the way up the sides of the endive. Bring to a simmer, then cover pan and place in oven. Let endive simmer in the oven for 25 to 30 minutes, monitoring level of liquid in the pan and adding water a tablespoon at a time if necessary. Endive is done when completely tender throughout when pierced with a skewer. Transfer endive halves to a cutting board, cut in half again lengthwise, and keep warm in a covered baking dish. Strain pan liquids into a small saucepan; you should have about 2/3 cup of dark, flavorful braising liquid. Reduce oven temperature to 325°F.

4. While the endive is in the oven, make the salt dough: in a large bowl, mix together kosher salt and flour. In a separate bowl, beat together egg whites and 1 cup water. Gradually add the liquid ingredients to the dry. Mix by hand, using a pinching motion to incorporate. Sprinkle with 1 tablespoon of water and mix. Continue adding water 1 tablespoon at a time just until a cohesive, kneadable dough has developed: the salt dough should be rather dry. Shape dough into a disk, wrap with plastic wrap, and refrigerate for at least 10 minutes.

5. Line a baking sheet with aluminum foil. Divide the dough into 2 equal-sized lumps. On a lightly floured surface, roll out first dough lump into a rectangle about 1/4-inch thick and 10 inches by 20 inches. Carefully transfer it to the baking sheet. Lay the salmon in the center of the dough and season with ground black pepper. Now roll out the second lump of dough into a 10-inch by 20-inch rectangle and drape over the bottom layer of dough to cover the fish. Seal by firmly pressing together all edges of the dough. Place baking sheet in oven and bake at 325°F for 20 minutes, flipping after 10 minutes. Remove pan from oven, flip fish once more, and let rest for 5 minutes.

6. While the fish is cooking, finish the sauce: whisk the endive purée into the braising liquid. Thinly slice the tarragon and add it to the sauce. Heat to warm through. Taste, and season with salt, pepper, and more lemon juice if desired.

7. Peel away the salt crust, using a knife to get started. (This dish makes a striking presentation. Why not carry it to the table on a platter and remove the crust in front of your diners?) Scrape off all whitish traces of crust from the exposed salmon flesh. Remove skin from salmon and discard. Carve salmon into 4 portions.

8. Just before serving, float olive oil on the surface of the sauce. If serving with Luxurious Potato Purée, dollop some potato purée on the center of each of 4 plates. Lay 2 endive quarters on either side of the potatoes, and perch the salmon on the endive. Ring the plate with sauce. Serve immediately.

MAINE LOBSTER WITH CLOUD EARS & SOYBEANS

Lobster heads, lobster roe, crunchy mushrooms, and a fancy-chef foam...this one will have you dabbing sweat off your forehead. Enlist the help of a sous-chef. Good luck!

- 2 ounces dried cloud ear mushrooms (also called "wood ears" and "tree ears")
- 2 tablespoons kosher salt for blanching soybeans, plus more to taste and for cooking lobsters
- 4 live Maine lobsters, each about 1 1/4 pounds
- 1 teaspoon chile paste
- 1 teaspoon chopped fresh garlic
- 1/4 cup chopped onions
- 3 tablespoons olive oil
- Ground pepper to taste
- 1/2 cup white wine
- 1 cup carrot juice
- 1/2 cup shelled soybeans (frozen are fine; look for edamame in Asian markets)
- 2 to 3 tablespoons unsalted butter

1. Set cloud ears in a small bowl and cover with hot water. Let stand 20 minutes or longer. Drain Tear or cut into bite-size pieces. Hold aside.

2. Bring a large stockpot of water to a boil and salt heavily. Drop lobsters into boiling water. (A trick for keeping the lobsters straight and tail meat unfurled is to skewer the live lobsters from head to tail.) Boil for 8 minutes and remove from water. When cool enough to handle, crack open the shells and remove the meat from the tails, claws, and knuckles. Chop into large chunks. Scrape out and reserve the tomalley (it's the greenish stuff located near the head) and any roe. Sever the heads from the bodies.

3. Make a chunky paste out of a combination of the lobster heads, chile paste, garlic, and onion. A food processor will make easy work of this; if you don't have a food processor, chop the ingredients with a heavy chef's knife.

4. Heat a wide-bottomed, low-sided pan with olive oil. When hot, add the lobster head paste Season generously with salt and pepper. Sauté, stirring constantly, until onions are translucent about 3 minutes. Add wine and cook until reduced to a third of its original volume. Add carrot juice plus enough water to just cover ingredients. Lower heat to bring sauce to a simmer, and simmer for 15 minutes.

5. While the sauce simmers, bring a medium pan of water to a boil. Add 1 tablespoon salt

- ○ sour
- ◐ salty
- ● sweet
- ◑ bitter

1hr 40 mins
TOTAL TIME

1hr 40 mins
ACTIVE TIME

DIFFICULTY

4
PORTIONS

RIESLING
KABINETT

Prepare an ice bath and dissolve into it 1 tablespoon salt. Immerse soybeans in boiling water and blanch 2 minutes. Transfer to ice bath with a slotted spoon and let chill 1 minute. Drain.

6. In a small pan over low heat, melt 2 tablespoons butter. Add reconstituted cloud ears, season, cover pan, and cook 5 minutes. Add soybeans and lobster meat. Hold over very low heat while you finish the sauce.

7. After the sauce has simmered 15 minutes, strain it into a blender, add lobster roe and tomalley, and pulse several times. Pour roughly half of this sauce into the pan with the lobster meat and vegetables. Keep over very low heat.

8. If you really want to wow your guests, turn the rest of the sauce into a vivid orange foam. You'll need an immersion blender. Transfer the sauce left in the blender to a small saucepan set over low heat and add 1 tablespoon of cold butter. Process with an immersion blender at highest speed, moving the blender in and out of the sauce to help incorporate air. Stop when you have a good amount of foam.

9. Mound lobster meat in shallow bowls and spoon a ring of sauce with soybeans and cloud ears around the lobster "islands." Finish with a cap of foam or, if you skipped step 8, more sauce. Serve right away.

sour

salty

sweet

bitter

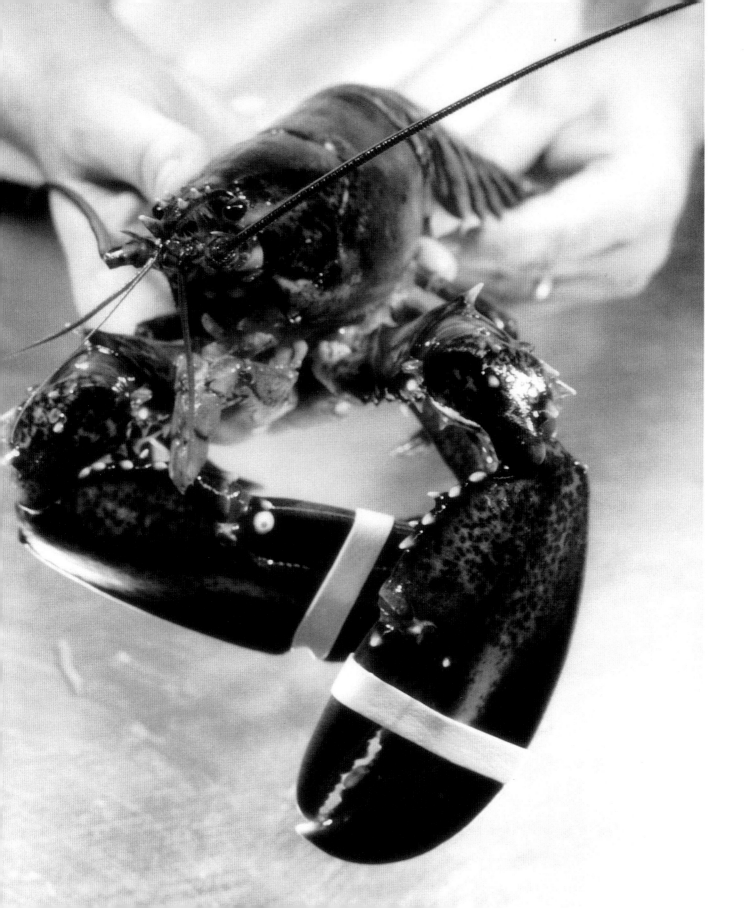

CHOCOLATE-CARAMEL PANNA COTTA WITH ESPRESSO FOAM & CARAMEL POPCORN

Boardwalk caramel corn meets a ubiquitous Italian custard. As a base, panna cotta is as versatile as ice cream; go ahead and invent your own flavors. The espresso foam provides a bitter edge to this otherwise sweet concoction. If you're short on time, skip the foam and serve strong black coffee instead.

- 2 1/2 cups heavy cream
- 3/4 cup whole milk
- 2 ounces bittersweet milk chocolate, preferably Valhrona 66 percent, coarsely chopped
- 1 1/3 cups sugar
  1 teaspoon unflavored powdered gelatin (1/2 packet)
- 1/4 cup popcorn kernels or 1 bag unseasoned microwave popcorn
  1 tablespoon corn oil (if popping popcorn in a pan)
- 1/2 cup crushed espresso beans
- 1/4 cup brewed espresso or strong coffee
- 2 egg yolks, lightly beaten with a fork

1. Combine 1 1/2 cups of the cream and 1/2 cup of the milk in a medium, heavy-bottomed saucepan over medium heat. When small bubbles appear around the liquid's edge, add chocolate and whisk until completely melted. Remove pan from heat and transfer mixture to a measuring glass or other container with a spout. Set aside. (Don't be concerned if a skin forms on the surface.)

2. Add 1/3 cup of the sugar to a high-sided saucepan and cook over medium heat, stirring continuously, until sugar has become a smooth, pale caramel. Remove pan from heat. Stand back from the pan to avoid spattering hot liquid, and pour in the chocolate mixture. Whisk to combine and to redissolve the caramel. Add gelatin and whisk until dissolved. Fill 4 individual 4-ounce molds, such as fluted metal brioche tins or ramekins, with the mixture and refrigerate until set, about 3 hours. These panna cottas can be made up to a week in advance.

3. Pop the popcorn in a microwave, air popper, or covered pan with corn oil.

4. Add remaining 1 cup sugar to a high-sided saucepan and cook over medium heat, stirring continuously, until sugar has become a smooth, pale caramel. Remove pan from heat and add the popcorn to the pan. Use a wooden spoon to quickly and gently coat popcorn with caramel. Turn caramel popcorn onto a sheet pan lined with parchment or wax paper and let cool to room temperature. Break into bite-size clusters. Stored in an airtight container, the caramel popcorn will stay crisp for several weeks.

5. In a small saucepan over medium-high heat, scald the remaining 1 cup cream. Add crushed

- sour
- salty
- sweet
- bitter

4 hrs 30 mins
TOTAL TIME

55 mins
ACTIVE TIME

DIFFICULTY

4
PORTIONS

MADEIRA

espresso beans and 2 tablespoons of the brewed espresso. Let steep, off heat, for 1 hour. Strain espresso cream through a fine mesh strainer into a clean saucepan. Add remaining 2 tablespoons espresso and remaining 1/4 cup milk, place saucepan over medium-high heat, and reheat liquid until almost scalding, whisking frequently. Place egg yolks in a medium bowl and temper them by vigorously whisking in 1/4 cup or so of hot espresso cream. Pass egg mixture through a fine mesh strainer into the saucepan containing the rest of the espresso cream. Tilt the saucepan toward you and lower an immersion blender just below the surface of the cream. With the blender on high speed, pass it in and out of the espresso cream to draw in air. Blend until foamy. If you don't own an immersion blender, try beating the cream with a whisk for several minutes.

6. Unmold panna cottas: dip each mold in hot water for 2 seconds, run a knife along the inner wall of each mold, cover with a dessert plate, quickly invert, and lift mold to release. Check espresso foam: if it has deflated, give it a few buzzes with the immersion blender. Spoon espresso foam around the base of the panna cotta and garnish each serving with several clusters of caramel corn.

THE FOUR TASTES

Sweet, salty, bitter, sour: these are the four tastes that register most vividly on the human tongue. The four tastes are primal and fundamental. Each on its own is unpleasantly intense, sapid, one-dimensional. A handful of raw cranberries tastes torturously tart, and a spoonful of sugar looks tasty only to a young child. But combine a little of each of the four tastes in one dish and you have something that's layered and balanced. Flavors—perfumes picked up by the nose—accessorize tastes.

For me, creating a successful dish is not a lot different than finding a missing integer in a math equation. If I start with bay scallops, which are intrinsically sweet, I'll rack my mind for the fill-ins. Bitter arugula, sour lemon juice, and a sprinkling of sea salt might be one combination I'll try. I'm sharing lists of sweet, sour, salty, and bitter foods so that you don't have to rack your mind. Whether you're creating your own balanced dish or looking for a substitute for an ingredient in a recipe, depend on these lists for ideas.

Sweet

Almond
Apple, sweet varieties
Apple cider
Applesauce
Apricot
Asian pear
Bacon, caramelized
Balsamic vinegar
Banana
Bay scallop
Beet
Bell pepper, ripe (red, orange, yellow)
Boniato (also "batata")
Burdock
Cactus pear (also "Prickly Pear")
Calvados
Candied ginger
Cane syrup
Cantaloupe
Caramel
Carob
Carrot
Cherimoya (also "custard apple")
Cherry
Cherry, grape, and pear tomato
Chestnut
Chinese red date (also "jujube")
Chinese or Thai sausage
Chocolate, sweetened
Clementine
Cocoa, sweetened

Coconut milk
Corn
Corn syrup
Crab
Cubanelle pepper (also "Italian Frying Pepper")
Currants
Daikon
Dates
Durian
Feijoa
Fig
Fraise des bois (also "woodland strawberries")
Fructose
Grape, table varieties like Concord
Guava
Hoisin sauce
Honey
Honeydew melon
Jicama
Ketchup
Langoustine
Lily bulb
Liqueur
Litchi
Lobster
Longan
Loquat
Lotus root
Madeira
Mandarin orange
Mango
Mangosteen
Maple syrup & maple sugar
Mirin
Molasses
Monstera (also "ceriman")

Nectarine
Onion, sweet varieties (Maui, Vidalia, Walla Walla)
Orange, sweet varieties (navel, Mineola, Valencia)
Papaya
Parsnip
Passion fruit
Peach
Pear
Persimmon
Pimiento
Pineapple
Plantain
Plum
Plum sauce, Chinese
Plum wine
Pomegranate
Port
Prune
Pumpkin
Raisin
Rambutan
Raspberry
Red bean paste
Sake
Sapodilla
Sapote
Sherry
Squash (especially acorn, sweet dumpling, butternut)
Stevia
Strawberry
Sugar (cane, beet, palm)
Sugar peas, both snap and snow varieties
Sweet banana pepper
Sweet potato
Tangerine
Treacle

Tomato
Vermouth, sweet
Water chestnut
Watermelon

Sour

Apple, tart varieties (Granny Smith, Stayman, Winesap)
Bergamot
Blackberry
Buttermilk
Cheese
Citron
Cloudberry
Cornichon
Cranberry
Cream cheese
Cream of tartar (also "tartaric acid")
Crème fraîche
Currants, black and red
Enoki mushroom
Goat milk and goat-milk cheese
Gooseberry
Grapefruit
Kaffir lime
Kiwi
Kumquat
Lemon
Lingonberry
Lime
Orange, bitter (blood, Seville)

Pickle
Pickled ginger
Plum
Pomelo (also "Chinese grapefruit")
Preserved lemon
Quince
Rhubarb
Rose hip
Sorrel
Sour cherry
Sour cream
Star fruit (also "carambola")
Sumac
Tamarind
Tomatillo
Ugli fruit
Umeboshi (Japanese pickled plums)
Verjuice/verjus
Vinegar, except balsamic
Yogurt
Yuzu

Salty

Anchovies (dried or fresh)
Bacon
Bresaola
Caper
Caperberry
Caviar
Chorizo
Clam
Clam juice

Dashi
Dulse
Fermented black beans
Fish sauce (nam pla or nuoc nam)
Glasswort (also "samphire")
Ham
Lox
Niboshi (Japanese dried sardines)
Nori
Nuts, salted
Olive
Oyster
Oyster sauce
Prosciutto
Roe (lobster, shad, or salmon)
Salt
Salt cod (also "baccalà")
Salt pork
Sardine
Sea urchin (also "uni")
Seaweed
Seeds, salted (pumpkin, sunflower)
Shrimp paste
Smoked salmon
Soy sauce
Tamari
Worcestershire sauce

Bitter

Angostura bitters
Arugula
Baking powder

Baking soda

Beer

Beet greens

Bell pepper, unripe (green)

Bitter almond oil

Bitter melon (also "bitter gourd")

Black walnut

Broccoli rabe

Brussels sprout

Caffeine

Calf's liver

Chicory

Chinese mustard green (gai choy)

Chocolate, unsweetened

Cocoa, unsweetened

Coffee

Dandelion green

Eggplant

Endive

Escarole

Frisée

Lima bean

Mustard green

Nettle

Orange marmalade

Radicchio

Spinach

Swiss chard

Tea

Tamarillo (also "tree tomato")

Tonic water (also "quinine water")

Turmeric

Turnip green

Watercress

SEASONAL CHART

JANUARY

Abalone
Black truffles
Blood oranges
Brussels sprouts
Burdock
Cardoons
Celery root
Chestnuts
Clementines
Coconut
Collard greens
Hedgehog mushrooms
Horseradish
Kale
Kumquats
Oysters
Passionfruit
Persimmons
Pineapple
Pomelo
Salsify
Sweet potatoes
Tangerines

FEBRUARY

Abalone
Black truffles
Blood oranges
Brussels sprouts
Burdock
Cardoons
Celery root
Coconut
Collard greens
Hedgehog mushrooms
Horseradish
Kumquats
Oysters
Passionfruit
Pineapple
Pomelo
Tangerines

MARCH

Blood oranges
Cardoons
Collard greens
Meyer lemons
Nettles
Oysters
Pineapple
Tangerines

APRIL

Artichokes
Asparagus
Cavaillon melon
Chantarelles
Fava beans
Green almonds
Meyer lemons
Morels
Nettles
Oysters
Porcinis
Ramps
Spring garlic
Spring onions
Tangerines

MAY

Artichokes
Asparagus
Blueberries
Cavaillon melon
Chantarelles
Dandelion greens
Fava beans
Fraises des bois
Green almonds
Kohlrabi
Mâche
Morels
Nasturtiums
Pea shoots
Porcinis
Ramps
Soft-shell crabs
Sorrel
Spring garlic
Spring onions
Strawberries
Tangerines

JUNE

Artichokes
Asparagus
Blackberries
Blueberries
Boysenberries
Cantaloupe
Cavaillon melon
Chantarelles
Cherries
Currants
Dandelion greens
Fava beans
Figs
Fraises des bois
Gooseberries
Kohlrabi
Litchi nuts
Mâche
Nasturtiums
Peaches
Peas
Pea shoots
Purslane
Raspberries
Soft-shell crabs
Sorrel
Spring garlic
Strawberries
String beans
Swiss chard
White truffles
Yellow summer squash
Zucchini
Zucchini blossoms

JULY

Apricots
Blackberries
Blueberries
Boysenberries
Broccoli rabe
Cantaloupe
Chantarelles
Cherries
Corn
Currants
Fava beans
Figs
Gooseberries
Kohlrabi
Litchi nuts
Mâche
Nasturtiums
Nectarines
New potatoes
Okra
Peaches
Pears
Peas
Plums
Purslane
Raspberries
Snow peas
Soft-shell crabs
Sorrel
Strawberries
String beans
Swiss chard
Tomatoes
Watermelon
White truffles
Yellow summer squash
Zucchini
Zucchini blossoms

AUGUST

Apricots
Blackberries
Boysenberries
Broccoli rabe
Cantaloupe
Chantarelles
Cherries
Corn
Currants
Eggplant
Figs
Gooseberries
Huckleberries
Kohlrabi
Litchi nuts
Lovage
Nectarines
New potatoes
Okra
Peaches
Pears
Peas
Plums
Purslane
Raspberries
Snow peas
Soft-shell crabs
String beans
Swiss chard
Tomatoes
Watermelon
White truffles
Yellow summer squash
Zucchini
Zucchini blossoms

SEPTEMBER

Apples
Artichokes
Broccoli rabe
Cantaloupe
Chantarelles
Corn
Cranberries
Crosnes
Eggplant
Figs
Gooseberries
Huckleberries
Kohlrabi
Litchi nuts
Lovage
Nectarines
Okra
Oysters
Pears
Peas
(Fresh) Pistachios
Plums
Porcinis
Pumpkins
Purslane
Snow peas
Spring onions
Swiss chard
Tomatoes
Watermelon
Zucchini

OCTOBER

Apples
Artichokes
Black trumpets
Broccoli rabe
Burdock
Celery root
Chantarelles
Coconut
Cranberries
Crosnes
Eggplant
Figs
Hedgehog mushrooms
Kohlrabi
Litchi nuts
Lovage
Oysters
Pears
Pheasant
Plums
Pomegranate
Porcinis
Pumpkins
Quince
Squash
Swiss chard
Zucchini

NOVEMBER

Apples
Bay scallops
Black trumpets
Blood oranges
Broccoli rabe
Brussels sprouts
Burdock
Celery root
Chestnuts
Coconut
Cranberries
Eggplant
Hedgehog mushrooms
Kale
Kohlrabi
Litchi nuts
Oysters
Partridge
Passionfruit
Persimmons
Pheasant
Pomegranate
Pumpkins
Quince
Salsify
Squash
Sweet potatoes
Swiss chard

DECEMBER

Abalone
Bay scallops
Black truffles
Black trumpets
Blood oranges
Broccoli rabe
Brussels sprouts
Burdock
Cardoons
Celery root
Chestnuts
Clementines
Coconut
Cranberries
Hedgehog mushrooms
Horseradish
Kale
Kumquats
Oysters
Partridge
Passionfruit
Persimmons
Pheasant
Pineapple
Pomegranate
Pumpkins
Quince
Salsify
Squash
Sweet potatoes
Swiss chard
Tangerines

SEASONLESS

All of these items are "seasonless" in that they are readily available all year round, and the quality and price remain fairly consistent.

Apples, Arugula, Asian mustard greens, Asian pears, Avocados, Bananas, Bean sprouts, Beets, Belgian endive, Bell peppers, Bok choy, Broccoli, Cabbage, Cactus pear, Carrots, Cauliflower, Celery, Chile peppers, Chinese long beans, Chives, Cucumbers, Daikon, Dates, Enoki mushrooms, Escarole, Fennel, Garlic, Grapefruit, Grapes, Green beans, Honeydew, Jicama, Kiwi, Leeks, Lemons, Lettuces, Limes, Lobster, Lotus root, Mangoes, Mesclun, Onions, Oranges, Oyster mushrooms, Papaya, Parsley, Parsnips, Pears, Pineapple, Plantains, Portobello mushrooms, Potatoes, Radicchio, Radishes, Rutabaga, Scallions, Shallots, Shiitake mushrooms, Spinach, Taro, Tomatillos, Turnips, Vidalia onions, Watercress, White (button) mushrooms, Yucca

INGREDIENT GUIDE
WITH SOURCES

WHILE NOT ONE OF MY CORE GOALS IN WRITING THIS BOOK, I'd be really pleased to learn that my readers are becoming acquainted with new ingredients as a result of *Flavor*. When confronted by the name of a food you're unfamiliar with, don't despair; flip right to this section. I'll tell you what the food is, what it looks like, and in what type of store you're likely to find it. Ten years ago, finding some of the ingredients called for in this book would have been a pretty big challenge for people living outside metropolitan areas. The Internet has changed that, of course. Look to the end of each food's entry for the names of Internet and mail order suppliers. These companies' website addresses and phone numbers can be found at the end of the guide. Highly perishable products will be available only locally. Above all, please keep in mind that there are few ingredients called for in *Flavor* that cannot be easily swapped for something more mundane.

ACACIA HONEY · Available in many supermarkets. *EthnicGrocer.com, iGourmet.com*

ALLSPICE, WHOLE · Spice stores. *Dean & Deluca, EthnicGrocer.com, Penzeys*

ALMOND FLOUR · Available in baking supply stores, or make by grinding blanched almonds. *True Foods Market*

ARMAGNAC · brandy produced exclusively in southwestern France. By law, Armagnac must be aged in oak barrels for no less than two years. Liquor stores.

BLACK MUSTARD SEEDS · Indian markets. *The CMC Food Company*

BUCATINI · Tube-shaped pasta popular in the regions of Sicily and Apulia. In Italian, bucatini translates as "small hole." Italian markets and pasta shops.

BUTTERFISH · Also "black cod" or "sablefish." A white, high-fat fish found in cold Pacific waters. Look for it at fish markets that carry pricey fish.

CHERVIL · Herb with tiny ruffled leaves and a delicate flavor. Try farmers' markets or growing at home. Substitute parsley. *The Golden Egg*

CHICORY · The root of a bitter green in the chicory family; tastes a lot like coffee. Coffee and health food stores/spice shops. *The Great American Spice Company*

CLOUD EAR MUSHROOMS(ALSO "WOOD EARS" & "TREE EARS") · Flat, ruffle-edged mushroom cherished in China. *The Golden Egg*

CORNICHONS · Tiny pickles imported from France. Markets stocking products from France should have them. *EthnicGrocer.com, The Golden Egg*

CRÈME FRAÎCHE · Cultured cream that is richer/less sour than American sour cream. Gourmet markets. Substitute: equal parts unsweetened whipped heavy cream and sour cream.

CUMIN, WHOLE · Cumin is popular in Indian, Mexican, South American, and Middle Eastern cuisines, so try markets catering to cooks from these regions. Spice shops.

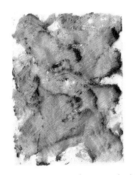

CURED SALMON · Salmon soaked in a saline mixture to draw out its moisture; quite different from smoked salmon. Fishmongers, gourmet markets, and (authentic) Jewish delis.

DAIKON · Asian radish resembling a huge white carrot. Buy fresh only. Easy to find in Asian markets and frequently stocked by urban greenmarkets.

DRIED SOUR CHERRIES · Middle Eastern merchants and stores carrying a wide selection of dried fruits. *Earthy Delights, Kalustyan's*

DUCK & GOOSE FAT · Available wherever other goose and duck products are sold. *Amazon.com, D'Artagnan, Dean & Deluca*

FENUGREEK · Spice shops. *EthnicGrocer.com, Penzeys, The Golden Egg*

FISH SAUCE (*nuoc mam* in Vietnamese; *nam pla* in Thai) · Pungent, salty condiment essential to the cooking of Southeast Asia. *Kitchen Market, Quickspice.com*

FLEUR DE SEL (including sel de Guerande) · Hand-harvested sea salt from Normandy. *EthnicGrocer.com, The Golden Egg, iGourmet.com*

331

FOIE GRAS. The enlarged liver of the Moulard or Muscovy duck or French-raised goose. Buy fresh only; safest to buy by the slice. *Cooking.com, D'Artagnan, The Golden Egg*

GAI CHOY · Asian mustard greens. Buy fresh only. Look for in Chinese markets.

GARAM MASALA · Blend of Indian spices; typically cardamom, black peppercorns, cumin, coriander seed, cinnamon, and cloves. *Kalustyan's, The CMC Food Company*

GRAPESEED OIL · A mild-flavored oil extracted from grape seeds; ideal for pan-frying and searing. Gourmet markets and ethnic grocers. *Cooking.com*

GREEN PAPAYA · The underripe stage of a large Southeast Asian papaya. Buy fresh only. Thai, Vietnamese, and Malaysian markets.

HANGER STEAK · Cut from the rear side, this is unique to the French system; a marvelous deep, rich flavor. In New York City, try Les Halles on Park Avenue South.

HOISIN SAUCE · A Chinese spiced soy-bean paste. Easy to find in Asian markets and increasingly available in the international foods sections of supermarkets.

INDIAN LIME PICKLE · Spicy, tangy Indian condiment of limes/lemons that have been macerated in oil with chile peppers and spices; in any Indian market. *EthnicGrocer.com, Kalustyan's*

JAMBON DE BAYONNE · Dry-cured ham produced in the Basque region of France. Jamon de Serrano (Spain) is similar and easier to locate in the U.S. *Tienda.com*

JAPANESE MUSTARD PASTE · As sweet as it is spicy; as with European-style mustards, a little goes a long way. I recommend S&B brand. *Quickspice.com*

JEREZ VINEGAR — Considered the king of sherry vinegars, this aged vinegar is produced exclusively in the southern Spanish town of Jerez. Gourmet markets. *Tienda.com*

JICAMA · Large root vegetable. Sweet and juicy; texture similar to a water chestnut's. Buy fresh only. Increasingly common in supermarkets and always available in Latin American markets.

JUNIPER BERRIES · The berry of certain evergreen juniper trees, popular as a seasoning for game like venison. Spice stores. *EthnicGrocer.com, Penzeys*

KAFFIR LIME LEAF · Leaf of the kaffir lime lends perfume to Southeast Asian dishes. Look in Thai, Vietnamese, Indonesian, and Malaysian markets. *Temple of Thai*

KIMCHEE · Spicy Korean condiment served with nearly every meal. Ranges from mildly spicy to extraordinarily hot. Available in any Korean market and many Japanese markets.

LARDONS · Diced slab bacon. Slab bacon is sold at some butchers and gourmet markets. Presliced smoked bacon cannot be cut into lardons because it is too thin.

LAVENDER, DRIED · Do not cook with lavender intended for home decoration or potpourri. Numerous lavender farms in the U.S. grow at least some of their crop organically. *The Spice House*

LEMONGRASS · A tall reed whose inner layers are redolent of lemon and flowers. Always available in Thai and Vietnamese markets as fresh whole stalks. *Temple of Thai*

LONG BEANS (also "yard-long beans") · Long, skinny beans with a mucilaginous texture similar to okra. Sold in knotted bundles in Chinese produce markets. Buy fresh only.

MÂCHE · Small, pale, delicate-flavored greens. Buy fresh only. Specialty produce markets. *Marché Aux Delices*

MIRIN · Sweetened rice wine used extensively in Japanese cooking. Japanese and other Asian markets. *EthnicGrocer.com, Kitchen Market, Quickspice.com*

MISO · Fermented soybean paste; darker color indicates greater fermentation/stronger flavor. Japanese and other Asian markets and health food stores.

MUSTARD OIL · Spicy, bright yellow Indian oil used both as a cooking oil and condiment. Indian markets. *Kalustyan's*

PECORINO CHEESE, FRESH · Unlike most pecorino cheeses, not aged. All is imported from Italy. Gourmet markets and cheese shops. *Ideal Cheese, iGourmet.com*

PHYLLO DOUGH · Once the sole domain of Middle Eastern and Greek cooking, but now becoming very popular as an easier alternative to puff pastry. Look in the freezer aisle.

PLANTAIN · Looks like a large green banana but is much starchier and less sweet. Plantains are the main staple of several global cuisines. Latin American and Caribbean markets.

RICE STICK NOODLE · Any Asian market. *EthnicGrocer.com*

SKATE · Member of the ray (as in stingray) family whose aquatic wings are edible. Inexpensive but hard to find. Try fishmongers carrying uncommon fish and Asian fish markets.

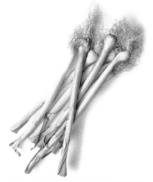

SPRING GARLIC, SPRING ONIONS · The just-harvested versions of the dried bulbs we see every day. Tender flesh, no papery skins, and milder flavor.

STAR ANISE · Beautiful, star-shaped pod of Chinese evergreen. Botanically unrelated to anise. Aroma combines licorice and cinnamon. *Amazon.com, EthnicGrocer.com, Kalustyan's, Penzeys*

SUSHI NORI · Square-shaped, dried seaweed used to roll sushi. Japanese and other Asian markets. *Quickspice.com, The CMC Food Company*

SZECHUAN PEPPERCORNS (also "red peppercorns") · Not a true peppercorn, but the berry of an Asian shrub. *Penzeys, The CMC Food Company*

TAHINI · Middle Eastern sesame paste. Mix well before every use. Middle Eastern grocers and health food stores will carry tahini. *EthnicGrocer.com, Kalustyan's*

TAMARIND · The tart, orange pulp of a tree pod, sold in many forms. Buy either liquid concentrate or paste. Grocers catering to Indian, Thai, and Mexican cooks. *Kalustyan's, Kitchen Market*

TARO ROOT · Large, hairy root native to the tropics. Creamy white with purple flecks. If you've eaten poi in Hawaii, you know taro! At Asian, Latin American, or Caribbean produce stands.

THAI BASIL · Distinct from other varieties of basil, with a strong anise character: imagine a cross between tarragon and globe basil. Buy fresh only. Thai and Vietnamese markets.

THAI CURRY · Comes in red, yellow, and green. Most are incredibly powerful, so always use sparingly. *EthnicGrocer.com, Kitchen Market, Temple of Thai*

THAI EGGPLANT · Round, firm, green eggplants the size of billiard balls. Buy fresh only. Thai and Vietnamese markets.

TRUFFLE · Large fungus that grows underground near the roots of certain trees. Expensive due to its scarcity and labor-intensive hunting methods. *Cooking.com, Marché Aux Delices, Urbani*

TURBINADO SUGAR · Raw, light brown sugar that has been steam-cleaned; look for "Sugar in the Raw" brand at gourmet markets and baking supply stores. *Cooking.com*

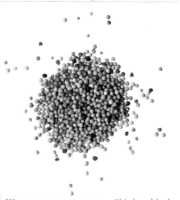

UNI (also "sea urchin") · The coral-colored edible portion of the spiny sea urchin. Sweet, briny, and somewhat musky. *Katagiri, Mitsuwa, Sunrise Mart*

VENISON · Nearly all is farm-raised. Venison is a low-fat alternative to beef. Gourmet markets and butchers. *Amazon.com*

WASABI PASTE · Though not made from wasabi at all, it is a decent imitation of the real thing. Look in any Japanese market. *Quickspice.com*

WHITE PEPPERCORNS · Skinless black peppercorns that have a milder and more neutral flavor. *EthnicGrocer.com, The Golden Egg*

WILD MUSHROOMS · The wildest of the wild include chanterelles, morels, porcinis, and hedge-hogs. Portobellos and creminis are not wild; they're versions of white button mushrooms. *Marché Aux Delices, Earthy Delights.*

YOUNG GINGER · Just-harvested, moist ginger with a pink tinge and relatively gentle flavor. Look for it in Chinese markets in the spring and early summer.

YUZU JUICE · The juice of a small Japanese citrus fruit. Available in Japanese markets. In the New York City area, two sure bets are Sunrise Mart and Mitsuwa Plaza in Edgewater, NJ. *Katagiri*

ZUCCHINI BLOSSOMS · In season mid- to late summer. Fresh only. Farmers' markets.

DIRECTORY OF INTERNET & MAIL ORDER SUPPLIERS

Amazon.com (portal for many Internet purveyors)
http://www.amazon.com

The CMC Food Company (Internet only)
http://www.thecmccompany.com · (800) CMC-2780 · (609) 861-3065 *fax*

Cooking.com (Internet only)
http://www.cooking.com

D'Artagnan (wholesale and Internet)
http://www.dartagnan.com · (800) DARTAGN

Dean & Deluca (retail stores and Internet)
http://www.deandeluca.com
Retail stores in New York City; Washington, D.C.; Charlotte, NC; Kansas City, KS; and St. Helena, CA · (877) 826-9246 · (800) 781-4050 *fax*

Earthy Delights (Internet only)
http://www.earthy.com · (800) 367-4709

EthnicGrocer.com (Internet only)
http://www.ethnicgrocer.com

Ideal Cheese (retail store, wholesale, and Internet)
942 First Avenue, New York City
http://www.idealcheese.com · (800) 382-0109 · (212) 223-1245 *fax*

The Golden Egg (Internet only)
http://www.the-golden-egg.com

iGourmet.com (Internet only)
http://www.igourmet.com · (877) 446-8763

The Great American Spice Company (Internet only)
http://www.americanspice.com
(888) 502-8058 · (260) 420-8117 *fax*

Kalustyan's (retail store and Internet)
http://www.kalustyans.com
123 Lexington Avenue, New York City
(212) 685-3451 · (212) 683-8458 *fax*

Katagiri (wholesale and Internet)
http://www.katagiri.com
(212) 755-3566 · (212) 752-4197 *fax*

Kitchen Market (retail store and Internet)
http://www.kitchenmarket.com
218 Eighth Avenue, New York City · (888) HOT-4433

Marché Aux Delices (wholesale and Internet)
http://www.auxdelices.com
(888) 547-5471 · (413) 604-2789 *fax*

Mitsuwa Marketplace (retail only)
Retail locations in Edgewater, NJ (formerly Yaohan Plaza); Arlington Heights, IL; and Costa Mesa, San Jose, Los Angeles, San Diego, Torrance, and San Gabriel, CA. Visit their corporate website at http://www.mistuwa.com for addresses and phone numbers.

Penzeys Spices (retail and Internet)
http://www.penzeys.com
Retail stores in several states; see website for locations.
(800) 741-7787 · (262) 785-7678 *fax*

Quickspice.com (Internet only)
http://www.asian--food.com
(NB: there are two hyphens between "asian" and "food") · (800) 553-5008

The Spice House (retail stores and Internet)
http://www.thespicehouse.com
Stores located in Chicago, IL; Evanston, IL; and Milwaukee, WI

Sunrise Mart (retail only)
4 Stuyvesant Street, 2nd floor, New York City
(212) 598-3040

Temple of Thai (Internet only)
http://www.templeofthai.com
(877) 811-8773 · (712) 792-0698 *fax*

Tienda.com (Internet only)
http://www.tienda.com
(888) 472-1022 · (757)564-0779 *fax*

True Foods Market (Internet only)
http://www.truefoodsmarket.com · (877) 274-5914

Urbani Truffles and Caviar (wholesale and Internet)
http://www.urbani.com

GLOSSARY

For descriptions of ingredients used in recipes, see the INGREDIENT GUIDE WITH SOURCES *that starts on page 330.*

AIOLI · A Provençal mayonnaise flavored strongly with garlic.

BARIGOULE · A dish described as "à la barigoule" includes artichokes or stuffed artichokes.

BATON · A cut of fruit or vegetable. The widest of the three stick-shaped knife cuts in classical French cuisine; the other two are julienne and allumette (also "matchstick").

BERGAMOT · Variety of orange used only for its aromatic peel. Bergamot is the dominant citrus note in Earl Grey tea.

BEURRE NOISETTE · Also "brown butter." Butter that has been cooked until light brown in color. Milk solids of a beurre noisette separate from the butterfat and take on a nutty flavor. (*See page 340 for process.*)

BISTEEYA · A traditional Moroccan bisteeya is a dome-shaped pie of spiced, ground pigeon meat, eggs, raisins, and pine nuts encased in phyllo dough.

BOUILLON · A broth made from straining the water used to boil proteins or vegetables. Used as the base of soups and sauces.

CARAMELIZE · To break down the natural sugars of a substance through cooking, thereby changing texture, color, taste, and flavor. Caramelization generates more than 100 chemical reactions.

CARPACCIO · An Italian dish of thin-sliced air-dried beef. In current usage, carpaccio may be used to describe any food served in very thin slices.

CEVICHE · Spanish spelling is *seviche*. A dish consisting of raw fish or shellfish marinated in or doused with citrus juice. Citric acid causes the fish to turn opaque, making it looked cooked. Despite appearances, raw fish marinated in citrus juice is still raw.

CHIFFONADE · A verb meaning to cut herbs and greens crosswise into extremely fine strips or shreds. Noun refers to such a cut.

CHINOIS · A cone-shaped strainer ideal for passing soups and sauces through. The word means "Chinese"; whoever first named this tool was reminded of the hats worn by Chinese field-workers.

CLAFOUTI · A tartlike dessert consisting of fruit—cherries are the most traditional—baked in custard. Clafouti originated in the Limousin region of southwest France.

CONFIT · Originally used to describe duck legs cooked in their own fat, now refers to any item that has been preserved by slow-cooking in a thick, viscous liquid such as sugar syrup or oil.

DEGLAZE · Anglicization of the French *deglacer*. Cooking method in which a small amount of wine, stock, or other liquid is added to a hot pan in which food, usually meat, has been sautéed. Concentrated juices or bits of food adhering to the bottom of the pan are then loosened and incorporated into the liquid.

FINES HERBES · Herb mixture consisting of chopped fresh chervil, chives, parsley, and tarragon.

FRICASSÉE · In traditional French cuisine, a dish of chicken that has been sautéed in butter and then stewed with vegetables. Has been used to describe other foods, such as vegetables, that are cooked in a similar manner.

GALANGAL · A rhizome native to Southeast Asia similar to ginger. Compared with ginger, galangal is larger, more aromatic, and spicier. A staple in Thai cooking; also common in Indonesian cuisine.

Deglaze Process

Beurre Noisette Process

GRIBICHE · A sauce made of finely chopped hard-boiled eggs, oil, vinegar, mustard, capers, cornichons (small pickles), and herbs like parsley and chives. Popular as an accompaniment to fish.

JUS · French for "juice." When used in the context of a meat preparation, jus refers to the flavorful brown liquid that meat releases during cooking. Meat jus is often used as the basis of quick pan sauces and gravies.

NAGE · A preparation of shellfish in which the fish is served in a pool of the stock used to cook it. From *nager*, French for "swim."

NONREACTIVE · In kitchen parlance, materials that won't cause a chemical reaction with acidic ingredients like citrus juice and vinegar. Stainless steel, glass, and ceramic are nonreactive materials. Aluminum and copper, on the contrary, are reactive and should not be used with acid.

RAGOÛT · A thick, rich stew. Can be a main dish or sauce. Pronounced the same as, but different in meaning from, the Italian term *ragu*, which is a meat sauce for pasta.

RAMP · *Allium tricoccum*. A wild onion resembling a scallion that grows in mountainous areas. Robust flavor and odor reminiscent of garlic. A true harbinger of spring, ramps have a short season that runs from late March to early May.

SHOCK · To immerse in ice-cold water food that has just been blanched or otherwise cooked. The sudden temperature change halts the cooking process and prevents further change in texture, color, and flavor.

SILPAT · Brand name for a flexible fiberglass sheet used in baking.

SOUBISE · One of the sauces in classic French cuisine, soubise combines onions, cream, and bechamel (milk, butter, and flour). My version uses only onions and butter.

SOUS VIDE · Refers both to the vacuum packaging of supermarket products and a method of cooking in which a food, conventionally a protein, is sealed in plastic and then poached. Pronounced "soo-VEED."

SWEAT · To coax the natural moisture out of an ingredient — onions and mushrooms are typical examples — by cooking in a covered pan containing a small amount of fat or liquid.

TEMPER · To bring the temperature of a sensitive liquid (eggs or chocolate are two common examples) closer to the temperature of a hot liquid. The purpose of tempering an ingredient is to prevent it from solidifying.

VELOUTÉ · In classic French cuisine, a white stock thickened with roux (a cooked flour-butter paste). Used with poetic license in this book to mean a velvet-textured sauce or soup. Pronounced "vel-oo-TAY."

WASABI · A pale green rhizome related to horseradish. Fresh wasabi has a floral aroma, multilayered flavor, and spiciness felt more in the nose than on the tongue. It thrives under very specific conditions, and attempts to grow it outside of its native Japan have been largely unsuccessful. Extremely expensive. Products marketed as "wasabi" powder or paste are not wasabi but green-tinted horseradish.

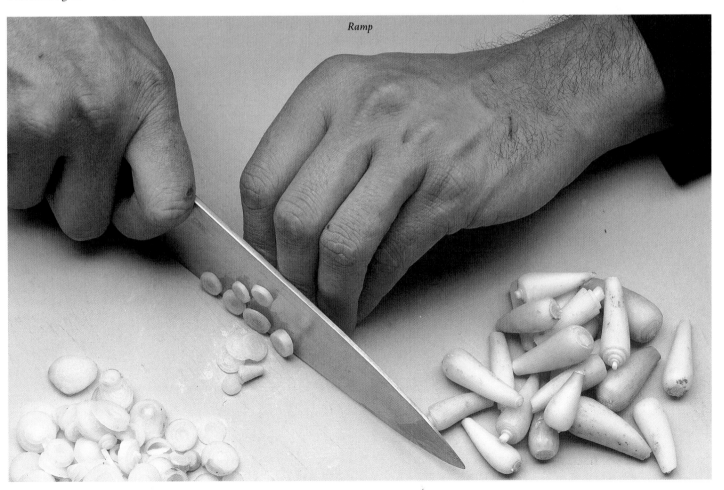

Ramp

Velouté

Chiffonade

INDEX